SO-BPI-548

HUMAN NEEDS AND POLITICAL
DEVELOPMENT

HUMAN NEEDS AND POLITICAL DEVELOPMENT

A Dissent to Utopian Solutions

by

Han S. Park

ASU WEST LIBRARY

JA
76
.P36
1984
WEST

SCHENKMAN PUBLISHING COMPANY, INC.
Cambridge, Massachusetts

Copyright © 1984

Schenkman Publishing Company, Inc.
P.O. Box 1570
Cambridge, MA 02138

Library of Congress Cataloging in Publication Data

Park, Han S.
 Human needs and political development.

 Bibliography: p.
 Includes index.
 1. Political sciences. 2. Social problems. I. Title.
JA76.P36 1984   306′.2   84-1433
ISBN 0-87073-997-2
ISBN 0-87073-998-0 (pbk.)

Printed in the United States of America

All rights reserved. This book, or parts thereof,
may not be reproduced in any form without written
permission from the publisher.

*For my late parents who
endured inconceivable hardships
of life with dignity.*

PREFACE

The more I travel and become acquainted with people living in a variety of environments, the more I see that human beings share many psychological attributes and behavioral traits. While we must recognize cultural variations and societal diversities in our complex global community, we must also realize that humans encounter the same recurring problems and often respond to them with similar strategies. Students of comparative sociological and political studies often unduly dramatize the peculiarities of different societies to the extent that any meaningful comparative observation is viewed as a case of over-simplification. Consequently, genuine efforts to form universal conceptions and to construct grand theories are hampered by fashionable cultural relativism and human subjectivity.

As an immigrant to the United States, I have often been subjected to the widely held notion that people of different origins manage their lives by their own unique norms and by values that are alien to the American experience. Unpersuaded by such a perception and convinced that all human beings share aspirations and behavioral goals, I have put my thoughts together by developing a paradigm which supersedes ethnocentrism and ideological biases. This organizing of thoughts has finally culminated in the present volume.

Initial ideas for the paradigm were conceived in the late 1960s when I was a graduate student at the University of Minnesota. I had the privilege there of working with one of the foremost sociologists of the century, Don Martindale. Also at Minnesota I was inspired by a number of other scholars including Mulford Sibley, Edwin Fogelman, Robert Holt, and Roger Benjamin. I thank them all. This paradigm evolved from a paper presented at the Inter-university Center at Dubrovnik, Yugoslavia in 1977, and I am indebted to the participants in the symposia, especially to Alex Inkeles, Robert Dubin, and Josip Obradović.

At the University of Georgia where I have taught since 1970, I have worked with a number of colleagues and outstanding graduate students. Their names are too numerous to mention, but a few deserve particular recognition: Gary Bertsch and Robert Clute for their encouragement; Dave Mason for his intellectual companionship; Shungo Kawanishi, Mahmood Monshipouri, Kyung-Ae Park, Ann Rowley, and Mahendra Srivastava for their efforts to examine concrete historical cases by utilizing various facets of the paradigm.

Finally, I desire to acknowledge my wife and children for their patience and inspiration. Without their support this project would not have been possible.

HP
University of Georgia
March, 1984

TABLE OF CONTENTS

HUMAN NEEDS AND POLITICAL DEVELOPMENT

INTRODUCTION

As we approach the year 2000, "the spaceship Earth" is beginning to show signs of mechanical malfunctioning as well as a breakdown of cooperation among the four billion or so fellow-travelers. Every day we see evidence of the deterioration of the planet's regenerative capabilities, as Nature's adaptive mechanisms, by which some semblance of environmental equilibrium is maintained, fall victim to the growing appetites of an ever-increasing population. At the same time, the conflicts that infect the body politic of the planet are becoming so volatile and serious in their consequences that we can ill afford to delay further the diagnosis and treatment of this trans-human malady. The state of the planet Earth and the prospects for its future have rapidly deteriorated, as its growing number of inhabitants have constantly waged their brutal internecine struggles for control over each other and for possession of "more" of everything the good Earth has to offer. The competitive ethos of industrial growth, with its concomitant explosion in the consumptive dimensions of contemporary lifestyles, has driven its inhabitants to bury their heads in the sand—"after all, we might find oil under there"—ignoring the health of the planet itself. Consequently, this human species which has thrived for so long in this global environment may well be on the verge of its final destiny of self-extinction. The passengers on the spaceship remain confined within their small, windowless cells, preoccupied with "private" affairs to the exclusion of the problems of their fellow passengers or the operating conditions of their planetary transport. And when they do venture out of their cells, it is all too often for the purpose of indulging themselves in further struggles over the control of yet more resources rather than in cooperative efforts to maintain the spaceship in working order.

1

Amidst this social malaise and planetary decay, we can no longer content ourselves with simply alleviating temporarily the symptoms of these problems, but must deal decisively with their causes.

During the past few decades, particularly since World War II, the world community has experienced a series of revolutionary changes in virtually every aspect of human life. The application of high technology to warfare and the competitive arms race during the Cold War have made human existence itself vulnerable and precarious in an ultimate sense. The expansion of the market economy beyond the political boundaries of nation states has inextricably intertwined the members of the world community in a complex web of mutual dependencies, rendering national governments largely impotent, if not obsolete, in a number of crucial policy-making areas. The succession of political authority by means of coups, revolutions, and foreign interventions has become more frequent than the use of "legitimate" mechanisms of regime change. The veil of political ideology, once so useful in concealing the more primitive and cold-blooded ambitions of nations or groups of nations, has lost some of its vital translucence and, hence, its effectiveness in beclouding the true motives of actors behind the shroud of noble, high-minded—but apparently transparent—ideals. The "ills" of industrialization are being felt everywhere. Air pollution, water pollution, and even noise pollution have emerged as the undesirable though unavoidable side effects of modern industrial society. The imminent exhaustion of energy resources, the decay of urban centers and the quality of life in them, and, most serious of all, the erosion of shared moral codes and institutions like the family that traditionally have reinforced them are scarcely the problem of any single nation. Indeed, they have become and are becoming ever-more endemic to all societies. As such, these pan-human problems cannot be resolved by any one nation's efforts; rather, cooperative efforts on the part of all human beings are desperately needed. If we fail to realize the seriousness of these and other problems facing *all* societies, and if we fail to deal with them effectively, the future of the planet is indeed bleak.

One major obstacle that must be overcome is the tendency of policy makers and academics to ignore the global character and impact of these problems. The tendency is to isolate these issues, and label them as the problems of either "developing" societies or of post-industrial "developed" societies. Hence, the former will be taken care of by the development process itself, and the latter can be isolated and dealt with by those societies that face them now. Consequently, solutions tend to be piecemeal, uncoordinated, and fraught with the exigencies of various unintended side-effects that feedback into the system to create a whole new set of symptoms while leaving the fundamental problems untouched. This shortcoming is at least in part in consequence of the intellectual perspectives that we apply when analyzing the problems of the world or some part of it. The tendency to view the world in terms of "developed versus underdeveloped," "modern versus traditional," "East versus West," and "North versus South" has not served us well either in academia or in the political arena. Such perspectives emphasize the difference between nations, the diversity of their problems, and the mutual irrelevance of each other's solutions. In an increasingly interdependent world, where the policies of any one nation inevitably reverberate through the community of nations, what is needed is a paradigm that helps us understand the common basis of our problems—no matter how diverse they may appear—and the shared interest in their solution. This, then, is the purpose of this book: to develop an alternative paradigm of social change and political development that can help us better understand not only the problems of the "developing" society but also of the "developed." To the extent that we can see the two as emerging from common human characteristics, we should be better able to deal with them simultaneously and in a mutually beneficial manner.

We shall begin in the first chapter by examining the current "state of the art" in the development literature. Our goal is to discern the theoretical inadequacies that remain and determine how they may be at least addressed if not resolved by an alternative conception of the common process of human social and political development. Chapter II shall examine some leading conceptions of political development as it attempts to develop a set of criteria by which the concept of political development should be defined. This will pave the way to an alternative definition of political development which might better satisfy the definitional criteria than the hitherto available definitions. Chapter III will develop a paradigm of developmental social change in such a way that the development process entails a series of stages where each stage has a unique pattern of institutionalization and life styles. This third chapter will only show the overall picture of the paradigm itself. Chapters IV through VII will deal with each of the developmental stages in order to explore more fully its properties. The final chapter will discuss a series of theoretical and empirical implications of the proposed paradigm, and suggest the need for a change in human nature and the growth of a world culture that would be more conducive to some form of global management of resources and values.

Chapter I

COMPARING LIFE SITUATIONS

STATE OF DEVELOPMENTAL THEORIES

As nations have become increasingly interdependent and the global community has emerged as an indivisible unit, a number of subdisciplines in each of the social sciences have made the comparison of different countries a routine and almost casual practice defying the boundaries of their own academic realms. Yet problems in the art and logic of comparing different "life situations" have at times appeared insurmountable. It remains clear that, in political science at least, no consensus has yet emerged among comparativists as to how to go about this awesome task. The traditional mode of analysis, characteristic of comparative government prior to the behavioral revolution in political science, has proved to be ill-suited conceptually for the analysis of the many newly autonomous nations of Asia, Africa, and Latin America. Traditional comparative analysis was developed in and for the comparison of stable, mature, industrialized societies. Consequently, it generally focused upon the formal institutions and constitutionally defined governing processes of mature Western societies. However, the relative immaturity of the political milieu and the persistent underpinning of indigenous culture and social structure meant that the traditional elements of comparison were inapplicable because the same institutional structures either did not exist or were less visible and much more intermittent, coming into being only in response to clear and present needs. Where comparable institutions could be said to exist, they were often not the strict structural or functional equivalent of their corresponding formal institutions in the nations of the industrial West (Almond and Coleman, 1960, pp. 3–26). As a consequence, a great deal of the activity of comparativists in recent years has centered upon the myriad of methodological as well as epistemological questions left unanswered by the existing literature in a discipline that is still in its own pre-paradigmatic infancy.

Hence, as a prelude to our own study of political development, we shall begin in this chapter with an assessment of the current status of comparative political science as a science. We must have some sense of where we have been, as a discipline, before we can decide where we ought to be going. What have been the major theoretical perspectives toward a "science" of comparative politics and development? In what ways have they proved lacking? Only when these questions have been answered can we expect our new direction to be free of the pitfalls of previous theoretical perspectives.

With these concerns in mind, we shall focus upon three related issues that are fundamental to any attempt at scientific comparison of "life situations" cross-culturally. First, we shall begin by exploring the *raison d'être* for such comparisons as we examine the question: "Why do we compare?" Second, we turn our attention to the issue of the feasibility of establishing comparability in the area of life situations as we ask ourselves the question: "Can we compare?" Third, we shall raise the rather unconventional question of "Should we compare as we do?" in an attempt to explore some of the implications of current practice in cross-national comparative analysis. As such, this chapter will address empirical and moral issues, as well as methodological and epistemological questions.

THE SYNDROME OF UNIVERSAL COMPARISON AND SCIENTIFIC REVOLUTION

Since the inception of the behavioral revolution, the student of political phenomena has often found himself forced to accept almost uncritically the (alleged) rules and objectives of "scientism." Otherwise, he could scarcely hope to keep pace with the rapid diffusion of new research technologies which has for some time characterized the development of the social sciences in general, and political science in particular. Within our own discipline, comparative studies have been, since the 1960s, geared toward scientific theory construction. Indeed, the pursuit of scientific knowledge as an unchallenged goal of comparative analysis has elevated the aim of universal explanation to the desideratum of virtually every serious researcher in the area.

Most recently, we have witnessed concerted efforts by a number of scholars aiming to generate universally applicable theories of political change and/or development. Beginning with the seminal work by Almond and Coleman (1960), in which they attempted to explain the political dynamics of several developing nations by applying to each the same conceptual framework (that of "structural functionalism"), the study of political change has emerged as an increasingly dominant trend in comparative politics. The desire to compare social life situations cross-nationally has developed as a response to the broader disciplinary transition generally referred to as the behavioral revolution.[1] With behavioralism, universally applicable explanation has become the ultimate goal, indeed the definition, of social scientific inquiry. Yet the comparativist faced a rather unique set of problems when it came to developing *universally* applicable explanations. The nations and cultures to which his theories were supposed to apply are so diverse, so ostensibly unique that he was hard pressed to devise even universal *concepts* with which to construct such theories. To render the basic conceptual elements universally applicable required defining them at such a high level of abstraction as to strip them of any substantive content. Given the conceptual difficulties inherent in trying to subsume such diversity under universal rubrics, it is not surprising that the theories employing these concepts were likewise so far removed from reality as to be virtually useless in explaining or predicting events in a given nation. The theories could accommodate *any* course of events after the fact; hence they were of no use in predicting one set of outcomes (as opposed to some other) before the fact. They remained little more than intellectual artifacts of a discipline in its infancy.

The diversity of life situations in the world, which is the comparativist's domain, could not be ignored. Hence, attention had to be directed toward accounting for this diversity while subsuming it under some complex of universal propositions that allowed one to make some sense out of this apparent miasma of cultural differences in life situations. With this understanding, the comparativist has adopted comparison of life situations as the methodological foundation of his science. As such, the comparison of life situations needs to be assessed in light of the status of the behavioral revolution itself. Only in this manner can we evaluate the feasibility, as well as the desirability, of such a mode of comparative inquiry.

Behavioralism, at least in political science, emerged as the dominant force redirecting the objectives and functions of the discipline during the middle of the twentieth century and especially after the Second World War. With the advent of the Cold War, the political scientist found himself totally incapable of contributing to the growing need for *uncertainty reduction* in the emergent nuclear age of the world political community. The desire to reduce uncertainty about political phenomena and to apply "scientfic" methods to political inquiry could hardly be accommodated within the framework of conventional studies of government. Here, a discipline totally unprepared to serve this emergent need had no other choice but to borrow and adapt tools and concepts from the neighboring social sciences (and even the physical sciences) and to imitate (or at least approximate) their methods, methodologies and epistemological structure. Only in this manner could the findings and recommendations of the political scientist even remotely assume the air of scientific certainty so urgently demanded by his clients and, eventually, his colleagues.

However, due to, among other things, the ontological differences between physical and social phenomena, the behavioralist's painstaking and prolonged effort to refine social concepts and generate precision in social measurements faced serious impediments from the very beginning. Since most of these methodological obstacles were unique to the social sciences, the more mature physical sciences could offer no ready-made solutions. And at the same time, the social and political environment the behavioralist was expected to explain was itself becoming more perplexing, its increasing complexity compounded by the kaleidoscopic mutability of the world community's make-up.

Eventually, the political scientist's capacity to comprehend these global anomalies fell so low that, according to Easton, he was forced to accept "eternal puzzlement about his life world as a condition of his life world."[2] In the post-war years, socio-political conditions and problems have intensified to the point of making real the grave possibility of human extinction by way of nuclear holocaust, ecological deterioration, or more subtly, by moral decay and social degeneration. In response to this crisis, conscientious students of politics have called for yet another revolution in the discipline, a revolution in which "problem solving" is inaugurated as the ultimate goal of political studies. It was in this context that post-behavioralism was introduced.[3]

By placing scholarly emphasis on resolving human and social problems, the post-behavioralist is forced to adopt an interdisciplinary approach. Indeed, the almost epidemic spread of policy and management oriented political inquiries, comparative or otherwise, can be seen as new trends in which research topics are chosen for their relevance to public issues, and science is simply a tool designed to contribute to problem solving and, eventually, to enhance the quality of "life conditions."

It is in light of this post-behavioral doctrine that we should now raise the question of why we felt the need to compare "life situations", as well as other units of comparison, in response to the behavioral era's supreme demand for universal explanation. But should we continue blindly to design instruments whose sole purpose is to allow construction of cross-culturally valid, universal explanations? If we are to accept the aforementioned objectives of post-behavioralism, I submit we must conclude that universal explanation can be meaningful only when it can help solve problems and thereby contribute to the enhancement of human life conditions. Can a comparative study striving for universally applicable explanations help us resolve salient social problems? Can it in any way enhance the quality of life conditions in the global community? These questions will be dealt with in the following sections.

In the name of "scientific" research during the behavioralist years, numerous efforts were undertaken to construct nomethetic theories for universal application. Most of these efforts can be seen as directed at searching for developmental paradigms designed to allow comparison of societies and life styles cross-culturally. Given the inadequacies of traditional approaches, with their emphasis on formal institutions, and given the cultural diversity apparent in the emerging world order, such a paradigm development seems to be an urgent need.

The search for a paradigm of development politics came to involve two more specific concerns: (1) the quest for approaches that focus upon the "realities" of political processes and life in the political community, regardless of the formal institutional context in which they might (or might not) occur; and (2) a concern for the explanation of the processes of change that have become so dramatically evident (and apparently inevitable) in the newly emergent nations. The first issue, a methodological one, involves the intrusion of the behavioral revolution into the field of comparative politics, whereas the second involves the emergence of the more specific, and increasingly pervasive, substantive concern with modernization and political development. Thus, the actual behavior of the incumbents of political roles became the new focus of analysis, and the explanation of "political development" or "modernization" as the process of change in society in general and the nature of these roles and their interrelationships in particular became the new goal of analysis.

The "Traditional-Modern" Dichotomy

The process of retooling and reorienting comparative politics, especially for the purpose of an analysis of change, quite naturally began with efforts centered on distinguishing Western from non-Western societies. The idea was that, if the industrialized West is "modern" or "developed" and the Third World is not, then we should begin by distinguishing these two "system types" as poles on a continuum. "Modernization" then becomes the *process* by which a nation moves from one end of the continuum to the other.

Hence, the first taxonomic endeavors aimed at constructing a traditional-modern dichotomy, or some similar variant (e.g., rural-urban, agrarian-industrial, western-nonwestern). The theoretical underpinnings of these efforts were largely derived from Talcott Parsons' elaboration of "pattern variables." Pattern variables refer to mutually exclusive value orientations, and the value system that constitutes a society's culture will tend toward one or the other ends of the several specific dimensions of pattern variables (Parsons, 1951, pp. 24–112).

The idea of pattern variables has formed the basis of a number of efforts aimed at distinguishing modern from traditional society. The basic elements, present in some form or another in most of these works, include the following: (1) ascriptive versus achievement based status, (2) functionally diffuse versus functionally specific roles, (3) particularistic versus universalistic values, (4) collectivity orientation versus self orientation, (5) affectivity versus affective neutrality. In each dichotomy the former member is taken as characteristic of traditional society and the latter is typical of modern society (see Bill and Hardgrave 1973, p. 52 for a brief description of each).

Authors who have utilized this dichotomy scheme are numerous. Sutton (1963) proposed an "agricultural-industrial" dichotomy. The former is characterized by ascriptive status norms, low spatial and status mobility, a simple and stable occupational system ("functionally diffuse") and a differential stratification system. By contrast, in the latter system type we find achievement norms, high mobility, a highly differentiated and functionally specific occupational system, and an "egalitarian" achievement based on stratification system. Similarly, Riggs (1957) extended Sutton's models for the analysis of administrative systems, using the polar opposites of *agraria* and *industria*. (It should be noted that Riggs later elaborates this model into a more dynamic system, involving the *fused, diffracted* and *prismatic* stages of social development. This will be discussed later.) Ward and Rustow (1964, pp. 6–7) provide a check list of characteristics of the modern polity which a traditional polity presumably lacks by using similar concepts.

Generally, then, the modern polity in contrast to the traditional polity is seen as characterized by rationalized authority, differentiated and integrated structures, mass participation and positive affect toward the system and, consequently, the capacity to process a high volume of inputs and accomplish a broad range of goals. Modernization, then, is the bridge across the Great Dichotomy. It is a lengthy, complex process that occurs in phases but ultimately revolutionizes social life in the traditional society (Huntington, 1971, pp. 288–289).

A number of problems have been pointed out with respect to the validity and the utility of the traditional-modern dichotomy. Rustow (1967, p. 12) notes that while modernity can be affirmatively defined in terms of the characteristics of industrial societies, "traditional society" remains largely a residual concept. That is to say, those characteristics ascribed to traditional societies are in many cases simply the logical antitheses of characteristics ascribed to modern societies. It is doubtful that all or any of the so-called traditional societies manifested all these traits. At the very least, history shows that there was great diversity in traditional societies.

A second crucial problem with the dichotomous definitions is that they fail to distinguish between what is modern and what is Western. Indeed, modernity is virtually synonymous with the characterization of twentieth century Western European and North American Society. In fact, the dichotomy represents an empirical distinction of Western societies from Third World nations. Those scholars who use the dichotomy as two poles on the universal process of change imply that the nature of Western society is the goal toward which all emerging nations aspire. As Holsti (1975, p. 829) notes, the evidence from the developing nations argues against this inference.

Furthermore, the implicit teleological character of the change process implies that once a society has modernized (re: Westernized), change ceases. Surely, the persistence of change in so-called "developed" societies argues against this idea. Indeed, such a teleological conception of development contains an element of circularity: Some prior conception of development is needed to explicate the characteristics of the developed society.

Structural Functionalism and the "Transitional Society"

With the growing realization that the traditional-modern dichotomy was of limited utility and accuracy, scholarly efforts began to center upon the idea of "transitional systems." This new focus emerged from the realization that all societies possessed attributes of both the modern and the traditional ideal types. However, the enchantment with Parsonian pattern variables and functional models remained.

In *The Politics of Developing Areas* Almond states his assumptions in terms of "four characteristics that all political systems have in common" and which thereby constitute the basis for the comparison of political systems (Almond and Coleman 1960, p. 11). He asserts that all political systems have *structures*, which he defines as the legitimate patterns of interaction by means of which the order of society is maintained (Almond and Coleman 1960, p. 11). Systems may be compared, then, in terms of the degree and form of structural specialization. These structures derive their *raison d'être* from their performance of certain *functions*, and as a further basis of comparison, Almond postulates that there are certain functions that apparently are performed in all systems. Almond's eight "universal functions" are, on the input side, (1) *political socialization* which involves the transmission of political culture from one generation to the next, (2) *political recruitment* whereby the new incumbents of political roles are selected and trained, (3) *interest articulation* by which demands are identified and transmitted from the society to the decision-making elite, (4) *interest aggregation* whereby these demands are consolidated into a manageable form for the elite to act upon, and (5) *political communication* which is the process by which information is transmitted within the political system and between the political system and its environment.

On the output side there are the functions of (6) *rule making*, (7) *rule application*, and (8) *rule adjudication*, which correspond to the legislative, executive and judicial functions in the democratic political system, as it is commonly conceived. Beyond this, Almond assumes that all structures, no matter how specialized, will be multifunctional in some sense and to some extent. And finally, all political systems are *"mixed"* systems in the cultural sense, in that no system is completely "modern," nor are there any "all-primitive" or traditional systems (Almond and Coleman 1960, p. 11). In general, comparison is made within this framework in terms of the probabilities of performance of the specified functions by the specified structures, and in terms of the differences in the style of their performance. Development is conceived of as the system's increase in the effectiveness of the performance of these functions (Almond and Coleman, 1960, p. 59).

The criticisms directed at Almond's initial formulation are numerous and multi-faceted. They deal with, among other things, the lack of definitional clarity evident through this framework, weakness in the logical structure of the model, and questions concerning its capacity to depict meaningfully the process of change that must be central to any model of development.

First of all, we should note that in several ways the lack of definitional clarity in this construction severely limits its potential value as an explanatory device. Holt and Richardson (1970, pp. 34–35) contend that Almond does not explicitly define several of the key structures in his framework, and those that he does define tend to be defined *in terms of the functions that they perform.* As long as this is so, there can be no probabilistic theory concerning the performance of a given function by a given structure, because that relationship is true by definition and therefore need not be tested empirically. Furthermore, Almond nowhere clarifies even what a function is, and his eight "universal" functions are defined at such a high level of generality that it is unclear what specific sets of empirical indicators could be used to measure the performance of these functions (Mayer 1972, p. 148). Since the increase in the effectiveness of their performance is what constitutes development, we must have some criteria by which to evaluate their performance if we are to explain development.

Besides these definitional problems, the explanatory power of Almond's model is also limited by Almond's use of the assumptions of "universal" functionalism. In particular, he never specifies why it is

these eight functions, and not some others, whose effective performance results in political development (Bill and Hardgrave 1973,
p. 213). In his first assumption, Almond states only that these functions
are apparently sufficient for the effective performance of the system; he
nowhere claims that their performance, and theirs alone, is necessary
and sufficient for the effective functioning of the system. While Mayer
(1972, p. 143) notes that the differences between "universal" functionalism, such as the former case immediately above, and requisite
analysis, as would be the latter case above, appear semantical rather
than logical, Almond can neither predict that the inadequate performance of these functions will result in system failure, nor infer their
inadequate performance from systemic breakdown unless he rules out
the possibility of other unspecified functions contributing to the effectiveness of the system (Mayer 1972, p. 148).

There are questions as to whether Almond's framework, as he describes it, really addresses itself to the explanation of political change.
It seems potentially suitable for the comparison of different systems at
different levels of development. But to compare the states of systems
in such a static sense is not to explain the *process of change* over time
in a given system. Thus, the model's conceptual scheme is in certain
ways ill-suited for the representation of change over time in a given
system. "Increasing effectiveness" of functional performance and
"structural differentiation" are the only dimensions of change that are
explicit in this formulation. Even ignoring the definitional problems
with the former variable that were discussed above, to define development as the quantitative increase along some single dimension of
change is perhaps to neglect the qualitative changes that occur in the
nature of the system as it develops. Development involves important
identifiable changes other than just the evolution of "more structures"
performing the same functions "more effectively."

Furthermore, having posited that there is a certain interdependence
among the eight functions that is not necessarily harmonic, Almond
fails to specify the nature of these interdependencies and therefore
cannot predict that an increase in the performance of one function will
not be deleterious to the performance of one of the other functions. In
other words, given the interdependence of the functions, unless it can
be shown that the increased performance of one does not in fact detract
from the effectiveness of the system by causing a decrease in the
performance of one or more of the other functions, then we cannot

assert unequivocally that development results from increases in the performances of the eight functions. Hence, Almond's failure to specify the interrelationships among his eight functions limits his model's capacity to deal with the process of change in a meaningful way.

In *Comparative Politics: A Developmental Approach*, Almond presents a much revised version of his functional model of development, with the changes contained therein representing an attempt to correct some of the theoretical deficiencies attributed to his earlier formulation. Most importantly, perhaps, he expands his set of functional categories and attempts to establish some sorts of relationships between them in an effort to infuse his model with the capacity to account for the dynamics of developmental change. In particular, Almond asserts that political systems must be evaluated in terms of three different "levels of functioning," which, ostensibly, are products of certain patterns of interrelationship among the various functional categories. On one level are the *capability functions* (regulative, extractive, distributive and responsive) which determine the performance of the political system in relation to its environment. On another level are the *conversion functions* (the input-output functions of the previous formulation) which are internal to the political system and involve the system's ability to meet demands (inputs) with authoritative decisions (outputs). The third level is that of the *system maintenance and adaptation functions* of political socialization and recruitment whereby the system ensures its own continuity (Almond and Powell 1966, pp. 28–30).

Under this construction of the model, political development is given impetus when certain environmental conditions give rise to significant changes in the magnitude and content of political inputs. Such changes are deemed "significant" when it becomes apparent that the existing structural and cultural make-up of the political system is incapable of satisfactorily processing the new demand load. In such a situation, political development occurs when the political system undergoes the processes of *structural differentiation and cultural secularization* to such an extent that the needed increase in systemic capabilities is achieved, so that the new demands can be dealt with effectively (Almond and Powell 1966, p. 34).

Such challenges to the functional capacity of existing structural and cultural patterns occur in the form of what Almond designates as the "developmental challenges" of *state building, nation building, participation,* and *distribution.* Almond defines each of these in terms of their impact upon and required responses from the three levels of functioning of the political system. Finally, he posits a sequence of their occurrence, although he claims no theoretical imperative for this particular order; it is simply that this is the order in which they have emerged in the political systems of Western Europe (Almond and Powell 1966, pp. 36–37).

By means of these changes in the logic and conceptual content of his model, Almond has ostensibly answered the criticism of system states—yet he is unable to explain the dynamics of a process such as development. The new model apparently addresses the question of the "what" and "how" of development: development is the acquisition of greater *capabilities* by means of the *processes* of structural differentiation and cultural secularization. And the definitional clarity of his conceptual framework is sharpened somewhat by virtue of the greater number of concepts that are now explicit in the model.

However, the model remains plagued by many of the same problems that elicited the criticism of the earlier formulation. Despite the expansion of his set of functional categories, the concepts—even the new ones—are still defined at such a high level of abstraction that they cannot be operationalized without robbing them of some of the richness and complexity they retain in a strictly theoretical context. To operationalize these concepts without retaining most of their meaning in the empirical context would lead to unfair testing of the generated hypotheses (Flanigan and Fogelman 1967, p. 82).

Thus, while he uses the idea of the three "levels of functioning" to propose some very general relationships between the functions, these relationships are as yet untestable, since the critical concepts cannot be operationalized. And what relationships he has proposed—i.e., between the adaptation functions of differentiation and secularization and the several capability functions—represent only the bare beginnings of the set of interdependence patterns that would be a necessary part of any full-blown functionalist theory of political development. Almond, recognizing this weakness in his formulation admits the theoretical necessity of such a thorough-going specification of the political relationships between functions:

> The theory of the political system will consist of the discovery of the relations between these levels of functioning—capabilities, conversion functions, and system maintenance and adaptation functions—and of the

relation of the functions at each level (Almond and Powell 1966, pp. 29–30).

Even the one relationship he proposed—that differentiation and secularization lead to enhanced capabilities—is of questionable validity, at least when the concepts are so vaguely defined. Bill and Hardgrave (1973, p. 73) pointed out that enhanced capabilities are by no means guaranteed by structural differentiation and cultural secularization. Differentiation without the concomitant integration of the new structural units may in fact reduce the system's capabilities. And cultural secularization may exacerbate rather than resolve system challenges by creating new demands (such as participation demands) at a time when the structure of the system is already overloaded with demands. To define development thus in terms of the instrumentalities of capabilities rather than capability itself is to cloud the distinction between political development and what Huntington (1965) has termed "political decay." Both are plausible outcomes of the differentiation and secularization processes; yet Almond ignores this, and therefore provides us with no additional criteria with which to predict which will occur in a given set of circumstances.

Thus, while Almond has here at least attempted to inject the needed dynamism into his development scheme, the conceptual problems that plagued his first model remain critically unresolved here, as are the logical problems inherent in the universal functionalism paradigm. Perhaps the heuristic value of his model has been enhanced, but its desired explanatory power cannot be realized until these methodological dilemmas are resolved.

David Apter's works on modernization constitute a second instance of a functionalist approach to development theory. However, Apter's use of the idea of "structural requisites" and his more empirically based classification scheme for transitional societies distinguish his use of the functional mode from that of Almond. And, as would be expected, the theoretical propositions he generates within this framework differ from those of Almond with respect to both the aspects of the development process that are deemed to be of analytical importance and the way in which these phenomena are conceptualized.

To begin with, Apter limited his analytical concern to the process of social development. He listed three preconditions for the inception of modernization: a social system (1) that can absorb innovation without disintegrating, (2) in which there are flexible, differentiated social structures, and (3) with the capacity to provide the skills and knowledge necessary for living in a technologically advanced world (Apter 1965, p. 67). It is this last condition that distinguishes modernization from development in general: what Apter alluded to is industrialization, which is the definitive economic and technological aspect of modernization. Hence, modernization is defined as the increasing complexity of social patterns resulting from the differentiation and integration of new functional roles, and, particularly, the spread and use of "industrial type roles in non-industrial settings" (Apter 1968, p. 334).

In order to analyze this process, Apter began by proposing a typology of transitional systems which in their fulfillment of the above mentioned conditions represent four analytically distinct alternative starting points for the modernization process. These "ideal type" constructs are distinguished according to whether they have a *pyramidal* or *hierarchical* authority structure, on the one hand, and whether their political actions are guided by *consummatory* (i.e., sacred or otherwise "ultimate") goals or *instrumental* (i.e., secular) goals (Apter 1965, pp. 19–24).

Secondly, he attempted to specify what activities must be performed in order for the system to maintain itself as a unit. He terms these "structural requisites" rather than "functional requisites," although it appears that what he meant to imply by use of this term is the institutionalization of the performance of what others would designate as functions. To illustrate this point, we note first that Apter's primary *structural requisites* are (1) the structure of authoritative decision making, and (2) the structure of accountability. These two correspond roughly to what Apter calls the "functional requisites" of government, which are "coercion" and "information." Thus, in Apter's paradigm, "functional requisites" are the minimum tools a political system needs in order to perform the functions implied in the list of structural requisites (Mayer 1972, pp. 157).

Apter later increases his list of structural requisites to include (3) the structure of coercion and punishment, (4) the structure of resource determination and allocation, and (5) the structure of political recruitment and assignment (Apter 1968, p. 29). These appeared in his earlier formulation as "contingent structures" or "analytic substructures" of government (Apter 1965, pp. 245–247).

Finally, within this conceptual framework, Apter attempts to derive theoretical propositions concerning the interrelationship between these structural requisites and the differences, by system type, in these patterns of interrelationship. Since modernization involves the proliferation of "modern" roles throughout society, Apter examines the relative ability of each system-type to foster such an expansion, and the major way of doing this is by affecting the society's stratification in such a way as to provide for the greater upward mobility of the "modern" roles and/or strata.

In assessing the explanatory utility of Apter's paradigm, Mayer (1972, p. 257) noted that because Apter's typology is based upon empirical rather than normative criteria, his scheme is capable of organizing and giving meaning to an otherwise amorphous and disparate group of political systems. To the extent that he can derive logically a precise set of developmental outcomes for each of the system types, his paradigm would represent a sound basis for the generation of testable propositions from which to construct a theory of development. And in fact Apter attempted to generate such scientific generalizations by linking characteristics of his "mobilization system" and "reconciliation system," on the one hand, with certain specified stages of the modernization process, on the other (Apter 1965, 1968).

However, the full explanatory potential of his paradigm is never fully realized, and for much the same reasons as those that limit Almond's model. Like Almond, Apter conceptualized the critical phenomena in his explanatory sequences at such a high level of generality that operationalization is all but impossible. Therefore, while he may be able to account logically for certain loosely defined relationships between system types and modernization phenomena, he cannot predict precisely defined outcomes from a given set of empirical preconditions unless the operational linkage is established reliably between the preconditions and the concepts in his generalized explanatory sequences.

And like Almond, Apter does not pay sufficient attention to the specification of the relationships between his structural requisites. How does the functioning of one structure affect that of another, and vice versa? Unless such relationships are specified, we can never evaluate meaningfully the overall performance of the system. All that can be said is that the requisite structures, as a group, are functioning adequately if the system is still in existence. But such a conclusion is of no analytical value, and simply accentuates the tautological implications of Apter's use of requisite analysis.

As for this idea of "structural requisites," it too creates certain logical problems for Apter's paradigm, even though it should allow Apter to avoid those problems associated with "universal functionalism." In particular, there is no theoretical justification for the claim that Apter's set of requisites, and not some other, is the only possible set of structures by which a system can maintain itself. Since Apter's chief concern here is the explanation of modernization, it would be reasonable simply to assume the validity of his requisites and test the validity of this assumption later when the explanatory potential of the model has been established to such an extent as to warrant a more thorough examination of this assumption. However, Mayer (1972, p. 158) contended that, at the very least, the postulate of structural requisites should be defined with enough precision as to allow operationalization for such testing. In this respect, Apter's requisites offer little empirical utility.

Even given the assumption of structural requisites, it appears that the explanatory power of Apter's paradigm is enhanced little, if any, by its inclusion. All that this assumption does is distinguish surviving systems from those that do not survive in terms of the former's performance (and the latter's non-performance) of all of the implied requisite functions. Since political scientists are, in general, concerned only with systems that have maintained themselves, this distinction is meaningless from an analytical standpoint. The assumption of requisites contributes nothing toward the identification and explanation of the differences among the various systems that do survive, and this is the central analytical concern of political science and comparative politics (Mayer 1972, p. 158).

Finally there is a certain teleological aspect of Apter's model that limits its ability to explain the process of modernization. Specifically, Apter, like Almond and Coleman before him, tended to represent the process of modernization in terms of the goals of the process. That is, most of his attention is directed toward describing the starting points of the process (e.g. his typology) and its end state, the modernized society, while saying little about the dynamics of the process by which a system moves from the former state to the latter. To list the elements of the desired *outcome* of a process is not to explain the process itself (Golembiewski et al. 1969, pp. 252–253). And since it is the *process of change* that is by definition the focus of development analysis, Apter's model can contribute little toward the realization of this central explanatory goal.

What may be termed a third instance of a functional approach to political development is contained in the work of the Social Science Research Council (SSRC). However, the framework with which they conducted their research was derived largely from Almond and Powell's *Comparative Politics: A Developmental Approach*. In essence the SSRC simplified and relaxed some of the analytical restrictions of Almond and Powell's model in order to allow a maximum amount of investigative freedom for the researchers in specific nations while still maintaining a general basis for the comparison and integration of the various findings.

In *Aspects of Political Development*, Lucien Pye summarized the approach employed by the SSRC. Briefly, political development is seen as the interaction of the processes of structural differentiation, the imperatives of equality, and the integrative, adaptive and responsive capacities of the political system (Pye 1966, pp. 45–47). Development, in terms of these three categories of variables, which together make up the *development syndrome*, occurs in response to one or more of six crises that systems must face in the course of becoming modern nation states. These crises are: (1) the identity crisis (i.e., nation building), (2) the legitimacy crisis, (3) the penetration crisis (i.e., state building), (4) the integration crisis, (5) the participation crisis, and (6) the distributive crisis. The particular pattern of a country's development will depend upon the sequence in which these crises arise and the ways in which they are resolved (Pye 1966, pp. 63–66).

Since this analytical scheme is intended as simply a guide to research and not a formal model, it is difficult to criticize it by the same criteria as were used above. However, the amount of "guidance" it can afford researchers is limited by the same conceptual problems that plagued Almond's model. Its lack of clear operational criteria means that the cross-cultural validity of any resultant findings must be extremely suspect, since different researchers in different countries have no basis upon which to evaluate the equivalence of their operational definitions. Relations between the elements of the syndrome are unspecified, and Pye's insistence on equating development with democratization (Pye 1966, p. 71) envelops the scheme in a cloud of ethnocentrism that must be avoided in scientific inquiry.

Dissatisfied with the largely descriptive and non-formal explanatory endeavors of the aforementioned studies, Fred Riggs attempted to construct a more coherent paradigm of political change (Riggs 1964). At a time when everyone was trying to devise some law-like statement of comparisons among nations, he developed a more structured concept of the "developing nation" when he proposed that all transitional societies go through the stage of what he called the "prismatic society." A prismatic society is one in which the social and political functions of institutions have been diffused but not yet integrated. Hence, the degree of development of a nation may be described and compared in terms of the extent to which its institutional functions have become rationalized and specialized.[4] Riggs defines political development as "a gradual separation of institutionally distinct spheres, and the differentiation of separate structures for the wide variety of functions that must be performed in any society" (Riggs in LaPalombara 1965, p. 122). He suggested that this is a rule of social change by which every society must be guided. As such, universal comparative theory, based on a clear conception of this common process, should be feasible. There are many who have chosen this "institutional specialization" concept as the unit of comparative inquiry, as we see from the works of Apter, Pye, Huntington, and Diamont.[5]

Riggs' framework suffers, however, from the fact that it fails to delineate the conditions that are both *necessary and sufficient* for changing from one state of affairs to another. Therefore, its value is restricted to its taxonomic utility since its explanatory and predictive capabilities have yet to be established.

Having discussed some examples of the functional approach to development, our task now should be to discern which criticisms appear to be common to all three examples and what problems can be said to be intrinsic to the functional mode of analysis in general.

One criticism that was alluded to above is the apparent ethnocentric character of the functions defined by all the authors. Almond and Coleman admit that their functional categories are derived from political systems in which structural specialization and functional differentiation have taken place to the greatest extent (Almond and Coleman 1960, p. 16). Apter's structural requisites and Pye's development syndrome (and his crises) appear to be of similar derivation. In so doing, these authors in effect deny the possibility that alternative differentiation patterns might evolve in contexts different from that of the Anglo-American democracies (Golembiewski et al. 1969, p. 254). It is in this sense that their conceptual schemes are ethnocentric and hence of dubious theoretical utility.

A second point that should be made is that all of these authors deal with "modernization" rather than political development in general. While this is not a criticism of their work, it should be noted because this fact limits the applicability of their findings to a certain historical period and set of international preconditions. That is, they might account for the "modernization" of "transitional" societies in an international (comparative) context in which the transitional societies are assumed to be moving toward the state of modern industrial nations. This assumption is no more plausible than assuming that India's tomorrow will be America's today. In short, their models are not universally applicable from a logical point of view, nor can they explain the development of "developed" (i.e., modern) societies.

Stage Theories of Development
Given the static bias of functional analysis, a number of scholars turned their attention to the construction of stage theories of development. In this manner, not only was the idea of change built into the theory, but qualitative changes could be represented, instead of the simple movement along a single dimension (such as increasing structural differentiation). Rostow (1960) proposed a five stage process of development as follows:

1. "traditional society": characterized by low levels of technology, a static, agrarian economy that is labor intensive.
2. "the preconditions of take-off": here, scientific discoveries (or the intrusion of the West) are translated into technological advances.
3. "take-off": self-sustaining economic growth is achieved through increased investment, industrialization, and the commercialization of agriculture.
4. "the drive to maturity": outputs begin to exceed the increased demand generated by population growth.
5. "mass consumption": the leading sectors of production shift to the production of durable consumer goods and service oriented activities.

The weakness of this model is that it is a theory of economic development, not political development; also, it is based largely upon one historical case (the U. S.) and is therefore time-bound and culture-bound.

Organski's (1965) stages of political development are similar to Rostow's and fall victim to the same criticisms. The stages of (1) primitive unification, (2) industrialization, (3) national welfare and (4) the politics of abundance are stages of economic growth again abstracted from the American case. The applicability of these two-stage theories to contemporary Third World nations is limited, as the value systems of these nations and the historical context of their developmental efforts are vastly different from those of the United States and the rest of the industrialized West.

Development and the Individual

Besides these grand theories that attempt to depict the development of entire political systems, there have been several works that focus upon the changes in individual attitudes, belief systems and more general world views that seem to accompany the societal transition to modernity. The attraction of this approach for the behavioralist is that it is more clearly and directly linked to changes in behavioral patterns because it does focus on the basic unit of behavior: the individual human actor. If developmental changes at the individual level can be accurately depicted in theory, then the broader systemic changes that occupied the structural functionalists become, in principle, explainable in terms of these individual level changes. Systemic changes—and especially the different patterns of such changes that so baffled the structural functionalists—can be accounted for in terms of the differing institutional matrices within which ostensibly universal patterns of individual development have occurred.

One of the earliest attempts at comparing different societies by a similar individual level conceptual framework is the work of Daniel Lerner (Lerner, 1958). Here, he used the concept of "empathy" or mobile personality as the common "yardstick" with which to compare and explain the developmental dynamics of several Middle Eastern countries. In other words, development was defined as the movement of individuals toward this personality characteristic. Lerner and his associates conducted a comparative study in Turkey, Egypt, Lebanon, Syria, and Iran. They found that there are regularities in the life situations of individuals in these countries, thus making possible "scientific" theory construction at a cross-cultural level of analysis. Although Lerner's general theory of modernization was not claimed to be a universally validated theory, his research suggested that the theory would be useful in affirming the universality of many specific propositions and hypotheses.[6] However, few of his hypotheses have been tested successfully in subsequent studies.

David McClelland, working from the assumption that economic development and modernization are ultimately explicable by the people's psychological motivations, particularly the *need for achievement*, attempted to assess various nations' development cross-culturally by comparing the content of children's books, taken here as a measure of the degree to which the culture is grounded on achievement-oriented values (McClelland, 1961). Here again, the author maintains that the direct relationship between achievement orientation and economic development may be suggested as an interesting hypothesis, but cannot as yet be enthroned as a proven theory.

A more ambitious comparative research project was conducted by Verba and Almond, culminating in the publication of *Civic Culture* in 1963. The project, also known as the "five nations study," attempted to compare the U.S., the U.K., Germany, Italy, and Mexico in terms of people's political perceptions and attitudes as revealed by survey research methods. While this work represents a much more serious attempt at systematic comparative research, the introduction of this work provoked considerable discussion and debate as to the meaningfulness and validity of their cross-national and cross-cultural comparisons.

These and other theorists who define political development in terms of individual predispositions appear to suggest that certain cultures are more "developed" than others, and individuals belonging to those cultures are assumed to be more developed than others who happen to be in cultural environments. As they specify the cultural attributes such as achievement orientation (McClelland, 1963), mobile personality (Lerner, 1958), participant behavior (Verba, 1963), associational sentiment (Pye, 1962), and instrumentality (Apter, 1965) as being the characteristic of development, they are simply describing what is known to be the Western Man. Thus, these individual-based conceptions of development can hardly contribute to a science that is expected to be universal and value-neutral.

DATA COMPILATION AND
EMPIRICAL GENERALIZATIONS

In spite of the persistent problems found in the various approaches introduced in the 1960s, young researchers who had no choice but to comply with behavioral expectations continued to demand more data rather than a more acceptable conceptual scheme with which to structure the use of their data. This type of demand has been as epidemic as the spread of computer techniques and statistical analysis methods. It has forced the comparativist to utilize extensively whatever qualitative data may be available, regardless of their linkages with theoretic terms. In order to comply with this demand, he was forced to compile the sort of numbers that were readily available.

In comparative research the compilation of cross-national data has involved an almost exclusive reliance upon aggregate data for comparative and international studies.[7] The growing use of massive volumes of data in comparative and international research has also necessitated the application of increasingly sophisticated statistical and other methodological techniques, thus giving the research output at least the appearance of universal generalizations. However, due to conceptual and theoretical clumsiness the contributions of such research were far from being valid or even convincing, despite their attempt at technical and methodological sophistication. For instance, several empirical studies on the conditions of democracy have come far short of reaching agreement as to what it takes to make democratic institutions work.[8] The validity of these studies utilizing cross-national comparative data has remained questionable as their generalizations have seldom worked out in reality.

As an important source of this validity problem, the problem of cross-national comparability of social and political indicators and measurements has received heightened attention by more alert researchers. Teune and Przeworski (1970), for example, introduced some possible means of conceptual renovation as they raised the question of comparability. By establishing "equivalence" and "shifting levels of analysis," we might be able to enhance the comparability of social indicators in some cases.[9] But the fundamental issue of establishing comparable units of analysis and measurement remains basically unresolved, even in conceptual and theoretical terms. When it comes to the reliability and representativeness (validity) of measurements and data, the current state of comparative and international generalizations might well be described as one of hopeless or at least persistent futility. One proposed way of restoring the cross-cultural comparability while still using comparative data is to utilize "longitudinal" analysis of historical data. This is essentially a "within system comparison," and it thereby avoids many of the problems inherent in equating measures across systems.[10] However, despite the apparent promise of this technique, the problem becomes as complicated as the cross-sectional comparative approach because the issue of longitudinal comparability emerges in addition to the unresolved problem of cross-sectional comparability: if there is a comparability problem between nations with different cultures and varying levels of "development," then there should also be the same problem in cross-time comparisons within the same unit of analysis. For instance, in comparing levels of communication, one might use the number of television sets as one measure, but the predominant means of communication in the past might have been radios and newspapers, and the meaning of these facilities as communications media may well have changed over time, thereby yielding little basis for comparison. This situation would be analogous to comparing a developing country with an industrialized society in terms of their relative communications achievement.

In spite of the unresolved and ever-puzzling problem of cross-cultural comparability, however, the need for cross-national comparison has steadily grown in breadth. The need for global yardsticks for comparing life situations is illustrated by the recent proposal for a Global Monitoring System which would facilitate comparative assessments of human rights practices.[11] Here again, the need for a common measurement in making comparative assessment is imperative; yet even the concept of human rights comes far short of achieving consensus on a universal definition, let alone specific indicators and measurements.[12]

In short, we find ourselves today almost conceding that a meaningful comparison of life situations cross-nationally and cross-culturally is unfeasible. Nonetheless, we are prevented from drawing this pessimistic conclusion by our increased desire to make universal comparisons in order to deepen our sociological understanding of an intricately woven global community. Unfortunately, our desire is unlikely to increase the feasibility.

COMPARING "LIFE SITUATIONS"

Toward a New Basis of Comparison
Much has been said about quantification, measurement, and indices of comparable indicators in the field of comparative and international relations during the behavioral era. Indeed, comparison has come to be conceived of as involving or leading to the sort of quantitative and uniform generalizations that enable us to talk about social and political objects in terms of "more or less." We notice this in the casual way in which terms such as *more* democratic, *more* developed, *more* industrialized, and *more* rational are used in the discipline. Here all nations and other units of analysis are placed in a comparative (and hence competitive) perspective where they are reduced to complexes of numerical values. These numerical values have successfully provided a powerful motivation for intense and continuous social and individual competition at all levels of social complexity. Individuals compete for higher appropriations of numbers (such as income) and nations compete for a superior position in various numerically-based hierarchies (such as GNP, military strength and the like). As the world becomes more intimately interactive in both the physical and cultural sense as a result of the sweeping phenomenon of industrialization, nations are competing more intensely for commonly valued economic goods.

As the limitation of world resources becomes more keenly felt, competition for the acquisition of such goods will become more intense and social conflict more probable. Supremacy in social as well as international competition will be decided solely by "who has how much"; and the who-has-how-much will not be known or agreed upon until a common comparative "yardstick" is worked out, a prospect that is not highly promising as discussed earlier.

Moreover, I reject the notion of universal comparison by quantitative standards only. Such a comparison has done more harm than good in enhancing the "quality" of life conditions. The common desire to maximize and universalize the process of industrialization, and the uncritical adoption of Western technology and other instruments for solving human problems have indeed accelerated the irreversible processes of urbanization and mechanization, but at a high cost. Widespread social dislocations and popular disillusionment have emerged as the all-too-frequent concomitants of rapid modernization in traditional societies. Indeed, they have become rich enough to build apartment complexes and plenty of high rise chimneys to demonstrate symbolically their great "achievement." But this has not come about without generating the notorious "ills" of industrialization. Many societies have become even more similar to each other, and even more are approaching (or at least aspiring to) uniformity. Old buildings—monuments to the uniqueness of traditional culture—are replaced with skyscrapers. Farmers are leaving their land and their extended kinship ties to migrate into cities. Crime rates in urban centers are increasing as rapidly as the population, both spurred by the influx of rural immigrants. More cars and factories are emitting their poisonous exhaust. Once-luxurious and rare commodities are mass-produced, and people everywhere stroll through the same Western style shopping malls in search of the same bargains. More startlingly, remarkably similar curricula are being introduced in schools all over the world, all of this assuring us of an even more competitive and homogenized lifestyle in the near future. And much of this pattern may be attributable to the largely uncontested myth of "the bigger, the better."

In response to the human and moral consequences of "the bigger, the better," an increasing number of social critics are proclaiming their slogan of salvation: "small is beautiful." This apparently humanistic movement seems to attract the largest number of sympathizers in the more advanced post-industrial societies.[13] It would certainly be premature to make any conclusive judgment on this desirable and hopeful movement, but if the notion of "small" is perceived only as being diametrically opposed to the quantitative concept of "big", the movement will probably not provide much in the way of solutions. Perhaps it will only provide some psychic satisfaction for those who lament the passing of the "good old days"; or it may excite some utopian thinkers who, like Saint Simon, Fourier, and Robert Owen long ago, insist that social self-management is not only desirable but also feasible. However, what is common in "the bigger, the better" and "small is beautiful" syndromes is their reference to size as being the criterion for appreciation. In this sense, they are not fundamentally different.

"Apples and Oranges": A Qualitative Comparison
Due mainly to the excessive concern with quantitative thinking, comparison is perceived to be possible, for example, only among apples, or among oranges. But, to pursue the metaphor, the possibility of comparing apples with oranges is ruled out by this definition. We in com-

parative studies have been led to believe that objects different in kind cannot be compared scientifically, and this principle has served to mandate our reducing everything to a uniform dimension of quality that allows comparison in terms of quantity. As a consequence, we have fooled ourselves into believing that we can make all oranges into apples and, further, that America is a huge delicious variety—the consummate apple; and Kunta Kinte's Mandingo tribal society by comparison is a pitifully shriveled, miserably rotten little apple. Thus, we seldom hesitate to define development and to rank countries by such measures as GNP, industrial output, and urbanization. Some even define development in terms of certain attitudinal and behavioral traits that are common only in selected Western societies.

When we eat apples, we tend to take it for granted that everyone else is and should be eating apples, and that we are better off than others, depending on the size or amount of apples we possess. We ignore the fact that there are fruits that can provide us what apples can. Yet pitiable is the undeniable fact that many people in the "non-apple eating" societies think that they need to change their dietary habits to achieve and maintain what the "apple-eaters" have, even if their physical metabolism is not prepared for apple consumption. Still worse, they keep eating apples even when they see that the apple is not necessarily the best fruit, even for the original apple-eaters themselves.

This apple-eating analogy may not appear so unreasonable when we observe what is occurring in the less developed societies, as well as what has happened in the post-industrial societies. Third World countries have been rapidly industrializing, and many of them are entering the threshold stage of industrial society. Such successful Third World development may be attributed to three decisive factors: technology transfer, abundance of human and natural resources, and the increasing economic reliance of post-industrial societies upon Third World nations.

People in industrializing Third World countries have undergone profound changes in their value systems in the direction of economic rationality and pragmatism. Technical training has become a much-desired educational commodity in societies where, traditionally, technical education was either nonexistent (in any formal sense) or held in low esteem. As their economies prospered, they were able to send trainees abroad and hire foreign technicians and teachers to transfer the advanced technology of the West. At the same time, they had natural resources with which to apply the newly available technology and a relatively inexpensive labor force to produce commodities that could compete favorably in international markets. Finally, and perhaps most important, the developed industrial societies gradually underwent an extensive change in their own economic structures when multinational corporate conglomerates emerged as the capstone of their (and the world's) economic systems. The multinational corporations have brought changes in the economic conditions of the world in general and Third World nations in particular. The Third World nations not only participate in the process of industrial production for the multinationals, but they provide the most important markets as well.[14] Thus, the development of a Third World economy is seen as a desirable factor for the sustained growth of developed societies, which forces all parties to maintain more cooperative economic relations with each other. Here the main beneficiary is the Third World, and it is hastily but uneasily reaping the fruits of modern society.

However, developmental changes in Third World nations, particularly in the form of industrialization and technological transformation, did not occur without the cost of cultural and social dislocations, the dislocations analogous to physiological disorders in man that follow a sudden change in dietary habit.

This critique of industrialization and modernization, however, should not be interpreted as being one-sided, for technological development has resolved many individual and social problems and has contributed to the improvement of life conditions. Improvement of health care by advanced medical technology, resulting in the prolonging of life expectancy and the reduction of infant mortality, and increases in literacy rates may be cited as examples of the desirable accomplishments of modernization and technological innovation. What deserves criticism is the tendency toward cultural uniformity, homogenization, and quantitative aspirations, while uncritically rejecting or altering traditional value systems in favor of this common "yardstick." Another deserving criticism is directed toward the behavior patterns of the people in the process of modernization in which every one is trying to get "apples", the fruit of Western society, resulting in more ruthless economic competition and social struggle.

What is even more tragic is the servile mentality of intellectuals both in Western and developing societies. Many intellectuals, particularly the comparativists, have long concluded that "apples cannot be compared with oranges," and that the only way of sustaining a comparative science is to find what is common in both fruits. In the absence of a common index, they believe that societies cannot be compared. As discussed earlier, such index construction has a long way to go. The way is not only long but fraught with obstacles. It is blocked because no one *concept* can retain the same meaning in different social and cultural contexts, and a sound and rich body of literature supports this rather pessimistic conclusion of "semantic empiricism" and even "epistemic empiricism."[15] A term—be it democracy, income, education, human rights, or any other social concept—needs to be given a "meaning" in order to become a useful concept; and "meaning" is given with reference to characteristic features in a specific context. Since this condition is endemic to social concepts, we must conclude that we simply don't seem to have the kind of concepts that the physical scientist uses in formulating physical laws.[16]

As I alluded earlier, the proposal to transcend quantity-conscious comparison was made not simply because such a comparison is unlikely or because we can set forth a more operable mode of comparison. Rather, my argument rests on the belief that we can compare oranges with apples as much as we can compare different apples or different oranges; and comparing apples and oranges would provide us with added dimensions and perspectives for comparative studies. Those who say that we cannot compare oranges with apples need only observe the housewife who rather routinely compares apples with oranges at the grocery store. Are we, who presumably are as intelligent and capable of abstract thinking as the housewife, conceding that we cannot develop an analogous logic of comparison while she goes on practicing such a logic so widely and so casually?

From Comparison of Things to Comparison of People: The Right Track

Returning to the episode of the housewife in the grocery store, when she chooses to buy oranges instead of apples, she is likely to have some reason. It could be that she has apples in her refrigerator or that she simply likes the freshly harvested oranges. In any event, she will compare the two fruits in terms of their relative *meaning* to her or her family, and the decision to buy oranges will indicate that she values oranges more than apples. Here, the comparison is in terms of the *human* conditions affected by the choices that are available. Thus, depending on the life situation of a particular choice maker at a given point in time, the same apple may be valued differently.

Likewise, a one-dollar bill may provide a varying range of goods and services for the enhancement of human existence in different societies depending on the functional value of the money in each. For instance, a man could get a haircut, shampoo and styling, a shave, a back massage, and even a shoe-shine for about a dollar in the country barber shop in China. For the same money, he could hardly have gotten even one side of his hair trimmed or one of his shoes shined in the United States. If the same service cost ten dollars in the U.S., the one dollar being used in China for that particular purpose should be considered equivalent to ten dollars in the U.S.

This idea of establishing equivalence is not new in the literature of comparative logic. What is newly emphasized here is the principle of using equivalent *human* situations or value objects as a comparative yardstick, not the instrumental mechanism of money. This is to say that comparing an apple with another apple should be done in terms of its relative utility to the apple consumer in a particular situation. Any number of objects can serve the same human purpose. Furthermore, any one object can fulfill a number of human purposes. An artist may view an apple primarily as a subject for a drawing. Hence he values the color and appearance of the apple rather than its taste or size. And to this artist, a smaller apple could well be more precious than a larger one. In this sense, there is no inherent meaning in the object of the apple itself; nor is any meaning of the apple held universally and constantly. This implies that any unit of a material resource can have a variety of meanings and significances depending upon its particular use in a given cultural context. Thus, its utility (even quantitative utility) should not be assumed to be constant, nor can it be carried over unaltered to a different social context. This would imply that a country with a greater GNP should not necessarily be regarded as a more *developed* nation. For this reason, I would submit that comparative studies ranking nations by aggregate indices of social and economic characteristics are grossly misleading, as these indices may be only spuriously related to the quality of human life conditions.

We should never forget that all social institutions and material resources that we exploit are to serve human beings, and their very *raison d'être* lies in their relationship with and utility to human beings.

When people are alienated, their resources and institutions are meaningless for them because they are not serving to enhance the quality of life. There is no business more urgent than that of putting human beings in the driver's seat where they belong.

Beethoven and Picasso: Another Dimension of Comparison

If someone were to ask you whether Beethoven or Picasso is greater, you probably would reply that the question is a meaningless one because there is little basis for comparison. You may be right. If our comparative units are like Beethovens and Picassos, comparative studies may well be considered impossible. If they truly are impossible, so be it. But more nonsensical things have happened in the area of comparative studies. Comparative analysts, preoccupied with the imperative of quantitative comparison, have busily engaged in comparing Beethoven and Picasso in terms of their weight, height, hair color, the size of their big toes, and so forth, omitting what is truly significant about them. Analysts have produced comparative statements on income, industrialization, occupation, urbanization, and consumption of petroleum in a number of countries. They have even developed correlations, regression coefficients, and a host of other impressive quantifiers. But what good are these "achievements" if they do not represent what is meaningful about different societies? It is deplorable to assume that America would become an India, should the values of her indices be reduced to the level of India's. We cannot assume that all there is to an individual is his income, occupation, formal education, his place of residence, and so forth.

However, avoiding or denying comparisons between Beethoven and Picasso does not provide a solution to the issue of comparability, although it may support the humanist provocation. As long as social objects—particularly humans—manifest qualitative differences, analogous to the case of Beethoven versus Picasso, some sort of comparative method is essential. Of course, they can be compared as apples with oranges in terms of perceived meanings. Thus, to a musician Beethoven might be considered the greater, and to a painter, Picasso. But we must not forget that there is a significant difference between the case of "apples and oranges" and the case of Beethoven and Picasso. The two men were great achievers, exceeding by far the average person's accomplishments. We do not consider the fruits to be the achievers in themselves, but means by which human achievement is made possible.

Here, I would submit that, if comparison must be made, human beings should be compared in terms of human achievements. Human achievement in this case ought not to be determined solely by popularity or material possessions. Rather, it has to reflect the transformation of human attitudes and behavior as well as the more tangible achievements that result from attitudinal and behavioral makeup. It is beyond the scope of this chapter to dwell on the issue of *measuring* human achievement, for it is not an easy issue to resolve. We need only to point out that several major attempts have been made to trace the pattern of human growth and that much more study needs to be done in this area. Attempts by J. Piaget (1952) in his assessment of cognitive development, Kohlberg (1969) in his proposition of stages of moral development, Erickson (1950) in his psycho-social theory of human development, and Maslow's (1954) need-hierarchy might be some examples of such relevant attempts. Beethoven and Picasso probably would be seen as great achievers according to most of these theories. And a great number of other musicians and painters might be rated at much lower levels of achievement.

Human achievement could be evaluated by the fulfillment of human potential in relation to the resources available to realize such potential. Hence Beethoven's achievement could be considered greater since he was not adequately provided with material resources and was later handicapped by deafness. If so, the developmental level of a society may as well be rated by the degree of actualization of the potentials that members of the community may possess in relation to a given level of resource availability.

SUMMARY

In accordance with the thinking of post-behavioralism in which resolving relevant *human* problems is singled out as being the most important task of political scientists, this chapter advances the proposition that comparing "life situations" ought to be done in terms of human situations themselves rather than material or institutional situations. This led to a critical review of some major trends in the field of comparative social inquiries. Our conclusion was that establishing a common yardstick (index) with which all societies may be objectively compared is simply an unrealistic aspiration, partly because of the somewhat unique nature of social concepts and behavioral sciences. Furthermore, I proposed that quantitative studies attempting to generate universal laws are not only unfeasible but, more important, morally and humanistically undesirable.

Having concluded that we need to radically reconceptualize the idea of "comparison," I attempted to show with specific examples that the concept may be expanded to include qualitative comparison as well. Such a new conception of comparison is conducive to dealing with human and social problems more intimately and is more feasible than the conventional quantitative mode of comparison.

Admittedly, much needs to be done by way of operationalizing the "qualitative comparison," and the present discussion did not go far in this direction. However, I would be content if I have contributed to the task of putting the practice of "comparing life situations" on the right track. How far the train will travel will depend on further efforts and studies, but a train on the right track and stationary seems better than a derailed train traveling in an unwanted direction.

FOOTNOTES

[1] For the nature of the behavioral revolution in political science, refer to David Easton, "Current Meaning of Behavioralism," in James C. Charlesworth, ed. (1967), pp. 11–31; also, Robert A. Dahl, "The Behavioral Approach," *American Political Science Review*, Vol. 55 (1961), pp. 767–772.

[2] David Easton, "A New Revolution in Political Science," *American Political Science Review*, Vol. 63 (1969), pp. 1051–1061.

[3] Ironically, it was none other than David Easton, known as a founding father of the behavioral revolution nearly a decade ago, who proclaimed the need for a new revolution of "post-behavioralism."

[4] The pattern of such transformations is discussed in his article, "Prismatic Society and Financial Administration," in *Administrative Science Quarterly*, 5 (June, 1960); also in F. Riggs (1964).

[5] Refer to D. Apter, "The Role of Traditionalism in the Political Modernization of Ghana and Uganda," *World Politics*, 12 (1960); L. Pye, "The Concept of Political Development," in *The Annals of the American Academy of Political and Social Science*, 358, 1–13 (1965); S. Huntington, "Political Development and Political Decay," *World Politics*, Vol. VVII, No. 3 (1965); and A. Diamant, "The Nature of Political Development," in J. Finkle and R. Gable, eds. (1966).

[6] Lerner in his postscript states that "we have not proven our theory of

modernization; we have only explained and exemplified the regularities it posits." (Lerner, 1958, p. 398).

[7] The first volume collecting comparative data on many indicators was B. M. Russell, H. R. Alker, Jr., K. W. Deutsch, and H. D. Lasswell, *World Handbook of Political and Social Indicators* (1964). The more recent version of this volume is C. Taylor and M. Hudson, *World Handbook of Political and Social Indicators*, 2nd ed. (1972). Also massive amounts of data have been compiled in A. H. Banks and R. B. Textor, *A Cross Polity Survey* (1964) and in A. H. Banks, *Cross Polity Time Series Data* (1971). Also noteworthy is the fact that there are numerous data banks throughout the country. Not to be overlooked is the public sector: The United Nations releases various kinds of statistics on a regular basis, as well as the World Bank, the State Department, and foreign government agencies.

[8] I found in an empirical analysis that different studies on conditions for democracy ended up ranking the same group of countries in a vastly different way, ranging from a rank-order correlation value of .04 to .97. See Han S. Park, "Socio-Economic Development and Democratic Performance: An Empirical Study," *International Review of Modern Sociology* (Autumn, 1976), pp. 349–361.

[9] For an excellent discussion on establishing "equivalence," see H. Teune and A. Przworski, (1970), especially Chapter 6.

[10] Flanigan and Fogelman made a concise and lucid discussion on the desirability of historical analysis; see their "Patterns of Democratic Development: A Historical and Comparative Analysis," in G. Gillespie and B. Nesvold, eds. (1971).

[11] For a symposium on the Global Monitoring System, see R. C. Snyder, C. F. Fermann, and H. D. Lasswell, "Global Monitoring System: Appraising the Effect of Government on Human Dignity," *International Studies Quarterly*, 20 (June, 1976); R. Young, "Toward a Global Monitoring System," *ISQ*, 20 (December 1976); also J. W. Hendricks, "The Problem of Outcome Evaluation: A Comment on the Proposed Global Monitoring System," *ISQ*, 20 (December 1976).

[12] For a concise discussion of these definitional problems of human rights, see H. C. Kelman, "The Conditions, Criteria, and Dialectics of Human Dignity: A Transnational Perspective," *ISQ*, 21 (September, 1977); also, Han S. Park, "Human Rights and Modernization: A Dialectical Relationship?" in *Universal Human Rights*, Vol. 2, No. 1, 1980.

[13] Works critical of the syndrome of "the bigger, the better" are numerous. To cite only a few: E. F. Schumacher (1973); R. A. Falk (1975); S. H. Mendlowitz (1975); Gerald and Patricia Mische (1977).

[14] A recent news release by the State Department commenting on American economic reliance on the less-developed nations states: "We are already dependent on those [less developed] countries as important markets for U.S. goods and services, as unique sources of certain imports, as the locus of profitable U.S. private investment, and as the recipients of mutually advantageous loans by U.S. banks . . . The U.S. has many reasons for encouraging the rapid growth and development of the LDCs [Less Developed Countries],

in addition to the obvious fact that—as they develop—they will provide larger markets for U.S. goods and services." (GIST released in August, 1978, by Department of State.)

[15] Both "semantic empiricism" and "epistemic empiricism" regard experiences as a determinant factor of concept formation as well as structure of knowledge.

[16] Among numerous references on the subjective nature of social inquiry, a few excellent sources may be cited: M. Weber (1949); E. Nagel (1961); K. Mannheim (1939).

REFERENCES

Almond, G. and J. Coleman, eds.
  1960   *The Politics of the Developing Areas* (Princeton, N.J.: Princeton University Press).
Almond, G. and G. B. Powell
  1966   *Comparative Politics: A Developmental Approach* (Boston: Little, Brown).
Almond, G. and S. Verba
  1963   *The Civic Culture* (Princeton, N.J.: Princeton University Press).
Apter, David E.
  1966   *The Politics of Modernization* (Chicago: University of Chicago Press).
Apter, David E.
  1968   *Some Conceptual Approaches to the Study of Modernization* (Englewood Cliffs, N.J.: Prentice-Hall).
Bill, James A. and Robert L. Hardgrave
  1973   *Comparative Politics: The Quest for Theory* (Columbus, Oh.: Charles E. Merrill).
Charlesworth, J., ed.
  1967   *Contemporary Political Analysis* (New York: The Free Press).
Erikson, E.
  1950   *Childhood and Society* (New York: W. W. Norton and Co., Inc.).
Falk, R. A.
  1975   *A Study of Future Worlds* (New York: The Free Press).
Finkle, J. A. and R. W. Gable, eds.
  1966   *Political Development and Social Change* (New York: John Wiley and Sons, Inc.).
Flanigan, William and Edwin Fogelman
  1967   "Functional Analysis" in James C. Charlesworth, ed. *Contemporary Political Analysis* (New York: Free Press).
Gillespie, J. V. and B. A. Nesvold, eds.
  1971   *Macro Quantitative Analysis* (Beverly Hills, Calif.: Sage Publications).

Golembiewski, Robert T.; William A. Welsh; and William J. Crotty
1969   A *Methodological Primer for Political Scientists* (Chicago: Rand McNally).
Goslin, D. A., ed.
1969   *Handbook of Socialization Theory and Research* (Chicago: Rand McNally).
Groth, Alexander J.
1970   "Structural Functional Analysis and Political Development: Three Problems," *Western Political Quarterly*, 23:3.
Hempel, Carl G.
1968   "The Logic of Functional Analysis" in May Brodbeck, ed. *Readings in the Philosophy of the Social Sciences* (New York: Macmillan).
Holsti, K. J.
Sept. 1975   "Underdevelopment and the 'Gap' Theory of International Conflict," *APSR*, 69:3.
Holt, Robert T. and John M. Richardson
1968   "Competing Paradigms in Comparative Politics," in Holt and Turner, eds., *The Methodology of Comparative Research* (New York: The MacMillan Co.).
Huntington, Samuel P.
Apr. 1970   "Political Development and Political Decay," *World Politics*
Apr. 1971   "The Change to Change," *Comparative Politics*, 3:3.
LaPalombara, J., ed.
1967   *Bureaucracy and Political Development* (Princeton, N.J.: Princeton University Press).
Lerner, D.
1958   *The Passing of Traditional Society* (New York: The Free Press).
Mannheim, K.
1939   *Ideology and Utopia* (New York: Harcourt, Brace and World, Inc.).
Maslow, A.
1954   *Motivation and Personality* (New York: Harper and Row Publishers, Inc.).
Mayer, Lawrence C.,
1972   *Comparative Political Inquiry: A Methodological Survey* (Homewood, Ill.: Dorsey Press).
McClelland, D.
1961   *The Achieving Society* (Princeton, N.J.: Van Nostrand Co.).
Meadows, D. H., et al.
1974   *The Limits to Growth* (New York: Signet Books).
Mendlowitz, S. H.
1975   *On the Creation of a Just World Order* (New York: The Free Press).
Mische, Gerald and Patricia
1977   *Toward a Human World Order* (New York: Paulist Press).
Nagel, E.
1961   *The Structure of Science* (New York: Harcourt, Brace and World, Inc.).

Organski, A. F. K.
1965   *The Stages of Political Development* (New York: Alfred Knopf).
Parsons, Talcott
1951   *The Social System* (New York: The Free Press).
Piaget, J.
1952   *The Origins of Intelligence in Children* (New York: W. W. Norton and Co., Inc.).
Pye, Lucien
1966   *Aspects of Political Development* (Boston: Little, Brown).
1962   *Politics, Personality, and Nation-Building* (New Haven: Yale University Press).
Riggs, Fred W.
1957   "Agraria and Industria—Toward a Typology of Comparative Administration" in William Siffin, ed. *Toward the Comparative Study of Public Administration* (Bloomington: Indiana University Press).
1964   *Administration in Developing Countries: The Theory of the Prismatic Society* (Boston: Houghton Mifflin).
Rostow, Walt W.
1961   *The Stages of Economic Growth* (Cambridge: Cambridge University Press).
Rustow, D. A. and R. E. Ward
1964   *Political Modernization in Japan and Turkey* (Princeton: Princeton University Press).
1967   *A World of Nations: Problems of Political Modernization* (Washington: Brookings Institute).
Schumacher, E. F.
1973   *Small is Beautiful: Economics as if People Mattered* (New York: Harper, Row).
Sutton, Frank X.
1963   "Social Theory and Comparative Politics" in Harry Eckstein and David Apter, eds. *Comparative Politics: A Reader* (New York: Free Press).
Teune, H. and A. Przworski
1970   *The Logic of Comparative Social Inquiry* (New York: Wiley Interscience).
Weber, M.
1949   *The Methodology of the Social Sciences* (New York: The Free Press).

Chapter II

DEFINING POLITICAL DEVELOPMENT

While the term "political development" has come to be the focal point of an entire body of literature in comparative political science, few terms remain as ambiguous in their usage as this one. Indeed, one might even say that political development theory remains one of the woefully "under-developed" areas of contemporary political science. Debate continues to rage in academic circles over such issues as to what specifically the term is supposed to refer, how broadly (or narrowly) it should be defined and with what purpose in mind (i.e., for purely descriptive analysis of Third World versus industrialized Western nations or for explanatory-predictive theories of political change). Indeed, many have even come to question whether political scientists at this point in time should continue to use it as a central, organizing concept in their attempts to deal systematically with the diverse problems induced by political change. Perhaps, they argue, political development is simply too broad a term to be defined in any precise and meaningful way; and therefore, we should abandon it as the focal point of our theories and concentrate instead on more concrete, narrow-range and theoretically manageable issues facing developing nations.[1]

Before taking a stand on this debate, we will examine some of the reasons for its emergence, and perhaps gain some insight into a proper strategy for resolving it. We can begin by pointing out that the continuing presence of criticism on the one hand and the ever-increasing use of the term political development on the other, may be attributed to

41

the paradoxical qualities implicit in the term itself; while the term appears to be universally applicable (nomothetic), its high level of generality allows almost unlimited variation in the conceptualization of the term.

"Political development," as a universally observable phenomenon, is particularly susceptible to the laws of scientific theory construction. Science, as an enterprise aiming at the construction of nomothetic (explanatory-predictive) theories, requires that the units of theory construction be conceptualizations of universally observable phenomena. Although there have been contending views of the meaning of political development, few would deny that every society is in constant change, and that "development" is a form of social change.[2] The requirement of conceptual universality is increasingly recognized by political scientists. Now most universities offering political development as a course tend to define it in terms of the process and dynamic of social and political change rather than the problems of a particular Third World region. While the problems of Asia, Africa, and Latin America may provide necessary data for the comparative study of the process of political development, the common issues of social change—such as integration, stability, and mobilization—constitute the basis of comparability in such a study, and thereby impart to it its explanatory-predictive power.

However, the conceptual universality of political development suffers from what might be termed its "operational diversity." A term that is so broad in scope thereby permits an almost limitless variety of definitions and conceptual schemes to be subsumed under the title "political development." The term needs to be defined in such a way as to give boundaries to that process about which a theory is to be constructed. However, as a theoretical construct, "political development" encompasses such a broad ranging process of social and political change that, for the purposes of theory testing, it can be indicated and measured only by an index of multiple concomitants. Since this index itself can be variously constructed depending upon the nature of the society (or societies) observed and the particular definition of the process that is used, a series of methodological problems emerge in the construction of such a theory, particularly with respect to its utility in making cross-cultural comparative analysis.[3]

In this chapter we shall examine the use of the term "political development" in order to more clearly specify these methodological problems, and thereby enable us to develop a set of criteria by which to define the term. These criteria should be such that, if the scientist observes them, his theoretical construct of the development process would be devoid of these particular methodological pitfalls.

SOME CRITERIA

The following set of criteria are formed by examining the concept from the perspective of the philosophy of science and in terms of the semantics of "development" itself.

Political Development as Ideal Type

Although a definition is commonly held to be a meaning subjectively assigned to a term, most scholars would agree that this idea of "subjective meaning giving" is not in itself a sufficient ground for definition.[4] As Kaplan (1964, p. 72) concisely states, a definition should also provide a set of terms *synonymous* as a set with the term defined so that the term and its set of descriptives are each replaceable with the other. In other words, a definition identifies the characteristic features that are *necessary and sufficient* to distinguish that term from all others. For example, a bird may be defined by listing all of its characteristic features, such as two-legged, feathered, warm blooded and so forth. But one can not say that bird is defined by simply indicating *some* of its characteristics, such as two-leggedness, that might be shared by other animals as well. The set of identifying characteristics must be sufficiently broad and informative to clearly define one and only one term.

This simple meaning of definition has seldom been carefully considered in defining the term political development, which needs to be defined in such a way as to delimit that process by which we are to construct an explanatory-predictive theory. Yet, as I noted in Chapter I, most definitional bases of contemporary developmental theories are merely partial descriptions of what is observed in the "Western" world. More specifically, they usually consist of descriptions of either "Western" man in terms of his personality traits—associational sentiment (Pye, 1963), empathy (Lerner, 1958), achievement orientation (McClelland, 1961), and secularism (Parsons in Mitchell, 1967)—or the institutional characteristics of economically advanced societies—bureaucracy (Eisenstadt, 1963), role-differentiation (Riggs, 1964), and social mobilization (Deutsch, 1961).

Definitions such as these have been criticized for being value-laden or Western biased. Furthermore, in defining political development in terms of the characteristics of certain selected (i.e. Western) societies, some preconceived definition (or at least perception) of development is unconsciously applied as a criterion for selecting the model society (or societies). In this sense, *a definition of development is bound to be used to define development.* As noted above, most contemporary studies of political development tend to view it as a *process* of social and political change. And while the economic achievements of many "Western" societies may in some sense represent some of the goals of nations that have only recently embarked upon this process, it is doubtful that "Western" society as a whole represents the fundamental ideal toward which less developed nations are focusing their developmental efforts. Holsti (1975, p. 829) notes that we have often confused the aspirations for better life with the assumption that everyone wants to adopt *all* Western institutions through Western forms of economic activity.

If a definition is to be derived through observation of selected real societies, the fact that a society is comparatively advanced economically does not necessarily mean that its political system is an ideal laboratory in which to observe the concomitants of a *politically* developed society. In the absence of causal links between economic and political development, it is conceivable that the goal of economic abundance could be achieved in a variety of political milieus. Therefore, one should avoid restricting observations to those economically advanced societies of the industrialized West.

In view of this problem with empirically derived definitions of political development, it may be suggested that a definition for the term be derived as an *ideal type.* The ideal type definition, as used here, is not intended as an accurate representation of reality, but instead highlights those aspects of reality that, for theoretical reasons, are deemed important. In this sense, it is used as a basis for comparison with that aspect of reality under consideration. That is, to what extent does the reality approximate the definitional construct abstracted from reality? A definition of development of this sort, then, is not intended as an isomorphic representation of the development process, but as a theoretical construct abstracted from that reality and emphasizing those aspects of the process that are felt, *a priori,* to have some importance in any attempt to construct a theory of development. In this manner, perhaps we can avoid the shortcomings, mentioned above, that seem characteristic of descriptive-empirical definitions.[5]

Political Development as "Explanandum"

Since definition may be viewed as subjective meaning-giving, any definition of a term is justifiable to the extent that it succeeds in identifying the term's unique *definiens* (concepts with which a definition is made). Therefore, there could be numerous definitions of political development without any particular one being inherently superior to the others, at least in terms of "subjective meaning-giving." Hence, we need some basis of selection, and toward this end, the criterion of utility might be suggested; the intended use of a definition should be an important consideration in determining of what it should consist.

If we acknowledge that scientific theory construction is the aim of social scientific inquiry, then it would follow that concepts should be defined in such a way as to be useful to the social scientist in carrying out this task. This task of theory construction, as alluded to earlier, may be viewed as an enterprise producing statements that are *universally applicable*, on the one hand, and *explanatory-predictive*, on the other. Although both of these ideas have been mentioned elsewhere in this chapter, a more thorough discussion of them seems warranted at this point in order to more fully explicate their implications for the defining of political development.

The question of universal applicability is widely acknowledged as a crucial methodological issue in empirical theory construction. The argument against the "ideologically biased" conception developed by Huntington (1965) and others is based upon the scientific requirement of universal generalization.

Perhaps the proliferation of such "Western" biased or culturally biased definitions in the "behavioral" era is attributable to the very premises of behavioralism itself. Social empiricism of the behavioralist orientation claims to be pursuing "factual" knowledge through observation. Yet, as alluded to earlier, it is just such an empiricism that provides the justifications for defining political development in terms of what is observed in the economically developed Western industrial societies. What is *observed* in these societies is generally considered developed, and the socio-cultural attributes observed in less affluent and agricultural societies are usually termed underdeveloped.[6] Such views violate the requirement of universal applicability. And it is in this sense that a certain value-neutrality be observed as a criterion for definition.

Along with the construction of nomothetic laws, explanation and prediction are commonly regarded as the core tasks of scientific inquiry. An adequate explanation requires logical conditions as well as empirical conditions; that is, as Hempel and Oppenheim suggest, an explanation consists of an *explanandum* (statements describing the phenomenon to be explained), *explanans* (statements which are adduced to account for the phenomenon), and a logical deduction linking the *explanandum* with its *explanans.*[7]

A definition of political development in this case becomes the *explanandum* that is to be linked to the antecedent conditions in such a way that the conditions are expected, according to a deductive framework, to produce the phenomenon called political development. Here, a definition of political development delineates the phenomenon to be explained. Hence, a utilitarian definition of political development for scientific analysis is one that, in boundarizing the phenomenon of political development, points to those conditions *(explanans)* from which a causal process (of political development) may be deductively ascertained. The Marxist theory of historical materialism and Rostow's theory (1952) of economic growth are examples of theories constructed for explanation and prediction; in defining their stages in the developmental process, these authors suggest the necessary and sufficient (i.e., causal) conditions for the achievement of each stage.

Development as an Organismic Concept
The term "development" has been most commonly associated with the organization of a living structure and the life processes. Thus, as Dale B. Harris (1957) maintains, a definition of development should involve as an essential aspect the idea of a living system. Now, if "development" is such an animate concept, "political" as an adjective of development should likewise be defined in terms of a living unit rather than a reified one.

A living being is one with inherent goals and propensities rather than assigned goals and imposed attributes. Whereas a reified unit such as a political system or a social system may seem to have apparent goals and functional imperatives, these goals are assigned or imposed upon the unit by its constituent human beings. Parsonian "functional requisites" (Parsons, 1949) that we discussed in the previous chapter are typical examples of such assigned goals. Thus, as long as development is a concept associated with living units, and "politics" is seen as a certain segment of the web of human interaction, "political

development" should not be defined in terms of institutional imperatives but a definition should be derived from the actual state of human
beings.

To say that the human being needs to be the unit of analysis is not
necessarily to endorse what is called "psychological reductionism." Obviously, political development is a macro-level process involving wide-
ranging types of social change. However, this fact does not preclude
defining political development in terms of human attributes and explaining it in terms of their changing dynamics. This apparently ambi-
valent suggestion is in fact the essence of the perspective known as
"methodological individualism."[8] The individual man in this case is
taken as the unit of analysis, but explanation of society as a whole is the
goal of analysis; that is, look at the individual to talk about society. No
pretense is made to solve the classical problem of the relationship of
the parts to the whole. It is simply assumed that the whole is explainable by the parts in the sense that there are no emergent qualities
of the whole that the individual cannot alter. The whole is exhaustively
accounted for by the sum of its parts. This obviously debatable perspective of methodological individualism might be minimally required
for any kind of inductive social study.

In spite of this, there are in the current literature frequent
definitions of political development which employ the institutional
setups of the political system as the *definiens*.[9] Although institutionalization may be an essential characteristic of modern society, institutions
themselves are not "living" units with inherent goals or motivations or
life cycles. Much of the sympathy for the "no growth" or "decay" concepts of social change and the widespread skepticism concerning the
idea of assumed progressive social change stems from the fact that the
human factor is largely neglected in the face of the growing use of
institutions as a unit of observation.[10] An institution such as a bureaucracy is neither inherently developed or underdeveloped; its development can only be judged as a function of its achieving its assigned
goals, goals which are assigned by human beings because they are
important to human beings. It should be emphasized that an institution cannot be evaluated in any other way, for it is a human invention
designed to pursue decidedly human needs.[11] For example, one would
not evaluate the institutional setup of a university as a way of determining the state of "development" of the educational system. It is what the
institution does, not what it consists of, that accounts for its "de-

velopment" or "underdevelopment." The obvious question, then, is what should an institution be doing? Of course, it should be doing what the human being, its inventor, designed it to do. What do we expect from the institution of government? This is a question we should confront in our attempt to define "political" and "development;" and the answer should focus upon the human goals that institutions are created to pursue, not upon the structural or other characteristics of the institution itself.

Without a doubt, developmental movements are affected by social institutions. An institution, as a human invention, is molded and characterized by the unique socio-cultural environment in which it occurs. Thus, it is not unreasonable to expect that different societies with different cultural and social attributes, while pursuing the same goal, are likely to formulate different forms of a given institution in order to maximize the institutional effectiveness in achieving this goal. That is, the criterion of maximum efficiency in pursuing social goals requires different institutional responses in different societies, even though the respective goals of the societies might be similar. A society's institutional arrangement is as much determined by the attributes of that society as it is dictated by the goals themselves. For instance, the extended family system in China might perform the function of socialization, much as the conjugal family does in the West. However, in addition, the extended family has also been known to perform various other functions such as economic production *and* distribution and educational advancement, that in the West require a multiplicity of secular institutions. Therefore, to compare the two family systems cross-culturally, to evaluate the respective levels of development is not only value-laden but also meaningless. By the same token, although both industrialization and agricultural enterprise may perform the same economic function (i.e., that of production), we cannot compare the two institutions cross-culturally because production may not be the only function performed by agriculture or industry in a given societal context. We must conclude, then, that as long as the same goal is pursued by different institutional means in different societies, institutions provide us with a poor unit of comparative analysis.

Development as Movement Over Time
As Dale Harris (1957, p. 3) emphatically maintains, development occurs only over time. More precisely, development occurs as movement

over time toward the desired state of the living structure. A development, then, may be described schematically as follows:

$$
\begin{array}{l}
\text{To} \underline{\hspace{6cm}} \text{Tn} \\
\qquad\quad \text{M1 - M2 - . . . -Mn} \\
\text{So} \underline{\hspace{6cm}} \text{Sn}
\end{array}
$$

where *To-Tn* represents the time needed for the state change from *So* to *Sn* which is accomplished incrementally through Movements *(M1 . . . Mn)*.

This structure of development implies, among other things, that a developmental theory should be designed to explain, as well as describe, the sequential movements that represent the change occurring between *So* and *Sn*. This means that it should account for the process of change in the same unit of analysis. Theories or definitions derived from and aimed at comparing various units of analysis at a given time would not be adequate for scientific inquiry into the developmental process.

As we survey the literature on political development, we find that until recently most theories intended to describe and explain the phenomenon of development have been formed by the comparison of different societies at a given point in time rather than by the comparison of different levels of development that occur in the same society at different points in time. For example, economic growth, perhaps the most common yardstick of development, has primarily been compared cross-culturally with the apparently meaningless measurements of GNP per capita, proportion of industrial production, and the like. It would seem much more meaningful in this case to measure the *rate* of economic growth within the same society.[12]

Then, it might be suggested, as a rule for development theory construction, to consider the rate as well as magnitude of change in the same unit of analysis.

Development as a Stage Concept

A movement in the process of development represents an incremental progression toward the achievement of a goal. One way to represent movement in this manner is through a stage theory of development. This seems warranted for a number of reasons, especially when it is "political" development that is the focus of the theory.

From a purely semantical perspective, since the development movements are incremental, the idea of a stage is a useful means of designating each of the increments in the sequential chain.

Furthermore, as concerns specifically "political" development, we must keep in mind that political development is an ongoing process. While a society may achieve its previously designated political goals, this does not mean the developmental process has been completed. Rather, it then becomes the task to formulate new goals and resume the developmental process which aims at their attainment. Here, a stage theory might be useful in that the stages could be used to designate each of the sets of goals, the sequential achievement of which constitutes the process of political development.

Unfortunately, however, not many theories concerning political development deserve to be called stage theories. There are several theories that suggest categories of development including John Kautsky's developmental categories (Kautsky, 1962) and Edward Shils' typology of transitional societies (Shils, 1962). In the strict sense of stage theory, no contemporary work, with the possible exception of Rostow's *Process of Economic Growth,* can equal Marxism as being a true "stage" theory. Excluding Rostow's work on the basis of its exclusive economic concern, Organski's work (1968) may be the best example of a stage theory of political development. However, as we saw earlier, it also suffers from a number of substantive and methodological problems.

A stage theory should not only maintain clear-cut boundaries between stages, but each stage upon its completion should provide the **necessary** and **sufficient** conditions for moving into the next stage. Put differently, a stage, when fully realized, should be able to *produce* the subsequent stage. Neither a genetic breakdown of various time periods for classificatory purposes nor a typology of development constitutes a stage theory of development. While Marxist stage theory incorporates the notion of inevitable causality into its logic of development, Organski's stages are much more flexible as the author admits:

> There is nothing inevitable about the stages here set forth, but it is striking that in all the world's many nations development has been in the same direction: toward industrialization, higher productivity, higher liv-

ing standards; toward political complexity, political efficacy, and increased dependence upon the state (Organski, 1968, p. 23).

Although the stages set forth by Organski—i.e., (1) primitive unification, (2) industrialization, (3) welfare state, and (4) abundance— appear to describe the historical pattern of growth of some Western societies, they fail to form the stage theory that we need for scientific analysis. First of all, Organski bases his theory upon a Western biased definition in which economic development is treated as being synonymous with political development. Second, he fails to account for the mechanism of transition from one stage to the next. Third, he chooses not to recognize the sequential characteristics of the process of change, thus failing to construct a true stage theory. And finally, like Marx and Rostow, he fails to account for the development of the "developed society": what after affluence? Economic abundance may indeed be what every society desires, but the abundant life style does not stop the society and culture from changing: witness the rapidly changing North America and other post-industrial societies.[13]

SUMMARY

We have discussed some of the problems that confront the researcher in defining political development. The crucial definitional criteria have been identified within the perspectives of the philosophy of science and semantics. They may be summarized as follows:

1) To satisfy the requirements of a definition, a definition of political development should identify the unique features of the terms that are necessary and sufficient to distinguish it from all other terms. An adequate definition is one in which the *definiens* and *definiendum* are mutually replaceable.

2) The type of society defined as developed or underdeveloped needs to be an ideal type in the Weberian sense, in which the nature of the society should be determined as a hypothetico-deductive construct rather than an empirically derived description of the observed society.[14]

3) A definition, as the initial stage of scientific theory construction, needs to be made in such a way as to facilitate the formulation of explanatory-predictive laws. In order for the explanation of development to be feasible, the developmental unit should be an entity that has inherent motivations toward the achievement of goals. Thus, a

human, rather than an institution, might be preferred as a unit of analysis.

4) Since scientific inquiry is a nomothetic enterprise, a definition should be universally applicable; it should define the developmental process as it occurs in all possible social settings.

5) The term "development" originated as a description of structural changes in living organisms, and it has commonly been applied to living systems. This suggests, as does criterion 4, that human beings need to be the unit of analysis in a developmental theory and that, therefore, the definition of political development should be in human terms.

6) The term "development" implies a type of change over time. Hence, an adequate theory of developmental process should be capable of explaining the mechanism involved in this change. This necessitates the use of longitudinal analysis of the same unit over time, rather than cross-cultural comparisons of different units at fixed points in time.

7) A developmental change over time involves various movements, incrementally proceeding toward certain goals. These increments can best be represented as stages in a process, rather than categories or types that are minimally linked in a causal sequence. Hence, a stage theory appears to be the most appropriate kind to account for political development, and the definition of development should be such as to permit this.

8) A stage theory should not only spell out the boundaries of stages but it should clarify the conditions for transition from one stage to another. This is minimally required if development is to be depicted as a sequential process of change.

9) In order to be nomothetic, a stage theory should account for the further development of what have been inappropriately termed "developed" societies. Here, some type of cyclical theory might be suggested as a more powerful one than a linear progressive theory under the assumption that development of human society is not to be terminated.

Admittedly, it is a difficult task for any definition of political development to meet all the criteria discussed above. But having a set of acceptable rules for an adequate conceptualization of the term will be helpful not only in developing such a conception but also in refining and assessing the leading current definitions (Appendix).

FOOTNOTES

[1] For a concise discussion on the relevance of political development to political science, see Karl von Vorys (1967).

[2] Helio Jaguaribe (1973, pp. 195–206) makes a systematic assessment of the leading views of the meaning of political development.

[3] Some of the methodological problems, particularly the problem of comparability, are lucidly discussed by Przeworski and Teune (1970, Chapters 3 and 6).

[4] References on the meaning of definition are unlimited. For illustrative purposes the following works may be cited: Abraham Kaplan (1964, pp. 72–73), May Brodbeck (1968, pp. 3–6), Alan C. Isaak (1969, pp. 59–77).

[5] This suggestion concurs with David Apter's view (1973, pp. 3–17) that a "normative-structural" or "normative-behavioral" research needs to be conducted for the process of modernization-development.

[6] The real problem of Western biased definitions, however, does not lie in the apparent moral prejudice implied in identifying the Western life style as developed; rather a bias itself violates the rules of science. A definition with an Eastern or Confucian bias might generate even greater discontent among Western scholars.

[7] They present a useful diagram to show the procedure of explanation. See Carl G. Hempel and Paul Oppenheim (*Philosophy of Science*, XV. pp. 135–175).

[8] For a concise discussion on methodological individualism, see J. Watkins (1957) and May Brodbeck (1968, pp. 280–303).

[9] Jaguaribe (1973, pp. 201–202) discusses some of such institutionally oriented definitions of political development when he assesses Deutsch, Pye, and Huntington. One might as well include Weiner (1965), Riggs (1968), and Diamant (1966).

[10] For a discussion on the human dimensions of political development, see M. Sibley (1966), R. Heilbroner (1974), C. Sederberg (1974), D. Goulet (1968, 1973), K. J. Holsti (1975), and most of Barbara Ward's works.

[11] For an example of such an interpretation of social institutions, see J. O. Hertzler, (1946, pp. 4–5) in which the author states: "Social institutions are purposive . . . formed . . . to satisfy individual wants and social needs bound up with the efficient operation of any plurality of persons." An applicliation of such institutional theory to the American society is made by Don Martindale (1960).

[12] Such concern about the use of historical data is becoming increasingly widespread as the inadequacies of earlier abstract models of political development become more apparent. Almond (1970) and Rustow (1970), for example, have both acknowledged that the need for blending earlier models and applying them to sequences of historical events, carefully noting differences in the timing and the rates of change. For an application of such a rate of change concept to a comparative analysis, refer to my work (1976).

[13] It is this apparent "dead-end" assumption built into many development theories that Huntington (1965, 396ff), Eisenstadt (1964), and Riggs (1968), among others, were critical and resentful of.

[14] For the concept of "ideal type," see Don Martindale (1963). For Max Weber's original conception of the term, refer to Max Weber (1949).

APPENDIX

What is Political Development?

Almond, G. (with G. Powell, 1966, p. 105)
"the increased differentiation and specialization of political structures and the increased secularization of political culture."

Apter, D. (1968, p. 2)
"a process which affects choice. . . . The modernization focus helps to make sense of the choices likely to be at our disposal."

Deutsch, K. W. (1961, p. 102)
"Social Mobilization (equivalently used with development) is the process in which major clusters of old social, economic, and psychological concomitants are eroded or broken and people become available for new patterns of socialization and behavior."

Diamant, A. (1966, p. 92)
"a process by which a political system acquires an increased capability to sustain successfully and continuously new types of goals and demands and the creation of new types of organizations."

Dorsey, J. (1963, p. 320)
"the changes in power structure and processes that occur concomitantly with changes in energy conversion levels in the social system, whether such conversion levels change primarily in their political, social, and economic manifestations or in various combinations of the three."

Eisenstadt, S. N. (1968, p. 184)
"The capacity of modern society to adapt itself to continuously changing demands, to absorb them in terms of policy making, and to assure its own continuity in the face of continuous new demands and new forms of political organization."

Goulet, D. (1968, p. 299)
"a crucial means of obtaining good life."

Huntington, S. (1965, p. 387)
"the institutionalization of political organizations and procedures."

Lerner, D. (1958, p. 50)
"Modern society is participant in that it functions by consensus."

Levy, M. (1965, p. 65, in Masannat 1973)
considers "any society more developed the greater the ratio of inanimate to animate sources of power and the greater the extent to which human efforts are multiplied by the use of tools."

Organski, A. F. K. (1968, p. 7)

"increasing governmental capability in utilizing the human and material resources of the nation for national goals."
Pye, L. (1966)
"the capacity to maintain a certain level of public order, to mobilize resources for a specific range of collective enterprises, and to make and efficiently uphold types of international commitment."
Riggs, F. (1965 in LaPalombara, 1965, p. 122)
"a gradual separation of institutionally distinct spheres, the differentiation of separate structures for the wide variety of functions that must be performed in any society."

BIBLIOGRAPHY

Almond, Gabriel A. (with G. Powell) (1966). *Comparative Politics—A Development Approach.* Boston: Little, Brown.

————— (1970). "Determinancy—Choice, Stability—Change: Some Thoughts on a Contemporary Polemic in Political Theory," *Government and Opposition,* Vol. 5, No. 1 (Winter 1969–70), pp. 22–40.

Apter, David E. (1968). *Some Conceptual Approaches to Modernization.* Englewood Cliffs, N.J.: Prentice-Hall.

————— (1973). "Norms, Structure, and Behavior and the Study of Political Development," in Nancy Mammond, ed., *Social Science and the New Societies.* East Lansing, Michigan: Social Science Research Bureau, Michigan State University, pp. 3–17.

Brodbeck, May (1968). "Methodological Individualism: Definition and Reduction," in her reader *Readings in the Philosophy of the Social Sciences.* New York: The Macmillan Co., pp. 280–303.

Deutsch, Karl W. (1961). "Social Mobilization and Political Development," *American Political Science Review* 55, pp. 493–514.

Diamant, Alfred (1966). "The Nature of Political Development," in Jason L. Finkle and Richard W. Gable, eds., *Political Development and Social Change.* New York: John Wiley.

Dorsey, John T., Jr. (1963). "The Bureaucracy and Political Development in Viet Nam," in Joseph LaPalombara, ed., *Bureaucracy and Political Development.* Princeton, N.J.: Princeton University Press.

Easton, David (1965). *A Framework for Political Analysis.* Englewood Cliffs, N.J.: Prentice-Hall.

Eisenstadt, S. N. (1963). "Problems of Emerging Bureaucracies in Developing Areas in New States," in Bert F. Hoselitz and Wilbert E. Moor, eds., *Industrialization and Society.* Paris: UNESCO.

————— (1964). "Breakdowns of Modernization," *Economic Development and Cultural Change,* XII, pp. 345–367.

————— (1968). "Theories of Social and Political Evolution and Development,"

56   *Han S. Park*

The Social Science: Problem and Orientations. The Hague: Mouton.
Goulet, Denis (1968). "Development for What?," *Comparative Political Studies,* Vol. I, No. 2, pp. 295–312.
——— (1971). *The Cruel Choice: A New Concept in the Theory of Development.* New York: Atheneum.
Harris, Dale B. (1957). "Problems in Formulating a Scientific Concept of Development," in his reader, *The Concept of Development.* Minneapolis: University of Minnesota Press.
Heilbroner, Robert (1974). *An Inquiry into the Human Prospect.* New York: Norton.
Hempel, Carl G. and Paul Oppenheim. "Studies in the Logic of Explanation," *Philosophy of Science,* XV, pp. 135–175.
Hertzler, J. O. (1946). *Social Institutions.* Lincoln: University of Nebraska Press.
Holsti, K. J. (1975). "Underdevelopment and the 'Gap' Theory of International Conflict," *American Political Science Review,* Vol. LXIX, No. 3, pp. 827–839.
Huntington, Samuel A. (1965). "Political Development and Political Decay," *World Politics,* 17, pp. 386–430.
Isaak, Alan C. (1969). *Scope and Method of Political Science,* Homewood, Ill.: The Dorsey Press.
Jaguaribe, Helio (1973). *Political Development.* New York: Harper and Row.
Kaplan, Abraham (1964). *The Conduct of Inquiry.* San Francisco: The Chandler Publishing Company.
Kautsky, John H. (1962). *Political Change in Underdeveloped Countries.* New York: Wiley.
LaPalombara, Joseph, ed. (1965). *Bureaucracy and Political Development.* Princeton, N.J.: Princeton University Press.
Lerner, Daniel (1958). *The Passing of Traditional Society.* New York: The Free Press.
Levy, Marion J., Jr. (1965). "Patterns (Structures) of Modernization and Political Development," *The American Academy of Political and Social Science* 358, pp. 30–40.
Martindale, Don (1960). *American Society.* New York: D. Van Nostrad Company.
Masannat, George S., ed. (1973). *The Dynamics of Modernization and Social Change.* Pacific Palisades, California: Goodyear Publishing Company.
McClelland, David C. (1961). *The Achieving Society.* New York: The Free Press.
Organski, A. F. K. (1965). *The Stages of Political Development.* New York: Alfred Knopf.
Park, Han S. (1976). "Socio-Economic Conditions for Democratic Performance," *International Review of Modern Sociology,* Vol. 6, No. 2, pp. 349–361.
Parsons, Talcott (1949). *Essays in Sociological Theory: Pure and Applied.* Glencoe: The Free Press.

Przeworski, Adam and Henry Teune (1970). *The Logic of Comparative Social Inquiry.* New York: Wiley—Interscience.

Pye, Lucian (1963). *Politics, Personality, and Nation Building.* New Haven, Conn.: Yale University Press.

———— (1966). *Aspects of Political Development.* Boston: Little, Brown.

Riggs, Fred W. (1963). *Administrations in Developing Countries.* Boston: Houghton Mifflin.

———— (1968). "The Dialectics of Developmental Conflict," *Comparative Political Studies,* Vol. I, No. 2, pp. 197–228.

Rostow, W. W. (1952). *The Process of Economic Growth.* Cambridge: Cambridge University Press.

Rustow, D. (1970). "Transitions to Democracy," *Comparative Politics,* Vol. 2, No. 3.

Sederberg, P. C. (1973). "The Betrayed Ascent: Modernization and Political Development in a 'No Growth' World," unpublished paper presented at the Southern Political Science Association Convention in New Orleans.

Chapter III

HUMAN NEEDS AND POLITICAL DEVELOPMENT:
A PARADIGM

POLITICAL DEVELOPMENT DEFINED

Political development may be defined in terms of the capacity of the political system to satisfy the changing needs of the members of the society.[1] This definition is proposed as one that will satisfy the definitional criteria for political development that were discussed in the previous chapter. First of all, the universal presence of human needs and the continuous effort on the part of mankind to satisfy these needs appear to be non-culture bound and non-time bound. More important, these phenomena may be said to be common to members of the "underdeveloped" as well as the "developed" society. Further, this definition might allow us to capture the important qualitative dimensions of developmental changes in that, during the course of development, the changes in human needs referred to in the definition may be analytically defined as being of a qualitative nature.

As for the criterion of scientific utility, this can be assessed only after the paradigm has been formulated and applied. Only then can we determine whether our definition enables us to develop a paradigm with which we can attempt to explain and predict the phenomena of political development. I shall turn now to the task of building such a paradigm, and to the extent that it meets the criterion of scientific utility, we can say that it has theoretical value.

58

ASSUMPTIONS

The proposed paradigm, as is the case with any paradigm in what Kuhn (1962) terms "normal science," presupposes a set of assumptions and conditions. The validity of these presuppositions may be debatable, and some may be time-bound, thus necessitating the constant re-evaluation of their validity. Nevertheless, they are assumptions necessary for the deductive structure of the proposed paradigm and are claimed to be valid in light of contemporary society and politics.

Assumption 1: Man behaves in such a way as to conscientiously and constantly pursue the optimum satisfaction of his needs.

This assumption is consistent with the much debated yet widely utilized economic conception of human rationality (Friedman, 1953). A more fundamental justification for this assumption might be found in the common definition of human behavior itself as being goal-oriented action. In addition, however, we will need to assume the presence of some structure of human needs as being a species-wide characteristic if we are to formulate laws and theories explaining human behavior from a developmental perspective and at a cross-cultural level. A further discussion on this assumed universality of the structure of human needs will be presented later.

Assumption 2: At any given point in time a society's developmental tasks may be determined as a function of the then-dominant needs of its individual members.

This assumption, in congruence with the perspective of "methodological individualism," defies any reification of a society or social institutions; the "whole" is explainable by its parts, and any emergent quality of the collective unit of society—such as General Will (Rousseau, 1762) or Social Fact (Durkheim, 1938)—is not recognized. This would also imply that the state of human nature, insofar as the pursuit of individual need satisfaction is concerned *(Assumption 1)*, is considered constant regardless of whether one is a part of a group or an independent actor.[2]

Assumption 3: The legitimacy of government (and politics) lies in its contribution to enhancing people's need-satisfaction.

Thus, a political system (in terms of regime type and institutional characteristics) changes, at least in the long run, in such a way that the emergent needs of the people (or, in practice, the ruler's interpretation of public needs) may be most effectively met.

This assumption seems plausible in view of the consensus among virtually all contemporary ideologies on seeking the ultimate foundations of legitimacy in the consent of the ruled. Unlike the ancient and medieval doctrines in which different regimes sought different bases of political legitimacy—some in the virtue of the Philosopher King and others in the name of Divine Providence—all contemporary governments since the inception of the Lockean principle of Social Contract have sought the consent of the people as the ultimate reservoir of political power.

This assumption is also consistent with some leading theories of politics, including Easton's view (1964, Chapter 8) that it is the ability of the system to survive by responding to changing demands that allows it to persist. In terms of the Eastonian systems model, we may posit that "support" as the basis of legitimacy is generated as a function of the regime's capacity to meet people's *demands*, i.e., the expression of their needs. Roland Pennock (1965, p. 420) has even more directly suggested that the goal of government and the political system is the provision of political goods to satisfy human needs. It is the fulfillment of needs that makes the policy valuable to man and gives it its justification in the eyes of the public. On this basis, we suggest that political legitimacy and, therefore, regime stability, are analytically determined by the difference in amount between support and demand. Thus, a legitimacy crisis occurs when the level of demand exceeds that of support.

THE STRUCTURE OF HUMAN NEEDS

For the incremental and conscientious pursuit of human needs (*Assumption 1*), man is likely to have his needs hierarchically ordered on the basis of their sense of urgency and desirability. As alluded to earlier, such an orderly pursuit seems to be implied by the definition of behavior itself: i.e., goal-oriented action. Some goals are more urgent than others, and we can expect these to be pursued prior to the pursuit of other, less urgent goals. The concept of preference ordering (Friedman, 1953) is a more formal version of this idea. At any rate, in view of our emphasis upon the qualitative dimension of the concept of development, some structure of human needs must be assumed in the interest of explanatory-predictive theory concerning the developmental dynamics of human behavior.

Conforming to most of the basic premises underlying Maslow's (1954) conception of the "hierarchy of human needs," as well as the psychological perspectives of cognitive development, we suggest here a four-fold hierarchical structure of human needs. They are (1) survival, (2) belongingness, (3) leisure, and (4) control.

The hierarchical nature of the order in which these needs are pursued is seen in the fact that not until one level of needs has been fairly substantially and continuously satisfied will the needs of the next level emerge as the primary motivational basis of behavior. Thus, the organism is dominated and its behavior organized by the lowest, in the hierarchy levels of needs, that is felt (consciously or unconsciously) to be at present inadequately satisfied.

Each of these four levels of human needs will now be explicated more fully, and in so doing, we hope the incremental and progressive nature of the process by which they are pursued will become more readily apparent.

(1) *Survival:* Without necessarily adhering to Social Darwinism, it may be accepted as an axiom that all living beings including humans *want* to stay alive. This need constitutes more than just a conscious choice to survive: it appears to be inherent in human nature, and thus, borders on the instinctive. It is needless to say that the emergence of all other human needs is contingent upon the presence of conditions for survival. Because most people value survival so highly, as Lenski (1966, p. 37) maintains, anything that facilitates survival is also valued highly. Maslow's physiological and safety needs are considered essential, and when denied become demanding of the individual's attention because they are the necessities for survival.

If, however, mere physical survival were the only and ultimate desire of humankind, we might be able to eliminate many social and political problems. But, unfortunately, humans want not only to survive but to survive "well." In this desire to survive "well," humans manifest additional needs.

(2) *Belongingness:* Once the chances of physical survival are believed to be good, a human being is expected to seek others with whom to identify. Ever since Aristotle's description of man as a social animal, many studies have verified the social orientation of human nature. This disposition may be termed the need for love and affection (Maslow,

p. 1957) or "associational sentiment" (Pye, p. 1965), but in some form the desire for subjectively meaningful interpersonal relationships exists as a basic human need, which is the force organizing the behavior of most people at a very early stage of human development.

(3) *Leisure:* As severe limitations of environmental resources could pose a direct threat to both primitive survival and the maintenance of basic levels of socialization, humans desire to maximize control over the environment in terms of the ability to extract necessary material resources from nature. But once having acquired sufficient resources to ensure survival and socialization, the human disposition shifts to the desire for a leisurely mode of living. A leisurely lifestyle not only requires free time but also involves the consumption of material goods in amounts beyond what is necessary for mere physical survival. The desire to have a longer weekend, to ride in an automobile instead of on a bicycle, to have an automatic dishwasher, a backyard swimming pool rather than going to the public pools, and the desire to extend paid vacations are all appropriate examples of the human disposition for leisure. These types of consumption patterns are dictated by one's "appetites" and not by the biophysical imperatives of survival or even the pressures for social esteem.[3]

(4) *Control:* As man possesses time and material resources and begins to manage a leisurely life, he will become preoccupied with the desire to maintain a "superior" life, superior primarily to other individuals. At this point, man will become more self-conscious about his social status, or at least such considerations will become a more salient aspect of his motivational life.[4] The subjective feelings of relative deprivation with respect to status values might be only marginally important to a person whose primary motivations are to survive. But a status-conscious person's social behavior is easily dictated by his sense of relative achievement in his community. The desire to own material goods symbolic of high social status is evident in such a person.

In this sense, this kind of material consumption associated with the desire for social control or self-esteem is the kind of consumption that might be seen as being what Veblen (1899) termed "conspicuous consumption." Consumers in economically advanced industrial societies might be more accurately described as such *conspicuous consumers,* whereas the material *needs* of peasants in agrarian communities, although similarly stemming from a desire for "material" goods, would be characterized more in terms of seeking such goods for the purpose of physical survival. We can distinguish between the two kinds of material goods more readily by recognizing that the goods, such as diamonds sought for the purpose of self-esteem or "social control," attain their value mainly from their scarcity and from the social status that is attributed to their possessor, whereas the goods, such as food, needed for survival are always wanted irrespective of their availability. The latter are valued in themselves rather than as the means to the attainment of some other social or interpersonal value.

This "social control" desire may be interpreted as a desire to win fixed-sum competitions. Social status is a relative value so that winning by some necessitates losing by others.[5] It is in this sense that we can say this desire may be morally undesirable but empirically undeniable. As Thomas Hobbes observed, man is a very rare animal with the instinct for killing. Even worse, only man kills not merely for survival but for "glory." With enormous capacity to control the environment, contemporary man suffers even more complicated social and political problems than ever before, these having arisen precisely due to his desire to extend the realm of his control to include other human beings. As Martindale (1962, p. 42) observes:

> More rarely the very abundance of nature places strain on society. Partners who have lived together during adversity find that success destroys what hard times does not.

THE INCREMENTAL PROGRESSION OF HUMAN NEEDS

It is necessary, at this point, to clarify our contention that these four common needs represent the incremental stages in a structure of human needs. Further, they are distinct from one another not simply in quantitative terms of the *amounts* of values required for their satisfaction, but also in terms of the qualitative nature of each need: that which is required for any one need's satisfaction is qualitatively different from that which is required for the satisfaction of any other need. No additional amount of food, beyond survival requirements, will serve to satisfy the emergent belongingness needs of the individual.

To further illustrate the developmental nature of this process of need fulfillment, similar stages in the growth of a child from infancy can be discerned as an analogical representation of these broader levels of human needs. As an infant, a child instinctively seeks the nourishment that is necessary for its survival. Thus, this first stage represents the most fundamental of human needs—survival.

Furthermore, it cannot be said to be a culturally bound trait that a newborn baby will usually sleep (a sign of physical satisfaction) when food and shelter are adequately provided, and the child will cry when such needs are not met. Before long, however, the same child will not be fully content with food and comfortable physical surroundings alone. He will soon desire the presence of other persons such as his mother and will demonstrate a desire to belong to groups—initially the family. It is at this stage of human growth that one seeks to develop an identity in relation to other human beings.

As the child feels physically comfortable and psychologically secure, he or she will demand and reach out for toys. Insofar as a child's desire for toys is concerned, there appears to be no cultural exception; however, where an American child may want a Superman action figure a Vietnamese child may desire to play with a toy gun to shoot "American imperialists." When a child plays with a toy, he demands to be left alone, indicating the need for free time.[6] And although a child is initially satisfied with the toys he has, as he develops extra-familial relationships with other children, he starts to compare his toys with theirs and to conclude that he needs more and better toys. This corresponds to the fourth level of human needs, in which competition arises over social and material values: the child wants to have the most and the best toys in the neighborhood. Thus, to the extent that this observation of children's socialization process is universally applicable, the structure of human needs might also be considered universal. As we maintain the universality of this human need structure based on considerations of child development, one might question the relevance of children's needs to the motivations of adult members of the society. It is my belief that adults are not much more "mature" than children in terms of needs, since we differ only with respect to the nature of needs. Instead of demanding the mother's presence to satisfy the need for belonging, the adult may seek lovers, peers, and memberships in unions, churches, country clubs, and political parties. In place of Tonka Trucks and Hot Wheel toy cars, the adult may desire campers, sports cars, and golf clubs. Indeed, the fact that an adult no longer attempts to possess more toys does not mean that he ceases to seek more money, more power, and more of just about everything than other people. The difference between a child and an adult in this regard is in instrumentalities and means rather than need structures. As a child outgrows the shell of the family, he will be exposed to a much more complex and often hostile life environment. Therefore instrumental means such as a family and toys can no longer serve the goal of maintaining a sense of psychological belongingness and a leisured life. In the same way, as the person's frame of reference expands, social competitition becomes more intense, and winning in such a competition requires more resources and human capabilities.

Yet another way of demonstrating the incremental-progressive nature of human needs might be found within the assumptions and propositions underlying the literature of social stratification. Although the stratification criteria seem to vary—some by prestige, others by wealth, and still others by occupation—major stratification scales (Warner, Edward Scale, NORC) appear to parallel the levels of human needs we have established in this chapter. The "unskilled workers" or laborers who are usually classified at the bottom of the social strata can be interpreted as motivated by survival. "Skilled" workers in Edward's category can be conceptualized as those pursuing economic opportunities in anticipation of social advancement. And the white-collar class may be viewed as a class that is inclined to explore a variety of hobbies and leisure modes of life. Finally, the professional and managerial classes may be interpreted as those who pursue the highest need of our need-hierarchy: self-esteem and social control.[7] If, as Duncan and Blau (1966) assert, the social stratification scales that are prevalent today are not only mutually compatible but also historically consistent, the general correspondence of our need-stages to the stratification scales could be an important aspect by which we might substantiate the progressive hierarchical nature of human needs. Additionally, to the extent that man is oriented toward status improvement regardless of cultural and historical background, we could assert this as evidence of the universal applicability of the incremental need structure.

Based on the premises discussed above, one can measure the level of development by the proportion of members of the society who seek different kinds of human needs. Figure 1 shows the "ideal type" cases of the developed, developing, and underdeveloped societies.

INSTITUTIONS AND HUMAN NEEDS

Ever since Huntington (1965) pointed out that decay as well as development is a possible outcome of a nation's developmental en-

FIGURE 1
Patterns of Population Distribution by Needs

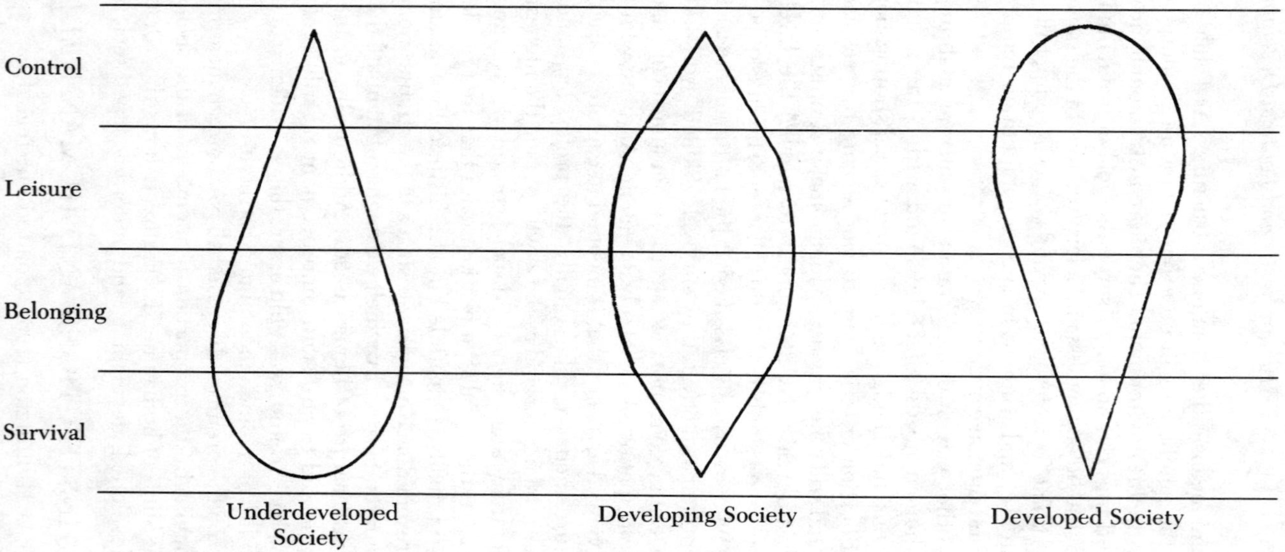

Control

Leisure

Belonging

Survival

Underdeveloped
Society

Developing Society

Developed Society

deavors, the idea of institutionalization has been an important concept for distinguishing the two sets of outcomes. Development requires not only that the regime acquire the capacity to respond to various types of demands from its environment. These capacities must also become institutionalized in the sense that they must exist as regularized, routinized mechanisms for dealing with these demands. In this manner, government develops the capacity to handle a larger demand load, as most demands can be processed through routine procedures. Furthermore, popular perceptions of government capabilities are enhanced, leading to a sense of security in the belief that, in the long run, government will be able to perform adequately. Hence, short-term fluctuations in government performance are less traumatic for both the government and its constituents, as they come to be viewed as simply minor, temporary deviations from an overall acceptable level of performance.

What is missing in most discussions of institutionalization is any explicit concern with *what* capacities must be institutionalized. It is not just any capacity that must become institutionalized, but the capacity to respond to specific types of substantive demands that is important. A government that has an efficient mechanism for regulating automobile traffic is not likely to survive unless it also has institutions that can guarantee sufficient gasoline to power those cars. What is needed, then, is some idea of *what* capacities must be developed and institutionalized.

In the context of our paradigm, a social institution will be viewed as a human invention intended to provide a regularized, routinized mechanism for the satisfaction of a particular human need. It is the capacity to provide the goods and services necessary for the satisfaction of specific substantive needs that is the *raison d'être* of institutions, and therefore, it is the nature of the needs that actually determines what regime capacities must be developed and institutionalized. In the same way, institutions can be expected to change in response to the changing nature of human needs. This is how they maintain their effectiveness in achieving institutional objectives. Thus, the sequence in which specific institutions emerge in a society should parallel the sequence in which the needs of their constituents (or clients) emerge.

When the most prevalent need among the members of a society is that of survival or, more concretely, obtaining food, we can expect the regime to give primary emphasis to the development of institutions associated with agricultural production and distribution. Government efforts to mobilize resources for policy performance will center initially on such things as land redistribution. Such policies are often used as a means of gaining and cementing the support of the rural population for the new regime. This was part of the Chinese Communist Party's strategy for winning popular support prior to their takeover and for maintaining that base of support after the revolution. The point that should be emphasized is that such programs are pursued in the early stages of post-revolutionary regime formation not simply for the purpose of maintaining the political support of the rural population, but also to ensure a stable agricultural sector which can provide the regime with a steady supply of products needed to fulfill the most basic survival needs of the rest of society as well. Only in this manner can the regime hope to maintain its as yet tenuous hold on political authority—by gratifying the most basic needs of its constituents.

Quite often, however, the reestablishment of the *status quo ante* in agricultural production is insufficient to ensure the continued capacity of the regime to provide for the adequate satisfaction of survival needs. Related policies will likely emerge, aimed toward agricultural research and development, increased mechanization of the agricultural sector and adoption of the latest in agricultural technology, public works projects such as irrigation programs, and projects such as road and railway construction that are the requisites of an adequate distribution infrastructure. These are some examples of the types of policies newly formed regimes are likely to pursue. The common thread linking them is that they are all examples of government mobilization of human and material resources for the purposes of ensuring the means of satisfying the more basic survival needs of the population.

Of course, not all nations are blessed with the resources necessary to attain agricultural self-sufficiency. For nations whose combination of population size and amount of arable land is such as to preclude self-sufficiency even at a subsistence level, institutions aimed at enhancing that nation's capacity to obtain agricultural products from other nations will be emphasized in the regime's policy-making. This is the situation that Japan has traditionally faced, with its relatively large population concentrated on a land mass smaller than California. Since the end of World War II marked a regime change in Japan, the differing responses to this dilemma exhibited by the two historical regimes may be instructive.

Under the Meiji regime, Japan became the foremost military power in Asia and used this might to subjugate Korea and Manchuria. Hence, territorial expansion through the use of military strength brought considerably more land under the control of the regime and thereby heightened its capacity to ensure the satisfaction of its constituents' survival needs. At the same time, Japan became increasingly effective in international trade. While the incursion of the West reduced China virtually to the status of a colony, Japan developed the institutional means to deal with the Western nations on a basis of equality in international trade. In this respect, its military might and trade capacity served as mutually reinforcing mechanisms to ensure its continued capacity to provide an adequate supply of agricultural products. Since World War II, with the abolition of the Japanese military, the institutions associated with its trade capacity have received increased emphasis. The result has been Japan's meteoric rise to second largest producer and exporter of manufactured goods, ensuring it the resources necessary to be one of the world's largest importers of agricultural products. Hence, given its relative paucity of domestic agriculture, Japan has proven capable of providing food in amounts far beyond what is needed for the physical survival of its population. And it has done so by evolving the institutional capacity to operate as an effective participant in international trade.

To promote the other conditions for physical survival, such as internal social stability and security from external threat, the institutions of the police and the military will be accorded primary importance. When security from violent threat is a salient concern guiding the conscious behavior of people in a society, the regime's response must involve the institutionalization of internal security in the form of a police force, and external security in the form of an effective military force. Given the early and intense primacy of such needs, it should not be surprising that many newly independent nations soon come under military rule after a brief period of tenuous, unstable civilian rule. The military's *raison d'être* is providing security from external threat and, along with the police, ensuring internal stability. Hence, the vacuum left by a civilian government that is unable to respond to the imperatives imposed upon it by the popular need for survival will soon be filled by those who control the institutions specifically designed for such purposes: the military.

In summary, then, in a society where survival needs are the most salient, we can expect government policy-making and institutional development to be centered on the areas of the military and police, and the agricultural sector of the economy. These sorts of conditions prevail in a newly formed nation or, more generally, in one that has experienced the takeover of a new regime. Especially when the regime change has occurred in a context of widespread civil and/or international violence will the survival needs of the populace be activated, as civil violence is life-threatening and the absence of an effective regime to satisfy even the most basic needs intensifies the popular sense of deprivation. The contending political faction that can best demonstrate its capacity to guarantee survival will be the one that stands to gain the most popular support, and will thereby enhance its chances of gaining political power.

As society attains a reasonable assurance that its survival needs will be met through the institutionalization of mechanisms that provide the necessary goods and services, the most prominent need level of the populace will shift to that of the belonging need. The emergence of such a need in a society on a broad scale requires an active, multifaceted program of socialization aimed at generating a sense of community and a measure of diffuse loyalty to the regime, or loyalty beyond what could be expected simply as a function of the tangible rewards provided by the regime. Institutions such as the family, religious groups, mass media and the educational system, as the primary agents of socialization, will be the focus of government policy-making, as the regime attempts to harness the power of these institutions in such a way as to make them agents of political socialization. It is at this stage that the importance of ideology also reaches its height. Ideology becomes a mechanism by which government attempts to institutionalize in the populace a belief system that is supportive of the regime and its goals and strategies. This belief system, then, is propagated by means of the various agents of socialization, especially those over which the regime can exercise some direct control, such as the mass media and the educational system. The family, religious groups and other more primary groups deal with belonging needs on a more personal and intimate level. They provide the individual with basic security in a sense of belonging which can then be translated into more general (and politically relevant) attachments to the broader political community.

It is these latter sorts of attachments that are most important to the regime. To the extent that they can be fostered, the resultant diffuse loyalty allows the regime some flexibility in its pursuit of further policy objectives. Loyalty to the regime is less exclusively contingent upon the immediate material rewards the regime can provide. Therefore, policies with more long-range objectives, requiring some measure of delayed gratification by the populace, can be pursued without risking a critical erosion of popular support.

Ideology, then, is the institutional mechanism by which the basis for such loyalty is propagated. The ultimate goals of the regime are spelled out, which permits justification of current policies (sacrifices) in terms of their efficacy in bringing about the ideal states spelled out in the ideology. Ideology provides a common political belief system for the people. It spells out their place in the current society as well as in the usually utopian future state of the society. As such, the common basis for political community becomes internalized in the members of society, and a sense of belonging in the larger society is generated on the basis of this shared political belief system.

The American case provides a striking example of the sorts of conflicts that emerge in the early post-regime-formation era and of the role an ideology performs in resolving these conflicts. While the revolutionary forces in colonial America constituted a minority, they managed to achieve a degree of solidarity during the revolutionary years. In the name of liberating the colonies from British rule, the revolutionaries set aside regional and interstate economic and political rivalries in order to deal with the British as a unified force.

However, once the revolution occurred and the British threat was eliminated, the tenuous unity of the colonies, formalized in the Articles of Confederation, became less than adequate for a nation no longer united against a common enemy. The old rivalries and disputes resurfaced with increasing intensity, and the nation of thirteen states was in danger of disintegrating into thirteen autonomous nations.

The Constitutional Convention was an effort to construct a new institutional foundation for the unity of the states. The new constitution provided the formal basis for the strengthening of the central government, while allowing a measure of autonomy for the states. The individual liberties guaranteed in the first ten amendments became the basis for individual loyalty to the newly formed regime. These documents, supplemented by the elegant defense of this government contained in the *Federalist Papers,* came to represent the American political ideology. Herein lie definitions of the purposes and limits of government as well as its structure, and more broadly, a conception of the nature of humankind in society and its appropriate form of government. As such, the documents perform the national integration functions of an ideology in that they spell out not only the formal basis of government but the reasons this particular form of government is worthy of citizen support.

To the extent that institutionalization of the mechanisms that lead to such integration is achieved, we can expect subsequent needs to emerge in the population. That is, if the regime succeeds in generating and maintaining a sense of belonging and political community among its citizens, the members of the community will soon shift to the next higher level of needs—the leisure needs. As the leisure lifestyle involves material consumption beyond what is required for survival, as well as free time in which to engage in such activities, institutions intended to promote automated mass production of consumer goods will be instigated. Thus, industrialization becomes the inevitable contemporary institutional concomitant of the leisure needs' emergence.

Government response to these needs can take a number of forms depending upon the character of the regime established in the first two stages. Under a highly centralized regime with state control of the economy, government planning institutions will be instigated. These organizations perform the task of translating broad policy guidelines into concrete production programs. Coordination of various industries and distribution of resources among them is undertaken with the goal of achieving an optimal return in terms of goods and services that satisfy popular leisure needs. In a market economy, institutions that regulate the market emerge in order to prevent any serious breakdowns in production or distortions in the allocation of resources to the several sectors of the economy.

An apparently universal concomitant of industrial growth is urbanization, or the increasing concentration of populations in urban areas. This in itself creates needs for government institutions, as public services must be provided for these populations. For example, where in a rural setting each farm unit can provide its own water supply with a well, it is impractical, if not impossible, for each family in a city to sink its own well. Hence, the government must provide such services or public goods as a matter of necessity, as well as convenience. A whole series of public services—such as water, sewage treatment, public transportation, and environmental control—will be demanded as needed auxiliaries to the growth of the urban industrial segment of a society. Failure to develop the institutional means to provide these services will, not only deter the growth and efficiency of the industrial sector, but will also eventually have a negative impact on government stability, as the regime's ability to provide for leisure needs fails to meet the levels of popular expectations.

As industrialization progresses, a growing number of people, especially those in urban industrial centers, will be able (even forced) to join the crowd of mass consumers. Those who achieve this stage of leisure lifestyle will, unfortunately, not remain content with these fruits of industrial life. There will soon emerge among them the next level of needs, the need for *social control*.

Those who seek social esteem tend to compare themselves with others. What they desire is "more" of the visible signs of status that would distinguish them as being more esteemed than "significant others." They want more of everything, and initially the "everything" happens to be money. Politically, such things as power or the relative advantage of one group over a rival group will be the sort of goals that become salient. These types of competition have a special zero-sum character in that one competitor's gain necessitates another's loss. Hence, the dilemma facing the regime is that it cannot simultaneously satisfy everyone's needs in this area. Thus conflict can only be managed; it cannot be totally resolved.

At this stage, institutions designed to manage such zero-sum conflict emerge. Political parties attain special importance as channels of such competition in politics. Interest groups emerge as institutional mechanisms to enhance the competitive advantage of their constituents in these conflicts. Labor unions develop from simple bargaining units to enhance workers' material lifestyle into political organizations that can make or break parties and candidates in an election. Their goals in this sort of endeavor is to enhance the workers' control over their work place and their voice in the general policy process of the political system. In short, the sorts of institutions that are ascendant at this stage are the ones designed to pursue power and influence that by definition cannot be possessed by everyone simultaneously.

In sum, members of a society pursue their needs by forming institutions, and the nature and type of prevalent social institutions at any given time can be described by observing the then-predominant human needs. When physical survival becomes the most pressing need, institutions pertaining to police and military, as well as those related to food production and agriculture, are regarded as primary. The family, churches, mass media and schools surface as important institutions when people seek groups with which they can associate for a sense of belonging. Industrialization, urbanization, and a market economic structure gain cultural and social supremacy when people desire to consume more than what is needed for survival. And political parties and interest groups develop when people strive for social recognition and esteem.

ATTITUDES, BEHAVIOR, AND HUMAN NEEDS

As people pursue their specific needs through institutions of a particular nature, their attitudes and behavior will be patterned in a changing, yet predictable, way. Thus, if we can tell the kind of need one is pursuing and the type of institutions with which one is likely to interact, we might be able to ascertain one's attitudes and behavioral predispositions at that point in time. As we now have postulated a set of relations between human need types and patterns of institutionalization, we could with greater simplicity specify some attitudinal and behavioral consequences of the various needs.

Obviously, when someone's minimum physical survival is threatened, any inconvenience imposed upon him or her would be accepted if such an imposition assures better chances of survival. Here, people will be inclined to be *submissive* and *compliant*—particularly to authorities.

Lawrence Kohlberg (1969, p. 379) describes this level of "moral development" as a "punishment and obedience" orientation, where the consequences of an action determine the value of the action. When survival is the dominant motivation, attitudes and beliefs about any sort of behavior will depend on the efficacy of that behavior for survival. Hence, a person may have little or no compunction about stealing food when starving, whereas the same person, with a fairly comfortable material lifestyle, may not even consider engaging in such behavior. That is, institutions relying upon coercion, such as law-enforcement and military agencies, can be most effective when the majority of the people in any given society are involved in survival-related activities and are therefore dependent on and submissive to such authorities.

However, in the subsequent stage, where humans desire a sense of belonging, attitudes and beliefs about behavior will be formulated with more of an eye to the response of "significant others." Initially, at least, one seeks the approval of those with whom one has immediate, and frequent contact: family, neighbors, fellow workers. Here beliefs are grounded in one's group affiliations and are as changeable as the groups. The task facing the regime at this point is to prevent this panoply of group-based beliefs from becoming the source of excessive group conflict. Group diversity is bound to generate belief conflict, and government, through the educational and mass media institutions, must attempt to minimize the differences by providing some broad belief system that can accommodate the various beliefs and thereby minimize the importance of differences.

At the individual level, values and belief systems are articulated as an attempt to justify group affiliations and social behavior. Here, education and religious experience serve to enhance one's ability to justify one's social existence in terms of more abstract principles and beliefs. At this point, one will develop a stronger sense of "we versus they" or "ours versus theirs," thus promoting organizational mind or "associational sentiment." It is the development of this psychological predisposition that facilitates the emergence and spread of ideologies, often serving power positions of a regime which otherwise might experience a severe setback in integrating the political community. The anticipated cultural and social fragmentation (a point we will elaborate upon further later) is mitigated by the regime's promulgation of a *common* set of abstract beliefs—ideology.

When members of a community shift their need level to one of leisure life as a result of the successful gratification of belongingness needs, we can expect that social change will be in the direction of industrialization, urbanization, and market economy. As people attach themselves to the spinning wheels of industrialization in which they become "cogs" in the wheels of production, they claim a small area of expertise and develop a rather segmented view of life. As the structure of industrial society is largely bureaucratic, the industrial person will also exhibit what is referred to as "bureaucratic mentality," characterized by impersonal, formalistic, and segmented relations toward others.[8]

Urbanization, on the other hand, is known to be destructive to traditional family and communal ties and social structure, and forces city dwellers to become self-centered and privacy-loving. It is one of the great ironies of history that people find themselves more isolated in the heavily populated urban centers than in a rural community where neighbors are often scattered miles apart from each other. It is quite common for an urban dweller not to know the people living next door, and he has little incentive indeed to know anyone with whom he or she has no functional interaction or economic interest.

Finally, market economy transforms human nature in a most powerful and profound way. In keeping with the dynamics of the market economy, people learn to be bargain-oriented and economically rational in that they pursue maximum payoff at a minimum cost. As the market transforms all values into the common quantitative yardstick of currency, people naturally seek "more" of everything, thus subjecting themselves to the simple value equation of "the bigger, the better." At the same time, the industrial person becomes a slave of "convenience" and automation. Here commodities are designed and redesigned to be convenient and time-saving. In this process of innovation of commodities in a market economy, mass media become the inevitable means of promotion for mass consumption.

Once mass consumption becomes a necessary condition for a continuously prospering market industry, the consumer will be capable of buying just about anything that can be mass produced because of the banking and credit systems. Thus, people without the actual resources to purchase their commodities will still be able to maintain their consumption level by using "plastic money" (credit cards) which most major companies and banking institutions are willing to mass produce and grant to anyone with a job. These mass consumers will soon become psychologically uneasy as their debts accumulate; thus they will become "precarious consumers" as well as "vicarious consumers."[9]

Most likely, the leisure-life pursuer in an industrial society will seek entertainment of all types. In fact, the concept of entertainment and instruments to entertain becomes broad and diverse, ranging from social parties to sports; and even politics comes to be considered a form of entertainment.

Finally, the competitor who seeks social recognition and esteem by winning competitions and conflicts will surface out of the leisurely class of mass public. By the time the acquisition of mass-produced commodities has made it difficult to distinguish the "winner" from the "loser," social recognition pursuers will look for those values, resources, and commodities that cannot be mass-produced or possessed by so many as to become meaningless. At this point, people will seek such things as power positions, rare collections, and reputations. As discussed earlier, this stage of development is characterized by a high sense of competition and by a game-loving personality. Games such as chess, bowling, baseball, horse racing, car racing and football are no longer for entertainment only. Participants in these games, either through actual physical participation or psychological involvement by associating with teams and players, will become deadly serious about the outcome of the game. Thus, games in a game-loving society tend to become professional, and players are rewarded with enormous recognition and material compensation. Rewards for winners, no matter how unreasonable the amount, are deemed natural, and the losers' sufferings are seldom seen as worthy of sympathy.

Just as games are played by rules rather than customs, game-loving people tend to maintain their lifestyles and sense of justice by means of the framework of detailed laws. It is not an accidental development that the court is becoming an integral part of life in America and other post-industrial societies. Every type of dispute is taken to court. Family relations, educational disagreements, and even love affairs are arbitrated in court—the ultimate umpire in social competitions and human games. Increasingly, we see evidence of the belief that what is legal is also right.

In sum, by examining the need-structure of individuals and the characteristics of corresponding institutions, we can ascertain behavioral and attitudinal characteristics at various stages of social change. Understanding psychological and behavioral predispositions is crucial as we attempt to discuss political characteristics and the policy directions of various types of political systems for the purpose of explanation and prediction, as well as the ultimate goal of problem solving.

STAGES AND POLITICAL DEVELOPMENT

We have established that certain types of human needs are likely to facilitate the development of certain institutions, and, as members of these institutions pursue their needs, certain attitudinal and behavioral traits will be formed. Assuming that styles of politics may be affected significantly by the nature of human needs and the demands placed upon the government *(Assumption 1)*, we can now infer political characteristics and policy preferences in different stages of social development by considering the human needs hierarchy and institution formation.

Specifically, we have established that human needs have a systematic, ordered structure in which the unique characteristics of the different needs result in institutional diversity as well as in a structured set of behavioral patterns. With the assumptions that a society's need-characteristics are defined as the aggregate of its individual members' needs *(Assumption 2)* and that a regime is to maximize its efforts in responding to the prevalent needs of the members of the society *(Assumption 3)*, we now can propose the structure of the process of political development. By determining to what extent the political system has capably accomplished its function of meeting these needs, a systematic process of development can be identified. The process may be seen as occurring in four distinct phases, with the government's response to each progressively higher level of needs constituting each of the four phases. These stages appear to represent much of the process of developmental political change, regardless of the regime type (ideological and structural) directing the process in any given instance. These stages may be called (1) regime formation (2) political integration (3) resource expansion, and (4) conflict management. Just as human needs are hierarchically ordered, these stages of political development are incrementally and sequentially structured. I shall explore further characteristics of each of these stages.

(1) Regime Formation
A new nation may emerge as a result of internal revolution, independence, or as a movement toward what Organski (1965) calls "primitive unification." In any of these channels, a regime comes to power by winning the competition between groups contending for political supremacy. This struggle for power may provoke intense forms of conflict such as civil wars or it may involve less extensive types of power conflict such as military coups. In either case, however, people will perceive their physical survival to be threatened. In times marked by the crisis of physical survival, as discussed earlier, people naturally want political stability of any kind, irrespective of the type of government, as long as the emerging regime can assure their survival. The question of regime "legitimacy" in this initial stage is largely irrelevant

or, at most, is regarded as being of only secondary importance: the "legitimate" regime is quite simply the power group that demonstrates its ability to quell domestic conflict. Thus, a regime may emerge from the power conflict often without any demonstrable evidence of popular support, an occurrence that would have been impossible within a peaceful form of political succession. However, once a regime is formed, it will attempt to solidify its power base and gain popular support. At a time when public needs remain largely at a *survival* level, the regime is likely to adopt policies that will help restore social stability and facilitate agricultural production. As people's attitudes tend to be compliant and submissive at this level of need development, the regime could easily develop a centristic form of leadership such as a military dictatorship. For in a military government it matters not how it rules but what it can do in providing social and political stability. Such leadership can often be effective in generating public support insofar as the public desires a more secure and safe environment. But it tends to be simplistic in other policy considerations. Thus, it may experience serious difficulty in responding to conflicting public opinions and in accommodating diverse organizations when such pluralistic development inevitably follows a period of social stability.

(2) Political Integration

Although historical experience in many newly independent nations indicates that a good number of military regimes never escape the vicious cycle of *coups d'état, a successful regime will adapt itself to the changing human needs and public demands by altering policies and ruling styles accordingly.* Since a regime has to deal with the problem of maintaining stability while coping with the emerging need for belonging, it customarily attempts to integrate mass belief systems and coordinate organizations by means of political socialization or ideological indoctrination. The very fact that there exists a simultaneous need for belongingness among the masses facilitates the regime's effort to politicize them with its norms, values, and beliefs in such a way as to enhance the regime's claim to political legitimacy. Thus, a regime at this stage is expected to adopt policies geared to political and civic education and to move from coercive control mechanisms to a more persuasion-oriented ruling style. Accordingly, policies in this second stage will be justified in terms of the value systems or ideologies promoted by the regime, a process which will naturally invite intellectuals to participate by assessing the ideological implications of policies. The integration efforts on the part of the regime will meet with varying degrees of success depending on the extent of incongruity between proposed policies and the more salient (often religious) cultural norms and inherited social structures of the public. The disastrous outcome of communist China's massive communalization movement, the Great Leap Forward Movement of 1958, for example, might have been in large part due to overly ambitious plans conflicting with existing cultural norms and Confucian social structures. The much too familiar problems of instability in Third World democracies (the Philippines, South Korea, Nigeria, Argentina, Mexico, Ghana, and Iran) are generally believed to be due to the discrepancies between their socio-cultural setting and the newly transplanted norms and institutions of Western democracy. Here, the success of political integration and stability depends to a large extent on how "radical" the regime's policies are, on the one hand, and how effective the regime is in political persuasion (indoctrination) on the other. At this stage the regime is particularly vulnerable to political unrest because the populace, by virtue of its being socialized, develops political opinions and articulates "demands" in exchange for "support" of the government, a situation which could easily lead to the expression of diverse, even conflicting, interests, often resulting in some form of political turmoil. Thus, political socialization by the regime must have as a goal the shaping of such popular demands into forms to which the regime has the capability and willingness to respond.

This new demand for socialization, to be sure, is a product of the completion of the first stage of regime formation; that is, when the regime has established itself in power, the people have the "right" to expect it to perform the functions that are the regime's *raison d'être*. Thus, the need for socialization could be pursued satisfactorily when the regime performs the task of political integration successfully. To the extent that the regime promotes the kind of environment conducive to meeting this need for socialization and psychological comfort, it attains *legitimacy* (i.e., the people's consent). At this point, political demand which has been created in the process of politicization will be accompanied by growing support for the regime, since, having eliminated its competitors, it can focus its effort upon the satisfaction of these new popular demands.

(3) Resource Expansion

As discussed earlier, a person is believed to have the inherent desire to engage in leisurely living as soon as the more pressing needs—physical survival and psychological belongingness—are met. In this pursuit of leisure, one tends to be more consumptive than productive in terms of material goods. A leisure class in any society is a class geared to material consumption in more fashionable ways.

And, since the amount of support for the regime is assumed to be contingent upon its effectiveness in continuously meeting people's needs, a successful regime must respond to this shift in the level of human needs. That is, having achieved political stability and national integration, the regime must recognize the shift in popular needs from socialization to leisure life, and respond with a program of resource expansion and mass production of consumer goods.

When the environment already has plentiful resources, the regime is not faced with the imperative of creating new resources. However, in almost all cases, the regime faces conditions of relative scarcity rather than abundance, and consequently, emphasis will be upon the increased production of goods and services. The need for resource expansion and mass production will force the regime to move as expeditiously as possible toward industrialization. For successful industrialization, the government needs to help develop an effective mechanism for resource and manpower mobilization on the one hand and for marketing commodities on the other. Here, the society will undergo rapid, and possibly uncomfortable, disequilibriating change in social structure and cultural life, as the traditional society will be forced to give way to urbanization and the formation of "Gesellschaft."[10] New problems, many of which are irreversible, will emerge in the processes of industrialization and urbanization. Such things as environmental deterioration and organized crime force the government to generate policies to cope with these problems. At the same time, people will desire a continuous supply of commodities at an affordable price, and consumer goods must be constantly refined and innovated to be ever more attractive to the leisure and convenience oriented public. Marketing, particularly advertising through mass media, will make a profound impact upon the consumers' cultural life, resulting in economic rationality and political apathy. This change in culture will certainly affect the styles of politics and policy priorities.

In the third stage of political development, political leadership and decision-making will be seriously affected by business cycles, and policies are most likely to be intended for the enhancement and protection of economic institutions. As alluded to earlier, successful economic development through industrialization requires the expansion not only of the market but also of the society's capability to mobilize material resources and labor power. Under conditions of relative resources and manpower scarcity, the regime may seek to extend and/or solidify its control over the economic sector. However, the regime must be able to secure, in some form, the consent of the people for such an extension of its power; and, as the definition of political development dictates, this must be done by showing the efficacy of such dictatorial control for the desired economic growth. Such a centristic mechanism of control can be an effective means of rapid economic growth by virtue of its efficiency in capital formation and social mobilization toward production. It is no secret in the minds of dictatorial and repressive leaders of many Third World nations (Nkruma of Ghana, Park of South Korea, Castro of Cuba, Marcos of the Philippines, and many other military leaders) that moral injustice can be justified by the resulting functional effectiveness. However, such a large measure of governmental control will be tolerated only if it can be shown actually to bring about rapid, extensive, and balanced economic growth: in short, dictatorship is accepted for what it does rather than for what it is.[11] As some sort of economic planning has been proven to be necessary for economic growth, many economically underdeveloped nations at this level of development are tempted to tolerate some form of centrist political system. However, as we will discuss in the following section, a centristic system could not maintain its high level of effectiveness in meeting human needs as people's need levels rise from the material dimension of leisure living to the social dimension of self-esteem or social control.

(4) Conflict Management: A Precarious Balance

In contrast to Rostow and Organski's utopian anticipations, economic affluence cannot be the final stage of social change, since leisure life or material consumption does not constitute the ultimate human desire.

As material resources become sufficiently abundant to guarantee a comfortable economic life, the level of human needs, in our need structure, is expected to change to that of social control. Social control, as discussed earlier, refers to the desire on the part of individuals to be "better" than other human beings. Although at this stage all citizens may have a comfortable life, in economic terms, they will perceive others as being "more comfortable" in some respect—either economically or socially. Thus, social competition arises in the form of competition for the control over what Easton terms "values," which, as mentioned earlier, include social as well as material resources.

The regime's task, then, shifts to that of resolving such conflict, actual or potential, through the *redistribution* of such "values," rather than the production of more goods, as would have been the case in the previous stage.[12] Therefore, it is expected that government policies deal primarily with the question, "who gets what, when, and why," rather than "how to maximize resource expansion." Usually the sorts of resources that are desired in this case are fixed or limited in amount, such as power positions and economic, social, or political privilege. Hence, politics in this stage may be characterized by conflict and competition. The final reservoir for conflict resolution lies in the irrevocable verdicts of the court, or some similar government institution, which is not associated with resource expansion or socialization.

However, the regime's task to satisfy all members of the society in this stage is even theoretically untenable because satisfaction by a winner in such a conflict necessitates deprivation by the loser, thus preventing the possibility of a society where the ruling elite will employ an overwhelming popular support. Furthermore, social conflicts are not going to be resolved due to the fact that, as the political regime recognizes the resolution of conflict as an effective demonstration of its capability, it may at times feel the need to *create*, rather than resolve, internal or external conflict in order to show its effectiveness in doing its expected job—the eventual resolution of conflict—and thereby generate support.

Because of these inevitable problems and dilemmas, social conflict can never be completely resolved, although it may be contained or prolonged. The precarious stability in the more advanced industrial societies appears to illustrate this point. Here, the regime's stability depends on the ruling elites' skill in the theoretically impossible job of maintaining the support of the "winner" without losing the loser's support entirely. This difficult job is being performed in post-industrial societies by one or more of the following strategies on the part of the ruler:

(1) Confuse the public by making conflicting issues so complicated

that people will be unable to develop sound positions on those issues;

(2) Interpret the implications of proposed policies in such a way that all parties may be led to believe that each is the winner;

(3) Maximize the political apathy of the middle class, often described as the "silent majority";

(4) Convert politicians into "actors" and "actresses" and distract the public with public images and personal appeals so that politicians can avoid taking public stances on controversial issues and yet draw mass support. Therefore, politicians in this fourth stage of development must possess superior acting ability and an attractive appearance, and they must not appear to have philosophical and ideological dogmas that cannot be compromised. Indeed, in some post-industrial countries, such as the United States and Japan, professional actors and comedians are even moving to the main stage of politics.

Nevertheless, the government and ruling elite in this stage will be required to maintain a precarious balance between sets of profoundly contradictory values and conflicting social forces, such as majority rule versus minority rights, liberty versus equality, and technological sophistication versus the preservation of humanitarian values. When such precarious balances fail to sustain their deceptive harmony, the "developed" society will, as all other societies, undergo serious institutional breakdowns resulting in legitimacy crises for the regime. Such a legitimacy crisis in turn could induce a regime change. The scope of the change may be limited to the replacement of the incumbents of government, or it could involve a total restructuring of social institutions as well as cultural values. The scope of such change will be determined by the level of institutional change in the political sphere that accompanies the regime change.

If a regime change requires changes only in the institutions that are germane to this stage of *conflict resolution*, the subsequent regime is expected to concentrate its efforts on this same task of conflict management. Hence, the political system, even after the regime change, maintains the same level of political development. On the other hand, if social institutions at all levels of the system are seriously affected by a regime alteration, the new regime will face the much more difficult task of starting off its developmental journey from an earlier stage. The implications of this reversal tendency in the developmental sequence will be discussed in the next section. Chart 1 shows the components of the paradigm: the stairs shown on top are intended to demonstrate the incremental nature of development. That is, a higher stage cannot be attained (or maintained) without a sustained foundation of lower stages.[13]

ON REVERSING DEVELOPMENT

The process of political development through the four stages, as we have discussed in this chapter, is reversible. If members of the society for any reason are unable to continuously maintain previously attained need satisfaction in their single-minded effort to pursue the emergent new needs, they might have to revert to an earlier stage in order to restore and strengthen the institutions of that stage. Only in this manner can their ability to satisfy previous levels of needs be maintained.

There are numerous environmental and contextual factors that affect not only the attainment of certain needs but also the maintenance of their satisfaction. For the first stage of regime formation, for example, a society's geopolitics, land conditions, population, and climate are all crucial environmental factors. These factors will surely affect the institutions of agriculture, police and military, and thus, status of the regime's continued stability.

The second stage, Political Integration, is most likely to be affected by levels of socio-cultural homogeneity. Ethnic plurality, linguistic diversity, religious incompatibility, and class structure will certainly intervene in the process of national integration. The more homogeneous the community, the easier the job of integration will be. One needs only to compare Japan and India in their tasks of national integration to illuminate the relevance and importance of these environmental variables.

As the society enters the third stage, where resource expansion is usually pursued through industrialization, a series of new factors will emerge as decisive contextual variables. The access of available natural (particularly mineral) resources, level of technological education, cultural aspect of achievement orientation, and susceptibility of the public to market economy are all important elements.

The most "developed" stage of conflict management will definitely be affected by all the contextual factors of the previous three stages. But even the most favorable environment in terms of those factors will never guarantee the achievement of this fourth stage because, as alluded to earlier, the "developed" society is destined to experience the problem of fixed-sum competition. That is, you cannot satisfy every member of the society insofar as someone's satisfaction is

CHART 1
Stages of Political Change

	Regime Formation	Political Integration	Resource Expansion	Conflict Management
Human Needs	Survival	Belonging	Leisure	Control
Means	Food Safety Security	"Friends" "Significant Others" Group	Hobbies & Toys Privacy Convenience	Influence Power Prestige
Institutions	Agriculture Police Military	Family Church (Religion) School (Education)	Industrialization Marketing Urbanization	Mass Media Interest Groups Parties
Attitude-Behaviour Traits	Pacifism Fate-accepting Compliant-Submissive Authoritarian	Altruism Cooperation Egalitarian Imaginative and Abstract	Consumptive Bargaining and Rational Entertainment Quantitatively oriented	Competitive Game-loving Legalism Bossism
System Character	Centrism	Ideological	Bureaucratic	Participatory
Leader-ship Type	Military-Coercive	Intellectual-Philosophical	Technocratic-Cooperative	Actor
Policy Preference	Production of necessities Law and Order Defence	Politicization Power Consolidation	Economic Growth Production of "conspicuous" goods Protection of Industry	"Just" distribution (Who gets What, and How?)

Symptoms	Stubbornness and Rigidity Uniformity Factions and Cliques	"Armchair Philosopher" Politicization of curriculum Purges Politics of Fear	"The bigger, the better" Environmental Decay Morality Confusion Loss of individuality	World of "fantasies" Mutual Distrust Legality replacing Morality
Probable Outcomes	Successive Military Coups	Totalitarian Control	Economic Reliance upon Others	Status quo (at best) Welfare System SLOW AND PAINLESS ROAD TO HUMAN EXTINCTION
Intervening Context	Weather Land Condition Geographical Location Culture	Social-Ethnic Structure Linguistic and Religious Homogeneity	Natural Resources Achievement/Ascriptive Orientation	All of the Factors at the Previous Stages

contingent upon others being deprived of satisfaction. At this point, the regime will face the subtle task of achieving an "adequate" distribution of resources if it is to generate and maintain the support necessary for political legitimacy. Here socio-political stability will at best be a precarious state based on the regime's skillful combination of siding with the majority without antagonizing the minorities. Often this skillful combination, as discussed earlier, is assisted by the growing apathy of the majority, the "silent majority," and the emergence of political issues and processes too complex for them to comprehend. But this precarious stability does not guarantee permanent tranquillity. When the regime fails to draw sufficient support (as in more stable societies), or when it fails to avoid serious minority dissension, a powerful transition becomes imminent.

The present paradigm dissents from the utopian notion that the "developed" state of society is an ideal end stage; nor does it assume the journey to development to be irreversible. Most major developmental theories, however, appear to suggest that a society becomes mature and often perfected when a certain level of development is attained. The Marxist notion of a classless and stateless proletariat society does not allow any other conclusion but that of a permanent utopia. Organski's affluent society seems to have no other goal but that of maintaining affluence permanently. Rostow's mass consumption state has a self-guiding mechanism to sustain its property indefinitely.

What comes after development? This question is indeed becoming ever-more serious, because the number of "developed" societies is increasing due to successful economic growth in various parts of the world. At the same time, we are faced with more profound and imminent problems with the fruits of development (pollution, apathy, technology, breakdown of primary institutions, etc.) than with the symptoms of underdevelopment. We at least have some ideas as to what can be done in conditions of underdevelopment, and we know what we should be striving for in an attempt to make improvements in such conditions; but we have little knowledge and no proven strategies to cope with the problems of the "developed" society.

As was hinted at earlier, the present paradigm sees the possibility of the breakdown of the "developed" society. In fact, this most advanced stage is inherently self-defeating due to the dilemmatic nature of the fixed-sum conflict situation imposed by that stage's predominant needs. The political system is bound to experience discontent among its losers. When an intense level of discontent develops among the greater portion of the people, the society will become susceptible to some sort of mass movement, perhaps a revolution. In most revolutions, as we have seen in the French, Russian, and Chinese revolutions, the reversing of development can go back to the very first stage where the people's most urgent desire becomes that of survival due to the life threatening conditions of revolutionary situations. In this case, a complete recycling of the four stages of development is likely if the existing institutions (military, social, economic, and political) are not acceptable to the newly emerging regime.

But when some of the previous institutional arrangements are utilized without major reformations, achieving the sequential stages for the new regime will be much easier and simpler. It could almost "skip" a stage in terms of time needed to fulfill the stage. On the other hand, when the newly formed government finds itself incompatible with all the existing institutions, a more thorough recycling of the developmental process might be expected. However, such a full-scale revolution is not a frequent phenomenon. The usual dissent movements in "developed" societies are more likely to be of a limited type, avoiding any drastic alteration of the basic characteristics of the political system. *The question of where (which stage) the system reverts to when a breakdown occurs can best be answered by observing which of the societal institutional objectives (security-stability, political socialization, economic development, optimal payoff) is placed in jeopardy during the transition to a new regime.* If, for example, a nation's security or stability is in danger due to the failure of the military or police, the system will revert to the stage where a regime formation movement is inescapable. When, on the other hand, the political socialization function breaks down resulting in social and ideological fragmentation, the system will certainly revert to a stage where the political integration function is re-emphasized. The Cultural Revolution of communist China (1966–1969) might be a good example of this type of reversion. The massive and overly ambitious drive for economic development embodied in the Great Leap Forward Movement (1958) resulted in a disastrous series of setbacks primarily due to the lack of sufficient political integration to warrant such large-scale communalization and radical economic goals. Subsequently, the frustrated communist leaders decided to wage a massive war against the fragmenting forces existing in the society, particularly the traditional Confucian elements and the "revisionists." One might also expect a "developed" system to revert to the stage of economic development when the economic condition deteriorates to the extent that the people's need for leisure life is deprived, and the economic institutions are incapable of coping with the problem. The years of the Great Depression in the once affluent societies of the industrial West might represent this phenomenon.

In short, the proposed paradigm recognizes the possibility of the reversal of the development process, and it also explains the conditions for the various kinds of reversal. Although it is important to bear in mind that developmental achievement is cumulative in that all the previous achievements must necessarily be sustained in order to avoid the possibility of reversal, the various paths toward "development" suggest that history does not repeat itself even if the developmental process has to revert to previous stages.[14] Figure 2 shows the possible developmental process and the paths for reversal.

SUMMARY

While the proposed stage theory of political development must for the present remain paradigmatic—being contingent upon the validity of the assumptions pertaining to the legitimate function of government and the specific structure of the human needs hierarchy—we can make a tentative evaluation of its potential theoretical utility. Inasmuch as human needs and need satisfaction will determine the nature of any form of politics, the paradigm could warrant the claims of universal applicability. Furthermore, it allows for a behaviorally-oriented analysis of the developmental process since human needs constitute the fundamental motivational basis of all human behavior.

It is the hierarchical order in which human needs are pursued that is the determinant of the "developmental" dynamics of this theory. By thus focusing on changes in the motivational basis of human behavior as a way of accounting for the developmental process, this theory avoids the ethnocentrism and other such limitations on the applicability of a developmental theory which are unavoidable when the developmental process is defined in terms of changes in systemic characteristics (such as institutional setups). Such phenomena must be viewed as systemic means to the accomplishment of more fundamental human goals; and since these means may vary cross-culturally and over time, it would seem wise to base our theoretical endeavors upon the more consistent phenomenon of human needs rather than upon such

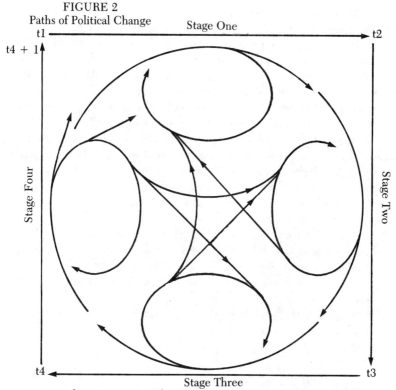

FIGURE 2
Paths of Political Change

systemic characteristics. The nature of human needs is much less susceptible to change than are the social means by which such needs are met.

Finally, this model assumes nothing as regards the inevitability of progress in the sense that it postulates the possibility—and indeed the probability—of political decay once the industrial and post-industrial stages of development have been reached and dilemmas have emerged to tax the political ingenuity of the regime.[15] In view of the notable lack of utopian societies in human history, this proposition seems not only reasonable but a necessary aspect of any theory of political development which claims congruence with reality. Furthermore, the present theory accounts for the reversal of the development process to other stages by pointing out the conditions for such decay and the extent of reversal to be expected with each degree of these conditions.

In short, it should be noted that the proposed paradigm focuses upon the dynamics of system level change, yet it explains this phenomenon in terms of certain behavioral attributes of the system's members. As such, it is a model broad enough in scope to incorporate theories of more specific sub-processes of the developmental phenomenon into the larger model, thus enriching its explanatory power. Theories of revolution and civil strife, of political socialization, of economic development, and of international conflict may all be constructed within the conceptual framework of this paradigm. In doing so, our understanding of these apparently diverse phenomena is increased by grasping a sense of their interrelationship. Thus, we propose this paradigm as a means by which political development—the change in a political system over time—may become the basis upon which to construct a truly scientific, cumulative body of knowledge about the political world.

In the following chapters, we shall explore more fully each of the stages in an attempt to explain a variety of political systems and social experiences through application of the paradigm. After devoting a chapter to each of the four stages, the book ends with a prescriptive analysis of "what after development?" pleading for changes in human social life which the author views as the only way out of the self-defeating "developmental" process.

FOOTNOTES

[1] Eisenstadt (1968, p. 184) offers a similar definition in that political development refers to "the capacity of modern society to adapt itself to continuously changing demands, to absorb them in terms of policy making, and to assure its own continuity in the face of continuous new demands and new forms of political organization."

[2] For definitions of methodological individualism, see J. W. N. Watkins, "Methodological Individualism and Social Tendencies," and May Brodbeck, "Methodological Individualism: Definition and Reduction," in May Brodbeck, ed. (1968).

[3] Lenski describes this kind of comfort as "creature comfort" when he discusses basic human needs. Refer to his work (1966: 38).

[4] For a good discussion of the thesis that man desires to have some control over other people, see Stanley A. Renshon (1974: 1–11).

[5] Dahrendorf characterizes conflict over social authority similarly as a fixed- or zero-sum situation. While the conflict he speaks of is essentially group conflict, he acknowledges that as mobility increases, this group conflict is

increasingly replaced by competition between individuals. See Dahrendorf (1959: 157–240, 171, 222).

[6] Jean Piaget, in his theory of developmental psychology, maintains that the sucking reflex as a hereditary physiological mechanism is used by the child as a means to adapt itself and be capable of gradual accommodation to external reality. This accommodation instinct is comparable to our "survival." He further discusses the phenomenon of assimilation as a basic fact of psychic life which is analogous to our second need, the need for psychological comfort. Refer to Jean Piaget (1963, Chapter 1).

Erik H. Erikson's conception of the Eight Ages of Man appears to confirm the fact that as a person becomes mature he or she develops views of him/herself relative to others (such as "inferiority, role confusion, isolation"). This development of "social self" is indicative of our need for self-esteem or social control. See his work (1950, Chapter 7).

[7] For stratification literature discussed here, refer to: Warner (1960); Alba Edwards (1938); National Opinion Research Center (1947).

[8] For general characteristics of bureaucracy, see H. H. Gerth and C. Wright Mills (1946).

[9] This "precarious consumption" is compounded by what Veblen called "conspicuous consumption" in which the consumer demonstrates his or her purchasing ability as an attempt to show off social status (Veblen, 1899).

[10] "Gesellschaft" represents values such as universalism, specificity, and neutrality as opposed to particularism, diffuseness, and affectivity which "Gemeinschaft" represents. Refer to Talcott Parsons (1937).

[11] For the justification of the dictatorial form of control in developing societies, refer to works by the leaders of Third World nations, compiled by Paul E. Sigmund (1962); also, John H. Kautsky, "The Appeal of Communist Models in Underdeveloped Countries," in his book (1968). Bruce Russett in an analysis of trends in world politics identifies the trend that most authoritarian nations are likely to be economically underdeveloped (Russett, 1965, pp. 138–144).

[12] Easton's definition of politics is appropriate for this fourth stage of development as he views politics as a process of "authoritative allocation of values." Refer to Easton (1965, pp. 96–97).

[13] One way of discerning the "ideal types" for the four stages is to observe the pattern of population distribution along the need hierarchy. Thus the ideal types might look something like the patterns shown in Figure 1.

[14] Indeed, this is in keeping with Maslow's characterization of the dynamics of the need hierarchy: the emergence of a new need does not mean that the previous need has disappeared; rather, it still must be satisfied, but the fact that it has been substantially and continuously gratified means that it is no longer the dominant concern of the individual. He is confident in his continued ability to satisfy that need, and hence his concerns shift to the next level.

[15] Huntington in his incisive assessment of the comparative study of modernization, development, and politics finds the literature wanting, still rife with "static assumptions," "teleological concerns," and "an evolutionary optimism reminiscent of the 19th Century." He states (Huntington, 1971: p. 294):

the modernization theory of the 1950s and 1960s has little or nothing to say about the future of modern societies; the advanced countries of the West, it was assumed, had "arrived," their past was of interest not for what it would show about their future but for what it showed about the future of those other societies which still struggled through the transition between tradition and modernity. . . . The theory of modernization thus rationalized change abroad and the status quo at home. It left blank the future of modernity. Modernization theory combined an extraordinary faith in the efficacy of modernity's past with no image of modernity's future.

REFERENCES

Apter, David E.
  1968   *Some Conceptual Approaches to Modernization.* Englewood Cliffs, N.J.: Prentice-Hall.
  1971   "Norms, Structure, and Behavior and the Study of Political Development," in Nancy Mammond, ed., *Social Science and the New Societies.* (East Lansing, Michigan: The Social Science Research Bureau, Michigan State University), pp. 3–17.
Blau, Peter M. and Otis D. Duncan
  1976   *The American Occupational Structure* (New York: John Wiley and Sons, Inc.).
Brodbeck, May
  1968   "Methodological Individualism: Definition and Reduction," in her reader, *Readings in the Philosophy of the Social Sciences* (New York: Macmillan Co.)
Dahrendorf, Ralf
  1959   *Class and Class Conflict in Industrial Society* (Stanford, California: Stanford University Press).
Durkheim, Emile
  1938   *The Rules of Sociological Method* (New York: Free Press, 1964).
Easton, David
  1965   *A Framework for Political Analysis* (Englewood, N.J.: Prentice-Hall).
Edwards, Alba
  1938   *A Social and Economic Grouping of the Gainfully Employed Workers in the United States* (Washington, D.C.: Bureau of Census).
Eisenstadt, S. N.
  1968   "Theories of Social and Political Evolution and Development," in *The Social Science: Problems and Orientations* (The Hague: Mouton).
Erikson, Erik
  1950   *Childhood and Society* (New York: W. W. Norton and Co., Inc).
Friedman, Milton
  1953   "The Methodology of Positive Economics" in Milton Friedman, ed. *Essays in Positive Economics* (Chicago: University of Chicago Press).

Gerth, H. H. and C. Wright Mills
   1946   *From Max Weber: Essays in Sociology* (London: Oxford University Press).
Goulet, Denis
   1968   "Development for What?," *Comparative Political Studies*, Vol. I, No. 2, pp. 295–312.
   1973   *The Cruel Choice: A New Concept in the Theory of Development* (New York: Atheneum).
Holsti, K. J.
   1975   "Underdevelopment and the 'Gap' Theory of International Conflict," *The American Political Science Review*, Vol. LXIX, No. 3, pp. 827–839.
Huntington, Samuel P.
   1965   "Political Development and Political Decay," *World Politics*, 17, pp. 386–430.
   1971   "The Change to Change," *Comparative Politics*, 3, No. 3.
Kautsky, John H.
   1968   *Communism and Politics of Development* (New York: John Wiley and Sons).
Kohlberg, Lawrence
   1969   "Stage and Sequence: The Cognitive Developmental Approach to Socialization" in *Handbook of Socialization Theory and Research*, David A. Goslin, ed. (Chicago: Rand McNally).
Kuhn, Thomas S.
   1962   *The Structure of Scientific Revolutions*, (Chicago, Ill.: University of Chicago Press).
Lenski, Gehard E.
   1966   *Power and Privilege* (New York: McGraw-Hill Book Co.).
Martindale, Don
   1962   *Social Life and Cultural Change* (New York: D. Van Nostrand Co., Inc.).
Maslow, Abraham H.
   1954   *Motivation and Personality* (New York: Harper and Row Publishers, Inc.).
N.O.R.C.
   1947   "Jobs and Occupations: A Popular Evaluation," *Opinion News*, 9.
Organski, A. F. K.
   1965   *The Stages of Political Development* (New York: Alfred Knopf).
Parsons, Talcott
   1937   *The Structure of Social Action* (New York: The Free Press).
Pennock, J. Roland
   1965   "Political Development, Political Systems and Political Goods," in *World Politics*, Vol. 18, No. 3.
Piaget, Jean
   1952   *The Origins of Intelligence in Children* (New York: W. W. Norton and Co., Inc.).
   1963   *Psychology of Intelligence* (New Jersey: Littlefield, Adams).

Pye, Lucian
    1965   "The Concept of Political Development," *The Annals of the American Academy of Political and Social Science,* 358.
Renshon, Stanley A.
    1974   *Psychological Needs and Political Behavior: A Theory of Personality and Political Efficacy,* (Riverside, N.J.: Macmillan Publishing Co.).
Rousseau, J.
    1762   *The Social Contract* (trans. G. D. Cole, E. P. Dutton and Company).
Russett, Bruce M.
    1965   *Trends in World Politics* (New York: The Macmillan Co.).
Veblen, T.
    1899   *The Theory of the Leisure Class: An Economic Study of Institutions.*
Warner, W. Lloyd, et al.
    1960   *Social Class in America: A Manual Procedure for the Measurement of Social Status* (New York: Harper and Row).
Watkins, J. W. N.
    1968   "Methodological Individualism and Social Tendencies," in May Brodbeck (1968).

Chapter IV

REGIME FORMATION

Regime formation refers to the process by which a new political system emerges. In this process, the incumbency of a new leadership will be identified, established, and defined. New rules will be promulgated to establish authoritatively which individual and group behaviors are tolerable and which are not. New political structures and institutions will be installed to replace the old, and above all, concerted efforts will be made by the leadership to solidify the populace in order to expand the scope of its capacity to control people and events and thus perpetuate its power position. Thus, a regime formation entails much more than a change in government personnel. It means a profound change in the nature of the political community itself.

TYPOLOGY

Regimes may be formed in a variety of ways. One of the earliest conceivable forms was "primitive unification" (Organski, 1965) in which tribal groups were consolidated under a common authority. Although all modern nations may have gone through this stage of primitive unification at one time or another, regimes are no longer formed in this way. Another type of regime formation which was rather prevalent during the dynastic era of political history, but is no longer an effective mechanism of regime change, is the hereditary succession of power. Although there may still be some monarchies remaining in the world today, their roles are mostly symbolic and ceremonial. With reference to the present topic, we can say at the very least they no longer serve as the institutional channel for succession and change in political leadership.

Modern regimes are formed through either election or revolution. As a common institution, the election often fails to produce a new regime but some elections do lead to profound changes in the nature of the political system. Although mass revolutions have been rather infrequent, their impact on the course of history has been extensive indeed. Mass revolutions, like sleeping volcanos, may not explode regularly, but when they do, their component behaviors and impacts become very difficult to assess scientifically. When a seemingly revolutionary change falls short of an extensive shake-up of the political system itself, thus resulting in a leadership change only, *coup d'état* becomes the appropriate concept with which to characterize such an event. Owing to its frequent occurrence, the *coup d'état*, which is usually instigated by the military, has become an important mechanism of regime change in post-World War II world politics.

In short, there are several different types of regime change in addition to "primitive unification," the original form of regime formation. Of these types, hereditary succession and electoral transition of power may be considered "legitimate" forms, as they proceed through existing institutions and according to rules based on widely shared norms and values. On the other hand, revolution and *coup d'état* are the extra-institutional or "illegitimate" means of regime change (Chart 2), as they occur in defiance of such rules and with the expressed purpose of altering, among other things, the rules of succession.

In this chapter, we shall examine each of these types with a more exhaustive discussion on revolution. Additionally, we shall examine the nature of the newly emergent political system itself, as we seek to illuminate some characteristic features of newly formed social and political institutions and their relationship to the indigenous cultural configurations of a society.

Hereditary Succession as a Symbol
In the modern era, as the basis of all regimes' claims to legitimacy has shifted from such principles of Divine Right or the Mandate of Heaven to some form of social contract, traditional hereditary dynasties have been replaced by various manifestations of republican government and people's democracies, all of which claim legitimacy on the basis of some type of mandate of the governed. Of some 150 nations, only a

CHART 2
Types of Regime Formation

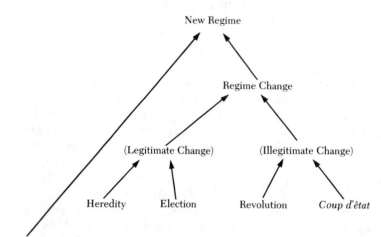

handful still maintain the system of inheritance, and few are intended to fulfill the function of power succession. Most of these nations retain their nationhood. The hereditary monarchs do not wield political power, nor do they personify public opinion or any popular mandate. In this sense, heredity is not a meaningful institution of power succession because in systems with such an institution political power resides elsewhere. To the extent that a state needs symbolic authority and desires to induce pride among the people for the history and heritage of the nation, the royal institution may be desirable and often functional toward that end. Nonetheless, succession through inheritance is no longer used in itself as an institution of regime change. This is not to disregard the fact that many reform movements and even revolutionary changes in the characteristics of political systems have evolved around replacement of rulers through the means of inheritance. The Meiji Restoration of 1868 in Japan was an example in which political reform was carried out by a warrior class, as it attempted to restore the power and authority of the royal family. But even in this case, the reformists did not start the restoration movement just for the protection of the royal institution; rather, the warrior class (Samurai), disenchanted with the feudal social structure and political order, used the idea of royal restoration to justify their "modernization" of other social and political institutions.

Election as a Mobilizing Mechanism

As we noted earlier, since the inception of the theory of Social Contract in the early seventeenth century, governments of all types have sought legitimacy for their exercise of political power in the name of the "consent of the governed." Thus, at least in theory, it would be unlikely that any government could prolong its claim to power without obtaining the continuous support, in some form or another, of its people. Although "popular support" and "consent of the governed" have been interpreted in a variety of ways by ruling elites of different political hues, no one would deny the importance of some minimal level of popular well-being as the ultimate basis of popular support and, therefore, of a regime's claim to legitimacy.

Thus, the popular election, as an institution by which candidates for positions of power are compared in terms of the levels of popular support each can generate, has become an effective, rational and widely used institution for the orderly transfer of political power. In reality, however, a regime change does not occur in so orderly a fashion unless the politics of the political system are guided by some form of constitutionalism and certain "rules of the game" that are deeply imbedded in the culture and political experience of the society. In other words, orderly change through elections is not expected in those societies where such culture and political experience are lacking, or where the masses are struggling for satisfaction of the most basic needs of physical survival. In such a society, the elite's claim to legitimate authority is tenuous at best, and electoral mechanisms themselves do not have the legitimacy that makes them institutions of orderly personnel change. Social and political pluralism as well as alternative parties and candidates are lacking and indeed may be outlawed. What opposition there is is likely to be revolutionary in nature, and seeks not only changes in government personnel from within a given elite group but replacement of the current elite group with an entirely different group. Under such conditions, those in power will use the election mechanism as a means to rubber stamp their own incumbency rather than as a means by which the popular support for one set of policies is tested against alternatives.

Thus, it should be to no one's surprise that in such societies elections have seldom served even as a means of government personnel change, let alone change in the structure of the regime and the political system itself. Where elections are taking place in the Third World, patterns of electoral behavior are often strikingly different from those accompanying elections in more mature pluralistic and polyarchical democracies.

One such unusual electoral pattern may be observed in the fact that people of lower socio-economic status are likely to be more "participant" in elections than people of higher education and income. This pattern prevails in many non-Western "democratic" societies (Verba et al., 1971). If indeed the inverse relationship between indicators of social development, such as education and income, and levels of electoral participation is the case, its implications for democratic development are quite serious. For instance, one could infer from this pattern that as the society successfully improves the socio-economic status of its populace, participatory democracy will inevitably decline. Yet, in the United States and most Western democratic societies we find that as people attain education and achieve higher socio-economic positions they tend to be more efficacious politically and better informed on political issues, and thus participate in elections more frequently and intensely. This "normal" pattern of electoral behavior is consistent with the general understanding that social and economic development will facilitate political democracy (Campbell et al., 1960).

The question is, why do people in many Third World and non-Western societies participate in elections less as they attain higher socio-economic status, particularly higher education? One prevailing explanation is that in such societies the institution of elections is not used primarily as an instrument whereby political systems or regimes may be altered or replaced. Rather, elections in these societies are used to mobilize the masses for the purpose of affirming the legitimacy of the existing government and its political structures and policies, thus solidifying the incumbent's power position. Here, elections are not used as a means by which the regime's performance can be judged by the people. The belief that voters in Third World nations may be mobilized by the government for generating maximum support, and that people with poor education and lower status are more easily subject to such government manipulation aptly describes this abnormal role of elections in these societies.

As the records indicate, few regime changes have resulted from lawful elections in societies outside the Western hemisphere. But the institution of elections has been employed in virtually every modern nation, including even totalitarian communist systems. This implies that elections serve some other purpose if not regime change. In countries experiencing difficulties in maintaining regime stability, often the occupants of the elite structure utilize electoral institutions for soliciting expressions of support for their claim to power or for expanding their power base. Particularly when the regime has just gained control over rival elite groups, it will need to prevent the possible resurgence of contending leaders. Thus, it is commonplace to find that purges and executions of opponents usually occur after a regime change; elections that might lend legitimacy to the rivals' claims and aspirations to power are not likely to be permitted.

In examining the functions of elections in emerging and unstable societies in this way, it is safe to conclude that the electoral system as a mechanism for regime succession is not a viable institution in these societies. In fact, many studies on the social conditions of democracy have suggested that the democratic electoral system is unsuitable for economically and socially underdeveloped countries (Park, 1976). A fuller discussion of the topic of the preconditions of democracy will be presented in Chapter V.

Military Coup d'État: A Vicious Cycle
An overwhelming proportion of Third World nations have experienced frequent regime change at the hands of the military, as shown in Table 1. Many of these countries do not seem to have any alternative but to remain in a vicious cycle of successive military *coups d'état*. In Bolivia, the turnover is so frequent that there have been some 190 irregular government changes since the nation's independence in 1825 (Kline, 184). Most of these regime changes instigated by the military involve only the circulation of government personnel and have little if any impact on the distribution of wealth and power, or on the social and political institutions of the country. However, each time a society undergoes a military coup the population must face a certain amount of political instability and uncertainty and often serious threats to their physical safety.

There seem to be several characteristics of newly independent and previously colonial countries that render them susceptible to successive military coups. An analysis of these factors may help us understand the dynamics of Third World politics, and approach problems in the area.

The Military as a Symbol of Nationhood. As a nation becomes politically independent from a colonial power, the first order of business tends to be the building of its own military machine. This is even more urgent when the people attribute the shameful experience of colonial rule to the former lack of military capability. Here, amidst the euphoria of independence, the people are often quite willing to give unconditional support to the building of the military. Symbolic features such as military uniforms, national anthems, and national flags are likely to reinforce and accommodate nationalist sentiments among the public. Thus, it is expected that in a newly independent nation, populist culture will be such that the strong institutionalization of the military will attain priority over the institutionalization of other political structures.

The Military as Mobilizer. Most Third World nations maintain a conscription army as a mechanism for military recruitment. In such a system, the army could be a *mass* organization which represents all segments of the society, and the government therefore can mobilize mass support through the army.

The army in the early stages of political development has a wide range of functions in addition to its primary role of national defense. These functions include the aforementioned political function of generating public support, as well as administrative functions of implementing policies by serving as a law enforcement agent, and even economic functions such as engaging in road constructions and other civil engineering projects. While performing these diverse roles, the military comes to command a great deal of power and authority beyond that associated with its defense function. This inordinate extension of its sphere of authority is facilitated further by the absence of any other large institutionalized political organization (with the possible exception of educational institutions, which we shall discuss in a later chapter). Thus, it comes to dominate civilian political institutions rather than simply serving as the enforcement mechanism for civilian policy makers.

The Military as a Modernizing Agent. In a society where a large proportion of the population is illiterate and has little motivation to train itself or to alter a lifestyle it has inherited for generations, military personnel often constitute the most skilled labor pool and thus, the leading edge of social change. In fact, military draftees in an underdeveloped society are taught to read and write and are provided with training in various technical fields which can be utilized in industrialization and other developmental social changes.

When a soldier is discharged from the military, he becomes an important opinion leader in his community and often exposes that community to information and ideas from outside the traditional community and its culture. Chances are that he himself will eventually migrate to an urban and presumably industrial locale and become instrumental in bringing other members of his family to the city, thus contributing to demographic changes in the society. The extent of the military's contribution to social change has to be enormous when the military is the primary large scale modernized mass organization, as is likely to be the case in any new nation.

The Military as an Egalitarian Institution. The institution of the military, with its rigid hierarchical command structure, is commonly known to be undemocratic. But in a newly independent nation the institution promotes achievement norms and provides democratic experience, at least to a greater degree than other traditional social institutions. Coming from a society that is primarily agrarian in its economy, feudal in its social structure and authoritarian in its political culture, the new soldier will experience a clear departure from the structural and cultural norms of the society. Every draftee, regardless of his social and economic background, is to be treated equally in that all receive the same uniform, the same amount of pay, and have the same obligations and duties. For the mass of the recruits this is a rather drastic and remarkable departure from their conventional social situation.

When soldiers are released from their military duties and return to civilian society, they often find it difficult to readjust due to their egalitarian experience and the new attitudes developed therein. As discussed earlier, many of them will leave their home communities for this reason and seek alternative lifestyles in urban settings. As urbanization is still in progress or has just begun, there is no "urban culture" as such to which the new migrants need to adapt. Rather, an urban culture will still be in the formative stages, just as the city itself is. In such a situation, those newcomers who have had military experience will have shared values and attitudes, as well as job skills, and thus will become the core segment of urban communities and the emergent "urban culture." Urban areas formed in this manner are more likely to be "egalitarian" and their new norms and values are fundamentally inconsistent with the traditional rural and agrarian culture.

These and other features of the institution of the military in Third World nations contribute to making that institution a pivotal developmental organization. All other institutions are likely to be centered around the military. Even in educational planning, national defense and the role of military will be given the highest priority. The economy will be decidedly affected by military needs. Every family will have someone serving in the army. Popular culture in the form of folk songs and stories and arts of all kinds will in some way promote military heroism.

In such a society, it would be highly unlikely if not impossible for anyone who does not have military leadership to emerge as a national political leader. This helps us understand why there has been in the Third World a strong political overtone in the military and why military leaders are most likely to dominate or even serve as politicians.

However, this still does not answer the puzzling question of why some societies have more stable military leadership than others. Many military-backed leaders around the world have enjoyed relatively stable and prolonged occupation of leadership positions, whereas many more have experienced short terms, and even shortened lives, as a result of their inability to control recurrent military coups. A cursory observation of regime changes around the world would suggest that there are some common characteristics among the more stable military regimes, and that these characteristics have helped the leadership in prolonging its power position. Among them we can cite (1) perceived or actual threat from outside; (2) the maintenance of a closed political system by controlling popular access to the outside world and by controlling communication among the domestic population; (3) developing an air of charisma for a leader through politicization of the masses around a cult or personality.

The crucial parameter for an effective military is its coercive capability, and, accordingly, the primary instrument for military control of political decision-making is its use of physical coercion. In domestic politics, however, coercive measures will not be effective for long, unless their use is seen as legitimate. In other words, in order to crack down on dissent and government critics, while at the same time building a stable foundation of popular support, the regime needs to employ some sort of justification for repressive action. Such justification is often found in claiming a threat to the nation's very existence, thus making compliance with government policies a necessity for the nation's survival.

Arousing the spectre of threat from without in order to solidify power within is hardly a novel strategy for a government or any other organization. Georg Simmel's study of organizational behavior espoused the thesis that organizational solidarity is likely to be enhanced when its environment is hostile. (There is also experimental evidence from small group psychology confirming this same phenomenon.[1]) Given the potentially severe consequences of foreign military attack, what a government must do to generate national unity is to create a minimally credible perception of foreign hostility. The actual magnitude or probability of conflict is less important.

Shielding information from outside, and controlling information flow within is essential to a stable military dictatorship, if for no other reason than the aforementioned purpose of provoking a sense of national crisis. To this end, a military regime imposes tight censorship on the media by allowing only a limited number of channels to serve as official, or functionally official, government organs.

Keeping the public selectively informed, misinformed or completely uninformed about world affairs is a common strategy of a repressive leadership to prevent riots and demonstrations or other anti-government opposition activities. By keeping the public incapable of comprehending public affairs and world politics the regime effectively maintains a closed society, and therefore is able to control people and events. It is often in the interest of the regime to retain the underdeveloped conditions of low literacy, governmentally constrained mass communication, and non-participatory political culture. In this sense, an ideal policy for perpetuating a military regime is to adopt a totalitarian form of government, since the most enduring military leaderships are found in totalitarian countries.

A military or militarist regime will seek to secure its power base by gaining some measure of mass support, either active or tacit, in its effort to eliminate power rivals, a process usually done in the name of the people. In this effort the regime will attempt to promote charismatic leadership through programs of indoctrination and political socialization. Such a leadership takes on a mystical, messianic quality that elicits widespread emotional popular support. In the post-independent Third World, charismatic leadership tends to emerge contemporaneously with the spirit of nationalism, and indeed the leader comes to be identified with the nation state itself and vice versa. Thus, to deny the leadership is to deny the statehood of the nation itself. In countries where the people still have vivid memories of the colonial experience, a growing ethos of nationalism, cystallized around the personality of the charismatic leader, can serve as justification for fierce suppression by the regime of any activity in opposition to the regime or its policies. The ability of the charismatic leader to generate such nationalism is greatest when he can claim to have played a crucial role in winning independence in the first place. Qualities of charismatic leadership have been found in such diverse but predominant personalities as Nehru of India, Mao of China, Sukarno of Indonesia, Nkrumah of Ghana, Nasser of Egypt, Kim Il-sung of North Korea, and Kenyatta of Kenya.[2]

From this evidence, we may suggest, first, that the presence of external threat, or at least the perception of a grave national crisis which might lead to the eventual dissolution or subjugation of the nation itself will help the military regime prolong its political life. It is not unusual that a regime facing the potential of domestic unrest will provoke external conflict, such as border skirmishes or military involvement in a self-proclaimed war, in order to arouse a sense of national emergency.

Second, a regime which implements an effective censorship program and insulates the public from sources of information external to the country is likely to stay in power longer than one in a more open society.

Third, when power is centered around one person, to the extent that he comes to personify the new national identity, the degree of charisma this person holds may be a predictor of stability of the government. However, the dilemma of charismatic leadership is that leaders die, and unless a leader can succeed in transferring personal allegiance to ongoing government institutions, the political stability is likely to dissolve when he dies.

In the foregoing discussion, we identified a few bases upon which a military regime attempts to prolong its political incumbency. Implicit in the discussion were the converse: namely, the causes of unstable military leadership. From this discussion, we might be able to discern a few propositions which may help us answer the crucial question of why some regimes never seem to escape the vicious cycle of military coups.

Even with a strong charismatic leadership in a tightly controlled closed society where people are politically inactive and nonparticipant, a regime can experience instability if its people are living in a state of extreme impoverishment without any alternative but rebellion. When people's minimum physical survival is threatened and the government is held responsible, the regime may be unable to prevent riots and uprisings. We shall turn to this question of revolutionary uprising later in this chapter.

Based on the paradigm outlined in the previous chapter, we can postulate a dilemma facing all military regimes, one which might be a key to explaining the phenomenon of successive military *coups d'état* in societies where the government is seemingly performing its role efficiently. The dilemma exists in that people in first stage societies will not continue to maintain their need level at physical survival once they are reasonably assured of basic human needs such as food, shelter, and protection from life-threatening conditions. A society with a military government that can assure satisfaction of these most basic needs will move into the second stage of political integration, when people's needs shift to belonging. In this case, the regime will lose its foundations of popular support not by being incapable of gratifying survival needs but rather because of a failure to address the newly emergent belonging needs. When the regime is inappropriate or incapable of adjusting its policy priorities to corresponding changes in popular needs and demands, it cannot retain the same level of popular support it generated in the first stage, even if it continues to be effective in delivering the basic services necessary for physical survival.

The military institution cannot easily adapt its policies to accommodate people's desire to enhance their social and psychological belonging. The military is an institution where values such as uniformity rather than diversity, command rather than compromise, and physical protection rather than psychological comfort are given the distinct priority. As has been aptly said, there are three ways of doing things in the world: the right way, the wrong way, and the military way. As such, professional militarism and military organization usually constitute a barrier rather than a facilitator to the second stage of social development. At a time when a regime suffers a low level of public support, it becomes vulnerable to power conflict, and a most likely form of power conflict in this early stage of development is one leading to a power struggle within the military itself. In the course of personnel and other shake-ups in the government, which are to be expected when eroding government support leads to anti-government activity in the society at large and power conflict within the regime, the once-secured basis of physical survival of the people will be threatened. As a result, the prevailing popular needs and demands will revert from the level of belonging to the more basic needs of physical survival. A new military government, which can successfully seize power in a coup, is bound to gain some support from the people simply by returning political stability and thus the capacity to ensure survival needs.

However, as soon as a new stability is achieved and the basic needs are assured, people will not lose any time in shifting their need level once again to that of belongingness, thus leading to another legitimacy crisis for the new regime if it too fails to adapt its policy priorities accordingly. When the effects of the power struggle are so extensive that the capacity to ensure survival needs cannot be revived easily and quickly after the coup, the government will enjoy a relatively prolonged period of minimal support for its rule, as the people's wounds from political turmoil and the struggle to survive gradually heal. A country like Bolivia which has recorded perhaps the greatest frequency of military coups is not a country whose people live precariously close to starvation, desiring merely physical survival. Rather, it is a country capable of providing at least the most basic services through its bureaucracy. For this reason, ironically, it might be more vulnerable to frequent coups, especially if these events leave the bureaucracy relatively intact. Indeed, as Table 1 shows, a great military involvement in politics exists in countries with relatively higher rates of economic growth, rather than the poor and stagnant countries. In short, what causes regime stability is not merely the efficiency of the government but to a large extent the degree to which it can anticipate and adapt to the changing needs of the public. This conclusion is not to suggest that all governments are inclined to respond to people's needs but, more importantly, that a government must *adjust* to the changing characteristics of popular demands if it is to draw public support, for it is the people's support that ultimately justifies political power. The military's rigidity, limited vision, and narrow range of capacities may thus be an important contributor to the phenomenon of vicious cycles of *coups d'état.*

Revolution: the Ultimate Change

A revolution represents the most traumatic and extensive form of regime change in that the entire political system is affected, including the lifestyle of the masses. A change in governmental structure or its personnel may be an important outcome of most revolutions, but it alone cannot constitute a revolution. A government change, in fact, is not only insufficient for a revolution but it is theoretically unnecessary. At times, we use the label "revolution" for an extensive social change forcing the society to alter its structure and people's lifestyle without governmental reorganization, as, for instance, in the case of the industrial revolution. In most cases, however, a revolution does involve governmental reorganization and overthrow of the incumbent regime through mass violence directed at the incumbent regime. A revolution, then, can be defined as a type of social change in which profound institutional changes force members of the society to alter drastically their lifestyle in a relatively short period of time.

In such a revolutionary process, it is commonly expected that many vital institutions will be dismantled and new ones formed. At the same time, a major proportion of the people find themselves socially dislocated and preoccupied with the tasks of relocation and readjustment to the new emerging institutional reality. Thus, political and social instability are typical symptoms of any revolution. In this section, we shall briefly examine the causes and dynamics of revolutionary social change as espoused by different authors, and attempt to synthesize their views and refine some theories for a more comprehensive analysis of revolutionary phenomena.

There are a good many theories of revolution and revolutionary activity. While there are varying views as to conditions for revolution, they all seem to agree that men rebel when they *feel* unhappy to the extent that they are willing to risk a drastic alteration of the existing power and authority structure on the basis of a belief that this is the only hope for an improvement in their situation. What might facilitate psychological dissatisfaction may vary, as evidenced in the economic determinism of Marxist theory, the political determinism of Lenin, and psychological determinism of Davies (1971). But the immediate cause of any revolutionary activity has to be the individual actor's attitudes and behavioral predispositions. One cannot explain revolution in any causal sense by direct use of aggregate social or economic variables, since a society or even a class as such cannot have a motive for taking an action. Only individuals have motives. This is not to suggest that we can or should deny the importance of social and economic conditions that are likely to produce a revolutionary state of mind among individuals. But our immediate analytical concern should be with the kinds of mind sets that might be conducive to engaging in revolutionary behavior. Social and economic conditions may be found to be the ultimate source of psychological discontent, but, in particular, certain social and contextual conditions cause revolutionary behavior through their impact on individual psychology and/or behavioral tendencies.

We shall examine a few premises and theoretical concepts that have been proposed as being valuable tools for the explanation of revolutionary behavior.

Frustration-Aggression. A basic premise in the frustration-aggression model is that revolutionary activity will occur when there is widespread frustration of some felt need or needs in society, and the government is viewed as being in some way responsible for this frustration. This premise is grounded in two psychological theories: frustration-aggression theory and theories of human needs as motivating forces of individual behavior. Frustration, following Gurr's discussion, "can be regarded simply as interference with goal-directed behavior" (1970, chapter 2). Aggression, an activity designed to injure the frustrating agent, is the individual's usual response to intense frustration. When the government is blamed for the frustration of large numbers of people in a polity, violent action aimed at the current regime will result. Thus, it follows that by knowing what needs are held in common and are prevalent at a given point in time, we can determine better which societal conditions are likely to produce such frustration.

For theoretical purposes we are conforming largely to Maslow's contentions, as we discussed in Chapter III. We maintain that all humans share the same basic needs, which dictate behavioral goals for the individual, though what counts for satisfaction of a given need may vary

TABLE 1

Selected Third World Countries Compared According to Degree of Military Influence in Politics and Growth Rate of GNP/Capita, 1965–1974

Degree of Military Influence		Less than 0		0.00–0.99		1.00–1.99		2.00–2.99		3.00	
Military regime	(34)	Chad, Equatorial Guinea, Mali, Niger, Somalia, Sudan	(6)	Benin, Burundi, Central African Republic, Ghana, Madagascar, Uganda, Upper Volta, Afghanistan	(8)	Chile, Haiti, Honduras, Ethiopia, Yemen Arab Republic	(5)	Argentina, Bolivia, Ecuador, Peru, Bangladesh	(5)	Brazil, Panama, Algeria, Iraq, Libya, Congo Republic, Nigeria, Rwanda, Togo, Thailand	(10)
High military influence	(23)	Uruguay	(1)	Egypt, Jordan, Lesotho, Zaire, Burma	(5)	El Salvador, Morocco, Sierra Leone	(3)	Colombia, Nicaragua, Paraguay, Syria, Philippines	(5)	Dominican Republic, Guatemala, Oman, Turkey, Cameroon, Gabon, Indonesia, South Korea, Pakistan	(5)

112

Low military influence (35)	(3)	(4)	(5)	(6)	(17)
	Bahrain	Guyana	Kuwait	Jamaica	Costa Rica
	Senegal	India	Qatar	Gambia	Trinidad
	Zambia	Nepal	Mauritania	Mexico	Botswana
		Peoples Democratic	Venezuela	South Africa	Liberia
		Republic	Guinea	Tanzania	Mauritius
		of Yemen		Sri Lanka	Swaziland
					Saudi Arabia
					Tunisia
					Ivory Coast
					Rhodesia
					Malaysia
					Singapore
					United Arab
					Emirates
					Iran
					Kenya
					Malawi
					Taiwan

Source: U.S. Arms Control and Disarmament Agency, *World Military Expenditures and Arms Transfers: 1965–1974,* (Washington, D.C.: USGPO, 1976).

Note: All growth rates are for the period 1965–1974 except the following: Guyana, Singapore, and Rhodesia (1966–1974); Botswana, Lesotho (1967–1974); Mauritius, Peoples Democratic Republic of Yemen (1968–1974); Equatorial Guinea, Swaziland (1969–1974); Bahrain (1971–1974); and Qatar, Bangladesh, United Arab Emirates (1972–1974).

across cultures. All behavior is a means for the fulfillment of these needs and desires, which acquire or assume a hierarchy of importance. Thus frustrations can occur at any level of social development since individuals may be frustrated for different reasons. A person can be frustrated, for example, because he or she is deprived of the basic needs of food, shelter, and security. Others can be equally frustrated because of denial of freedom or belonging. Still others can be discontented because of continuous failure in securing power positions.

This model thus requires, as Davies correctly observes, "the assessment of the state of mind of a people" to predict the source and level of frustration and, hence, the probability of revolutionary activity (1970, p. 146). While it is possible at times to actually collect information on an individual's state of mind through the use of interviews, an extensive direct inquiry into the "state of mind" would be impractical. Furthermore, levels of frustration in the populace would be changing their needs and desires change and as societal conditions chang₍ necessitating constant reassessment of the situation. It would therefor be desirable to determine what social conditions lead to frustrations ₍ individual needs.

Obviously the most basic need of humans and other organisms is the need for physical survival. But in individual terms, satisfaction of this need is not necessarily related to the level of aggregate or average wealth in the society. We would not want to say that the poorer a society is, the more likely there is to be frustration of basic needs and therefore the more likely there is to be revolutionary activity. While the frustration statement might be true enough, revolutionary activity will probably not take place in the most economically backward societies. As Davies notes, in such societies the physical and mental energies of people are totally occupied with the tasks of merely staying alive (1970, p. 136). Starving people do not join guerrilla armies, nor can they afford to take time out to throw rocks at government officials. On the other hand, in advanced societies with considerable wealth, the great majority would risk losing physical comfort by engaging in revolutionary activity. Therefore, it should be in transitional societies that we are more apt to find the types of political strife typically subsumed under the term "revolution." It is these societies that are undergoing the so-called "revolution of rising expectations." Hence, it is in the context of transitional societies that we shall examine two alternative theoretical constructs of revolutionary causation: the "J-curve" and the "U-curve."

The "J-Curve"

In his seminal work "Toward a Theory of Revolution," James Davies proposed a theory of revolution based on the psychological concept of "rising expectation" and the social variable of declining achievement (Davies, 1963). He postulated that human discontent will be intensified as one finds a growing discrepancy between one's expectations, which tend to increase constantly, and one's actual achievements, which tend to be lagging below the expectation level. The gap between the two variables, however, will not necessarily lead to a revolution as long as it remains within a "tolerable" range. However, when uncontrollable changes in the society, such as economic recession, cause a rapid decline in the level of one's achievement, the result is a dramatic increase in the gap between expectations and achievement. When people find that the gap cannot be tolerated, a "revolutionary state of mind" emerges among members of the society, inevitably leading to an actual revolution (Figure 3). In an effort to demonstrate the applicability of the "J-Curve" theory of revolution, Davies cites three cases, including Dorr's Rebellion, the Russian Revolution, and the Egyptian Revolution of 1952.

However, while, as a conceptual model, this theory is both intuitively appealing and apparently rich in potential explanatory power, Davies acknowledges that his "J-curve" model cannot explain all instances of revolution. And while he does tentatively limit its applicability to so-called "progressive" revolutions, he nowhere specifies what is meant by the term "progressive," nor does he examine why his theory should be limited in applicability to revolutions of this type. Indeed, this limitation seems based upon some perceived commonality in the espoused goals of the three revolutions that Davies uses as test cases of his model's validity (Davies, 1971).

In order to more fully realize the explanatory potential of Davies' model, we must first specify the "types" of revolutions—in terms of the social preconditions and psychological causes—to which the Davies model is applicable. Toward this end, we shall examine the assumptions—both implicit and explicit—of the Davies theory in order to more precisely delimit the scope of the model's empirical applicability;

FIGURE 3

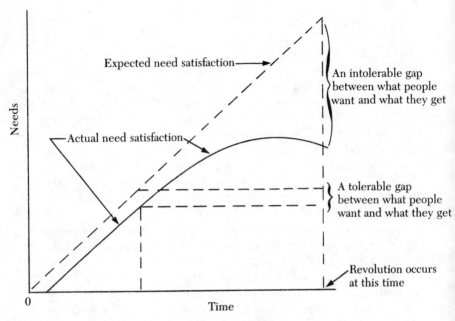

Source: Davies 1971, p. 135

subsequently, we shall propose an alternative explanation of the causes of revolution that, in terms of the scope of its applicability, will stand as a complement to the Davies theory. That is, rather than a denial of the Davies "J-curve" thesis, this alternative explanatory model is hypothesized to be applicable to certain types of serious civil disturbance that, while definable as revolutions, are in fact not within the empirically specified domain of the Davies model. What, then, are these assumptions and how, specifically, do they limit the applicability of the "J-curve" model?

As alluded to earlier, Davies' central thesis is that "revolutions are most likely to occur when a prolonged period of objective economic and social development is followed by a short period of sharp reversal" (Davies, 1971, p. 136). This proposition is deduced from the contention that the former period (of socio-economic development) will engender in a people the expectation of continued ability to satisfy their needs—needs which are themselves continually rising and expanding—and that the frustration of these expectations that occur in the latter period (of decline) will give rise to a revolutionary state of mind.

Thus, according to Davies, a certain trend in socio-economic conditions is assumed to engender in individuals feelings of dissatisfaction; and, in the absence of complete socio-economic deprivation, collective dissatisfaction will find social expression in revolution. However, several scholars (most notably Ted Gurr) have identified at least one other variable that is relevant to determining whether the dissatisfied state of mind, even when generalized into the requisite "social mood," will seek overt social expression in the form of revolutionary behavior. Even if the general state of life conditions is such that, for the population as a whole, minimum physical survival is assured, dissatisfied people are less likely to revolt if they perceive the government as having the capacity to put down the rebellion. If the probable costs of a revolution, in terms of human lives, are perceived as being extremely high, the masses may develop serious doubts about their chances for successful revolution and, consequently, not attempt such an uprising. Thus, the government's "coercive potential" is of relevance to the last link in the causal chain between the social mood of dissatisfaction and its overt expression as revolutionary behavior (Gurr, p. 1968).

A second and perhaps more crucial assumption in the Davies model is that expected need satisfaction will continue to rise even after there has been a sharp decline in the level of actual need satisfaction. The validity of this assumption is essential to the logic of the model since it is in this manner that the frustration that gives rise to revolution is created. Frustration is here conceived as the gap between expectations and achievement. It is our contention that this assumption is valid only under certain conditions. On the basis of this limitation of the model's applicability a more thorough analytical conception is proposed.

The three revolutions that Davies uses as test cases—Dorr's Rebellion, the Russian Revolution and the Egyptian Revolution of 1952—are marked by a seven-year, three-year, and two-year period, respectively, of sharp reversals in the level of popular need satisfaction. And for the latter two (the Russian and Egyptian cases) the period of *general* decline is twelve years and four years, respectively, with brief periods of minimal recovery temporarily defusing the revolutionary potential of these situations (Davies, 1971, pp. 138, 142, 144). Yet throughout these several years of decline, the popular level of expected need satisfaction is assumed to be increasing, or at least not decreasing.

We would argue that the continued rise in expectations in the face of several years of decline in objective socio-economic conditions may be conceivable only under certain conditions, and that, therefore, the applicability of the "J-curve" model is limited to cases that manifest these conditions.

What, then, are these conditions? The continued rise in expectations would occur only in a society in which the preceding prolonged period of objective social and economic development was characterized by *qualitative* socio-economic development such that the fundamental social fabric of the nation had undergone broad and profound change.

In this light, the paradigm sketched out in Chapter III might well be used as an ideal theoretical framework for specifying qualitative dimensions of social development, as it depicts social change in terms of qualitative dimensions of individual human needs. Furthermore, the paradigm as a stage theory of development specifies the sequence of qualitative changes in human needs and social development. As alluded to earlier, Davies' assumption of the continued rise in expectations in the face of several years of decline in objective socio-economic conditions is plausible only if the preceding period of development was one of *qualitative* change in the basic fabric of society. In the context of the development paradigm, then, we can conceptualize this qualitative change as the procession from one stage in the developmental process to the next. That such a progression constitutes a qualitative change in the patterns of social behavior is deduced from the fact that the motivational basis of such behavior has changed; a qualitatively different set of needs has emerged as the basis of people's expectations, and the decline in conditions threatens not only their ability to satisfy these emergent needs but eventually, the satisfaction of the previous levels of needs as well.

Thus, the "J-curve" model would be applicable in cases where the period of development has carried the people to the completion of one stage in the development process and into the beginnings of the achievement of the next stage. The subsequent decline would not lead to revolution as long as the accompanying conditions of deprivation involved only the loss of the more newly acquired kind of needs. Now, the new needs will dictate patterns of social behavior but since people have no basis in past experience to expect the satisfaction of the new types of needs, they are unlikely to develop false expectations regarding their fulfillment.

However, once the decline threatens the continued satisfaction of the qualitatively different and now substantially satisfied needs of the previous stage, revolution will break out. Perhaps of relevance here is Maslow's assertion that a person who has enjoyed fairly substantial and continuous satisfaction of a need is most able to tolerate a brief period of deprivation with respect to that need. To extrapolate somewhat from Maslow's reasoning, it appears plausible that while people in such situations may be able to tolerate current deprivation of that need, on a social level, they are unlikely to placidly accept the prospects of a prolonged or indefinite period of such deprivation, especially when they do not see themselves as responsible for the conditions that make the continued satisfaction of these needs appear uncertain.

Here, "intolerance" can be conceived of as a situation in which expectations are not adjusted downward with the decline in objective conditions. The completion of a stage in the development process implies that the people feel secure in their continued ability to satisfy the corresponding level of needs within existing social patterns. Their expectations remain high in this respect. Therefore, they will "tolerate" what we analytically define as the "gap" between expectations and satisfactions so long as this discrepancy is considered temporary.

However, once the prospects appear dim for the rapid recovery of the threatened level of needs, the "gap" between expectations and achievement will become intolerable, and a revolutionary state of mind will start to emerge among the people. Since the regime is considered ultimately responsible for engineering the social change necessary for the satisfaction of popular needs, it is the regime that is seen as being ultimately responsible for the disruption of existing social patterns to the extent that the previously gratified needs can no longer be satisfied on a steady basis. Likewise, the regime has demonstrated its inability (or unwillingness) to provide the means for the satisfaction of the newly emergent needs. Therefore, the regime is held responsible for popular frustrations and hence becomes the target for revolution.

For illustrative purposes, we can turn to Davies' own example of the Russian Revolution. After the emancipation of the serfs in 1861, their resocialization into new patterns of social life was not even remotely achieved until the early part of the twentieth century. Finally, after several abortive and impractical attempts at agrarian reorganization based on the private ownership of land, a system of rural communes was established which apparently removed the subordinate relationship of the serf to his former master without placing upon the serf the inordinate burden of having to buy his own land. Industrialization was proceeding, although much of it was imported and foreign-owned, and the people were granted a Duma with certain legislative powers (Treadgold, 1964).

The new patterns of social organization reintegrated the peasantry into society, and the popular demand for value control, in the form of greater political participation and a better standard of living was recognized to some extent by the Tsarist regime. However, the decline in socio-economic conditions which began prior to World War I was one of quality as well as quantity. The rural commune system was broken up by the Stolypin reforms, and private ownership again became the basis of rural social and economic organization; the Duma was stripped of all power and became, at best, a debate forum and at worst a rubber stamp organization to grant an air of "legitimacy" to the measures of Tsar Nicholas II and his advisers. In short, the qualitatively different patterns of social, political and economic life which had been recently achieved became jeopardized. The prospect of a return to traditional Tsarist absolutism with all its accoutrements engendered in the people a revolutionary state of mind. Expectations remained high yet qualitatively different from what could be achieved under the existing degenerating social conditions (see Figure 4).

Given the above limitation on the social conditions under which the Davies model is applicable, the type of revolution which *is* explainable by this model can be clarified. Since Davies claimed that his model explains "progressive" revolutions, perhaps we should specify this as a type of revolution characterized by the desire for a qualitatively different type of political regime. This is a logical corollary of our limiting the model's applicability to societies that have undergone profound qualitative social change.

While a threat to the previously satisfied needs finally spurred revolution, the needs of the next stage—which emerged just prior to the decline—actually shaped the goals of the revolution. A revolution is "progressive" in the sense that its espoused goals are in terms of the emergent level of needs. That is, people have experienced the satisfaction of the previous level of needs and are confident in their ability to regain that capacity. However, the regime may have never demonstrated its ability to facilitate the satisfaction of the newly emergent needs. Therefore, what is needed is not simply a change in regime

FIGURE 4
STAGES OF DEVELOPMENT

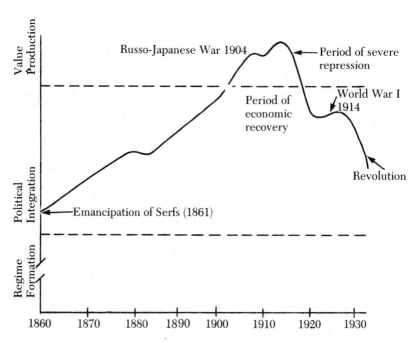

Source: Adapted from Davies 1971, p. 142

personnel but a change in the nature of the regime and its relationship
to society. In other words, a *type* of regime that can respond to the new
type of needs is required. When society's needs become qualitatively
different, the policies of satisfying those needs should also be qualitatively different, especially when the old socio-political patterns have
not yet proven themselves effective toward this end.

The "U-Curve"

As an alternative model of the causes of revolution, we propose one
which accounts for various types of revolutions occurring under different socio-economic conditions from those associated with the Davies
model. This new model is based upon the proposition that *revolutions*

FIGURE 5

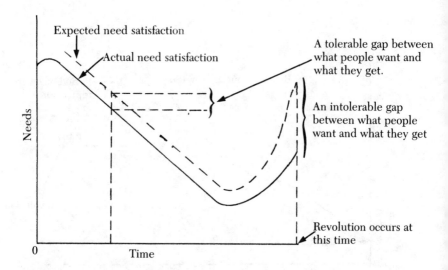

Expected need satisfaction

Actual need satisfaction

A tolerable gap between what people want and what they get.

An intolerable gap between what people want and what they get

Needs

0

Time

Revolution occurs at this time

are likely to occur when a prolonged period of socio-economic decline is followed by a brief rise in these conditions (see Figure 5).[3] Since the hypothesized preconditions are different from those in Davies' theory, we would expect that revolutions explainable by this model are likewise of a different kind than those subsumed under the "J-curve" thesis. Therefore, this "U-curve" model, rather than denying Davies' theory, acts as a complement to it, accounting for phenomena definable as revolutions, but occurring under varying conditions and having different objectives (i.e., of different "type") from those that accompany revolutions that occur in societies not undergoing qualitative social change and which aim at something less than the complete restructuring of political authority.

The justification for the set of limitations imposed on this theory is specified in terms of our paradigm of social development. We propose that immediately prior to the long period of decline, if the society had not undergone profound qualitative social change of the type represented by the progress from one stage of development to the next, the "U-Curve" is a useful explanatory framework. However, if such change had occurred, then the Davies theory would be applicable and thus predict the outbreak of revolution much sooner after the onset of the recession. For the "U-Curve," the society should have made significant progress toward the completion of its present stage of development such that the subsequent long period of decline should then be one of decline in the *quantity* of the means for satisfying the characteristic needs of that stage. The satisfaction of the previous level of needs is not threatened because if it were then either the Davies model would apply and predict the outbreak of revolution prior to the recovery, or the recovery itself would defuse the revolutionary potential of the situation rather than crystallize it, as this new model implies.

Thus, the fundamental patterns of social behavior have remained what they were prior to the decline, in the sense that the same basic need as defined in the hierarchy is still predominant. It is simply that the means available for satisfying these needs have diminished in amount, rather than in kind.

Since the decline here refers to a reduction of the means for satisfying current unsatisfied needs, expectations should adjust downward as objective conditions decline. This hypothesis is consistent with our analysis of expectations in the "J-curve" model: while the newly emergent needs remained a salient aspect of social behavior, expectations with respect to their adequate satisfaction were lowered in the presence of a decline in the means for gratifying them. Furthermore, this proposed adjustment of expectations seems likewise consistent with Maslow's suggestion that a person who has been habitually deprived with respect to a particular need will require a longer period of need fulfillment before he will feel secure about its continued satisfaction. That the given developmental stage has not been completed means, in this analytical context, that the people are not fully confident that existing social patterns are adequate to satisfy the needs characteristic of this state. On this basis, then, we propose that expectations do adjust downward when the decline is confined to one stage in the developmental process.

How, then, does the recovery lead to the outbreak of revolution? As alluded to earlier, the fact that there is a prolonged period of decline with respect to the satisfaction of existing needs implies that prior to the decline, significant—though not sufficient—progress had been made toward the substantial and continuous satisfaction of these needs (i.e., toward the completion of this developmental stage). Hence, while expectations have, during the decline, adjusted downward, they were, in fact, prior to the decline, at a relatively high level. And if the decline has been sufficiently prolonged and profound so that significant gains in satisfying these needs have been lost, then the time required for complete recovery to previous levels of satisfaction will be rather long. We would argue that since existing social patterns once led to significant (though not sufficient) satisfaction of these needs, then once recovery begins, the accompanying rise in expectations will outstrip the rise in objective conditions. Expectation will at least approach this previous level at a faster rate than if they had never been at this higher level. In other words, the rise in expectations will presumably outstrip that of objective socio-economic conditions when this period of objective rise is seen as a "recovery" (that is, when it has in fact been preceded by a decline, so that improvements are seen as the regaining of lost ground) rather than as "progress," strictly defined (which is to say, when the gains are such that the society has never experienced them at any prior point in time). If the period of decline has been so long that an equally extended period of time is required for complete recovery, then the increasing "gap" between expectations and achievement—the result of expectations rising faster than achievement—could conceivably reach the "intolerable" proportions which constitute the crucial aspect of the revolutionary state of mind before complete recovery defuses popular dissatisfaction.

This analytical treatment of the dynamics of expectations can at present be regarded as a hypothesis. However, it accounts for why in this model the "intolerable gap" between expectations and achievements should occur during the rise in objective socio-economic conditions, rather than during the decline. This explanation is consistent with the treatment of expectations in the Davies model as it has been located in our common analytical framework of the paradigm of development. In our proposed model, existing patterns of behavior formerly leading to significant satisfaction of the given level of needs provide more of a basis for the people to expect that they can again achieve such levels of satisfaction than if existing social patterns had *never* demonstrated such a degree of efficacy. On this basis, then, the hypothesis that during the recovery expectations will rise more rapidly than achievement is held to be at least deductively plausible.

As for the type of revolution that will occur under these conditions, the preceding discussion provides a clue to the characterization of such revolts. Since, as previously stated, existing social patterns permitted the substantial (though not sufficient) satisfaction of current needs, the people will be less likely to seek drastic altering of socio-political patterns. The regime as it existed had once created conditions conducive to the satisfaction of current needs. Therefore, the aims of the type of revolution predicted by the "U-curve" model will likely be restricted to little more than changes in the regime's personnel. What is needed is a set of political leaders who can restore to full capacity the pre-existing and previously effective social patterns.

Since this "U-curve" model is perhaps not as intuitively acceptable an explanatory scheme of revolutionary causation as the Davies theory, it would be useful here to present, for illustrative purposes, a brief analysis of a specific instance of revolution which is held to be within the empirical domain of the "U-curve." By construction of this analysis, using the terms and the logic of the "U-curve" thesis, we hope to establish, at least tentatively, the plausibility of the model as a useful explanatory device. In view of the model's proposed analytical complementarity with Davies' theory, it should not be surprising that the example to be used is China's Boxer Rebellion, a rebellion of the "type" which is not subsumed by the "J-curve" theory, according to Davies' claim.

How, then, does our proposed new model fit the case of the Boxer Rebellion? In a sense, the Boxer Rebellion represents China's last desperate attempt to defend its traditional way of life against the profoundly disruptive impact of the West (Purcell 1963). As such, it represents, in the terms of our model, an attempt to restore the traditional imperial system of socio-political relations to its former strength so that China could at least regain its status as a truly sovereign nation, even if she could no longer be the "Central Kingdom."

Thus, the decline in social conditions in China during the nineteenth century is seen as one in which the people's *need for belonging* was inadequately responded to by the regime (see Figure 6). Although at its height in the eighteenth century, the Ch'ing (Manchu) dynasty had made great strides in gaining the support of the Chinese people, the fact that the Ch'ing was a "foreign" (hence, "barbarian") dynasty made their acceptance by the Chinese rather tenuous. As was the case with other "foreign" dynasties (such as the Mongols), the Ch'ing was accepted as a legitimate dynasty only to the extent that they adopted the Confucian-based Chinese culture and political system and maintained the supremacy of China as the "Central Kingdom".[4]

In the nineteenth century, the increased economic aggression of

FIGURE 6
STAGES OF DEVELOPMENT

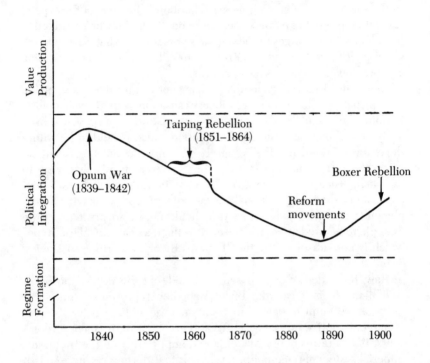

Great Britain, France, Germany, the United States, and even Japan presented China as a nation and the Ch'ing as a regime, with a new type of challenge to their culture and political sovereignty. When the Opium War (1839–1842) demonstrated the inability of the Ch'ing regime to maintain the political sovereignty of China, it was only a matter of time before the Chinese people were to act upon their resultant discontent, and revolt against the dynasty.

However, the anti-Ch'ing revolts that followed upon China's defeat in the Opium War were all eventually put down, although not by virtue of the strength of the Ch'ing but through the material aid and military leadership of the Western forces in China, who perhaps saw the maintenance of the all but impotent Ch'ing as being essential to the continued success of their economic encroachments in China (Li 1971). The fact that the Western nations did play a direct if not decisive role in the defeat of the Taiping (1851–1865) and Nien (1851–1868) rebellions undoubtedly intensified the anti-foreign sentiments that pervaded the Chinese people's growing disillusionment with the Ch'ing dynasty.

If China's decline is viewed as the Manchu regime's inability to achieve the political integration stage of development, then, in terms of our model, in what way was there a rise in these conditions immediately prior to the Boxer Rebellion? After China's defeat in the Sino-Japanese War (1894–1895), several reform movements occurred, culminating in the Hundred Days Reform, instigated by the more progressive elements in and around the Ch'ing government. These largely institutional reforms were designed to increase China's capacity to deal with the West on a basis of equality (militarily, economically, and technologically). Elements of "western learning," such as western science and mathematics, began to be incorporated into the educational system so that mastery of the Confucian Classics was no longer the sole criterion of educational attainment (Teng and Fairbank, pp. 133–154). Since educational achievement remained the primary legitimate basis of political recruitment, the result of these reforms was to open the path toward upward social mobility to a broader spectrum of the Chinese people. The rather expensive, time-consuming and increasingly impractical Confucian education had often been beyond the means of most Chinese families, and consequently, the ostensibly open status system of China was in reality much more rigid. It was only the educated, wealthy gentry who could afford the costs of the education so essential to the attainment of political office and social status. The reforms were aimed at changing this, and evidence suggests they were somewhat successful in this respect. In the years immediately prior to the Boxer Rebellion there was a steady increase in the number of new degree holders who came from rather humble social backgrounds (Ho, 1962, pp. 92–125). This represents an increase in the satisfaction of the popular needs for belonging in that the social basis of political recruitment expanded to include previously excluded elements of the social strata. Furthermore, this was accomplished by changing the content of the educational system in such a way as to make it more responsive to China's need to strengthen herself in the face of the aggressiveness of the West.

However, there is one aspect of the Boxer Rebellion that must be mentioned and accounted for, as it makes this rebellion rather unique in comparison with other "revolutions." We refer to the fact that the

Boxer Rebellion as a mass movement was *anti-foreign* rather than anti-Ch'ing, and in fact had at least the tacit support of the Ch'ing government. Thus, it was not an "anti-government" revolt in the sense we usually conceive of a revolution. However, a closer examination of this aspect of the Boxer Rebellion should clarify why it is in fact a "revolution" (as we defined the term) and not an international war, even though the target of the revolt was the foreign powers in China and not the indigenous regime.

As a matter of fact, the Boxer movement itself began as an anti-Manchu as well as an anti-foreign revolt, originating among, and for a while confined to, secret societies of the type that arose regularly during the periods of dynastic decline in China's history. However, as the Boxers actually gained the official sanction of the Ch'ing government for their sporadic anti-foreign activities, the movement expanded into a more broadly based mass uprising of a more exclusively anti-foreign nature (Purcell 1963). Indeed, the support that the Boxers gained from the Ch'ing government can be seen as an element of the rise in conditions that the "U-curve" model proposes as immediately preceding a revolution. It was this support that apparently crystallized popular discontent into a singularly anti-foreign sentiment and thus gave the movement an appeal that extended beyond that of the rather esoteric and extreme doctrines of the original Boxer secret societies. At issue was the question of China's political sovereignty, and while the maintenance of such was, analytically speaking, the central developmental imperative of the Ch'ing dynasty, the fact that the challenge to the Ch'ing regime's capacity to perform this function was essentially foreign in origin, and the fact that previous anti-dynastic, anti-foreign rebellions had failed, lends credence to the idea that the Ch'ing's support of the Boxers represents a rise in conditions that immediately preceded and caused the expansion of the movement into a mass-based anti-foreign rebellion.

Thus, we argue that the anti-foreign character of the Boxer Rebellion should not be construed as an indication that it was an international war rather than a domestic revolution. The Boxers were far from being pro Ch'ing, both in their beginnings as secret societies and later as a more broadly based movement. Indeed, there is considerable evidence that the Ch'ing government's support of the Boxers was more a product of the Empress Sowager Tz'u-hsi's political opportunism and desire to divert popular discontent away from the regime than the result of any sincere desire on her part to respond to popular needs. The goal of the rebellion was the restoration of China as a sovereign nation under the traditional imperial political system and not the revitalization of the Ch'ing dynasty *per se*. This is in congruence with our characterization of the "type" of revolution predicted by the "U-curve" model, even if the targets of the Boxers were the elements of foreign influence in China. This influence was the source of the Ch'ing's weakness and therefore, the Chinese people's discontent. Thus, it is only logical that the foreign forces in China should become the targets of the rebellion.

In sum, in assessing the theory of revolution by Davies in the context of the paradigm introduced in this book, we specified certain limitations on the applicability of his theory of the causes of revolution. Specifically, the theory can be applicable at certain points in the process of social and political development as described. And, concomitantly, its applicability has been limited to a certain type of revolution, as defined in terms of our paradigm of development. Also, we have proposed an alternative explanation of the causes of revolution that is applicable under different socio-economic conditions and to revolutions that are more conservative in their aims. Should these propositions prove valid, an understanding of the causes of revolution should be greatly enhanced, for this new theory represents, in effect, an implicit refinement of Davies' already powerful thesis and a complementary explanatory device applicable to those revolutions acknowledged by Davies as being outside the range of his model's analytical scope.

Thus far, we have discussed extensively what appear to be some promising models for explaining revolutionary behaviors in various societies experiencing different stages of developmental change. Both the "J-curve" and the "U-curve" theories combine the psychological factor of aspirations and the societal dimensions of achievement. Now another set of concepts which have been used extensively in the literature of revolution will be introduced. These use the more societal-level premises that revolutionary behavior originates from the actor's relationship with the society.

Relative Deprivation: Relative to What? While the concept of relative deprivation is germane to almost all theories of revolutionary activity, its operational definition is seldom agreed upon. Following the more orthodox definition of relative deprivation found in the Marxist tradition, Davies (1959, p. 283) defines it as "when a deprived person compares himself with a nondeprived person, the resulting state will be called 'relative deprivation'." In this case, the person compares himself with others. Ted Gurr (1970, p. 24), on the other hand, suggests that "relative deprivation is defined as the actor's perception of discrepancy between their value expectations and his value capabilities"; thus, one's status in the social hierarchy becomes relatively significant.

Several meaningful definitions, each depicting important aspects of the revolutionary state of mind, deserve our attention. Analytical distinctions between these definitions and their implications for the study of revolutionary behaviors are discussed below.

Social Comparison: Marxist and Non-Marxist Perceptions

As described above, a common conception of relative deprivation is that one is comparing one's situation with that of other people considered to be "significant others". Thus, a person's sense of deprivation or gratification is entirely dependent upon how he compares himself with others. Similar dynamics seem implicit in Marxist theory in that the proletariat may find itself deprived as a result of the bourgeoisie's enrichment.

This sort of social determinism has been the foundation of Marxist and other socialist revolutions throughout the world. An application of Marxist theory to European history demonstrates how the thesis of "relative deprivation" has been used as the sole basis of revolution.

Among other phenomena causing extensive social change in the eighteenth and nineteenth centuries, the industrial revolution was a decisive factor that forced the European economic structure to undergo the dramatic process of division of labor. Despite all the moral ills, including the "alienation of man from things," the new structure of division of labor did contribute to productivity increases and eventually mass production. While this was going on, the capitalist economic system, governed by its laws of supply and demand, compelled those who did not own the means of production (the laborers) to rely totally on the mercy of those who did own and control them. Since the value of commodities in capitalist economy is determined by the laws of supply and demand rather than by the amount of labor invested in their production, the people who were in a position to control the means of production and thus, to manipulate supply and demand, were able to accumulate what Marx referred to as surplus value (market value minus labor value). This unwarranted profit, according to Marx, inevitably enriches the "haves" by means of impoverishing the "have-nots." This process will lead to an unbridgeable polarization of social classes. On the premise that economic structure is the basic structure that determines the nature of all other social and cultural super-structures, Marx predicted that the class polarization would necessarily lead to the development of distinct and mutually incompatible relations between the two classes. As a result, in a mature capitalist system where the "haves" are profit-motivated and the "have-nots" are im-poverished to the extent that they can no longer tolerate the injustice, a proletarian revolution will become imminent. Marx was naive in believing that if and when such a rebellion takes place, the small number of the "haves" will be helpless in defending themselves against the huge masses, according to an iron law of history.

History did not follow the path of Marxist projections. There are ample reasons for this. In the process of modern industrialization, a large middle class emerged which did not belong to either of the two polarized classes. The social class structure in both transitional and post-industrial societies was more open to class mobility than Marx had anticipated. Also, technological development provided the oppressors, in some societies, with highly mechanized and sophisticated weapons with which they could more easily suppress mass rebellions. Further-more, there were other flaws in the basic premises of Marxist economic determinism.

It would be unrealistic not to recognize the impact Marxist views have made on the course of history. We have to admit that it is Marxism and its variations that have caused more revolutionary social changes throughout the world than any other single idea or theory. The Rus-sian, Chinese, and Cuban revolutions as well as numerous rebellions in Asia, Africa, and Latin America, have indeed been Marxist revolutions of sorts. Ironically, none of the revolutions occurred in a mature capitalist country, contrary to Marx's expectations. In fact, no revolu-tion has occurred in any society as a result of capitalist maturity. How-ever, the apparent humanist message that condemns social and economic inequality inherent in capitalist systems appealed to "rela-tively deprived" masses in the underdeveloped and developing regions of Russia, China, Eastern Europe, and the Third World.

Extending the premise of "relative deprivation" by social comparison, one might attribute global insecurity and international conflict to the disparity and inequity among nations. Authors such as Galtung have long adhered to the view that world peace cannot be maintained as long as we fail to bridge the gap between rich nations and poor nations. This view seems to be at least intuitively plausible and appealing when we consider two facts: (1) rich nations are maintaining their affluence in this deeply integrated global economy at the expense of poor nations who are forced to supply raw materials and cheap labor; (2) due to the development of worldwide communication networks and the increasing communicative capability of Third World nations, poor countries are keenly aware of their situation and are increasingly determined to protect their national interest by exhibiting a high degree of nationalism. These factors will undoubtedly spur the sense of "relative deprivation" on the part of Third World countries. In fact, the emergence of a New International Economic Order with a potentially explosive North-South confrontation has just about replaced the conventional ideological axis of the East-West tension. Thus, revolutions in Third World countries, still poor and struggling in the Southern hemisphere, are more likely to be nationalist in their motivations, with their targets outside the country. The most recent revolution in Iran, although it may appear to be a religious upsurge, is indeed a nationalist revolution against the common enemy: the United States. Revolutions in Southeast Asia, such as Vietnam and Kampuchea, can also be best characterized as nationalist movements rather than Marxist revolutions.

At any rate, the concept of relative deprivation through social comparison helps us understand many revolutionary activities in different societies. It is not only theoretically appealing but analytically very useful. However, the social comparison does not fully account for the basis of relative deprivation, as one's comparison of himself with others is not the only basis for comparison.

Temporal Comparison

While one may feel deprived or gratified relative to other people, one also may feel deprived or gratified by comparing the present situation with a past situation. One may find it gratifying to have made a big improvement over a period of time even if one's present situation is still worse than that of others. By the same token, one could surely be unhappy and feel a deep sense of deprivation when one's present situation shows little improvement over time, even though one's situation is currently better than that of others. For this reason, status improvement in the form of pay raises and other rewards is necessary to keep people happy and maintain a stable political system regardless of the level of affluence in a particular society.

In a developing society where people experience rapid improvement in their lifestyle, we often find mass support for the regime based on its effective role in bringing about such improvements, even if the people still are far from affluent and even if the regime fails to promote social and economic equality within the country. In fact, a rapidly developing transitional country with self-sustaining economic growth is most likely to have increasing disparity between the rich and the poor, and yet the regime may enjoy widespread mass support, as has been the case in South Korea since the 1960s. Anyone who visits China today will find the Chinese to be very poor, their living accommodations marginal, recreation facilities virtually non-existent, and the mechanization of agriculture almost invisible, yet he will be struck by their genuine sense of happiness, particularly on the part of older people. It will only take a cursory conversation with a Chinese to figure out why they are happy: they will tell you that they are happy because they remember those bad days before the revolution.

The two bases of comparison, social and temporal, are not mutually exclusive at all. On the contrary, one may be able to explain the revolutionary mind more completely by combining these two bases. One may compare himself with others; that is, compare one's rate of improvement with that of others over the same period of time. For instance, the rate of pay increase might be a basis for social comparison, although the rate itself is a temporal (time-embedded) concept. This kind of comparison will expand the explanatory power of the concept of "relative deprivation" itself.

Spatial Comparison

In addition to the social and temporal comparison, social psychologists, notably Brickman and Campbell (1971), introduced yet another basis of comparison that may explain some cases of relative deprivation. This kind of comparison is referred to as spatial comparison. In this case, one compares some areas of one's achievement with other areas of one's own achievement. Relative deprivation will result when one dimension of achievement is seriously lagging behind other achievements. For example, a well-educated black American with a highly paid and prestigious job who is compelled to live in a poor housing project may be dissatisfied due to the gap in his areas of achievements.

This basis of comparison may be particularly useful in studying the attitudes and behavior of people who have discrepancies between their achievements and ascriptive statuses, such as a racial and ethnic minority that has succeeded economically, but still faces socio-cultural discrimination in the United States. The status of minority people in this regard is surprisingly similar throughout the world. We find many situations analogous to the American black minority in the situations of alien nationals in China, Japan, and ethnically heterogenous African nations.

In fact, the state of mind with respect to relative deprivation is rather complex in this case because the "spatial comparison" is often combined with the other two bases, social and temporal. Thus, a black American may find himself experiencing a perplexing mixture of relative gratification and relative deprivation: he feels gratified when he compares himself with his own past, and deprived when he sees himself in the spatial comparison terms. In this case, *whichever may prevail in a given situation at a given time will dictate his behavior pattern.*

In this section we have discussed some bases of relative deprivation and relative gratification. What is suggested here is that a state of human mind with a propensity to rebel is a complex one needing a synthesis of all the bases of comparison.

The Tunnel Effect: Alternative to Relative Deprivation. Albert O. Hirschman (1973) in a fascinating analysis of "tolerance for income equality in the course of economic development" proposed a concept which questions the basic premise of relative deprivation. According to this concept, called the "tunnel effect," a person may find himself happier when he sees other people making progress, thus keeping himself further behind if he expects that their progress will benefit himself and, as a result, he too will improve some day. To elaborate this concept further, Hirschman uses an analogy:

> Suppose that I drive through a two-lane tunnel in the same direction, and run into a serious traffic jam. No car moves in either lane as far as I can

see (which is not very far). I am in the left land and feel dejected. After a while, the cars in the right begin to move. Naturally, my spirits lift considerably for I know that the jam has been broken and that my lane's turn to move will surely come any moment now. Even though I still sit still, I feel much better off than before because of the expectation that I shall soon be on the move.

The "tunnel effect" thesis seems to be particularly applicable to a society where class mobility is possible, and people are achievement oriented. If McClelland's (1961) observation is correct that people in economically developed countries are likely to be more achievement oriented than people of less developed countries, the tunnel effect thesis may be more useful in studying economically affluent nations, whereas the relative deprivation thesis would be more valid in poor countries. The transitional developing nations with a capacity for rapid economic growth are those which usually experience income inequality, however. Yet, as Hirschman observes, people in such nations tend to have a greater tolerance for inequity because of the tunnel effect. Consequently, there seem to be conflicting views as to what kind of society is more likely to be subject to the premises of the tunnel effect. Nevertheless, the thesis of the tunnel effect offers a significant validity and explanatory utility for certain people who are achievement oriented.

In this section, we have discussed some social and psychological bases of revolutionary activity, and concluded that assessing the "revolutionary mind" requires a careful analysis of its referents from premises of relative deprivation and tunnel effect. The state of mind conducive to revolutionary activity is the result of an extremely complex mental process. To understand it, a genuinely interdisciplinary analysis is imperative, as the "revolutionary mind" is likely to be a product of a wide range of variables at all levels of social complexity.

INSTITUTIONALIZATION AND CULTURAL FORMATION

We have discussed that the process of regime formation may involve different channels such as hereditary succession, election, military coup, and revolution. Once a regime is formed in which a ruling elite is identified, the political system will undergo a process of institutionalization intended to solidify the power base. In this institutionalization process, some institutions are given more emphasis than others, based on the degree to which an institution is vital to generating the necessary resources and values for the survival needs of the people.

In this initial stage of development, three institutions are likely to be considered vital, and institutionalization or institutional rehabilitation will be centered around them: the agriculture, the military, and the police. They are crucially important as they generate food, protect the society from external aggression, and maintain internal stability. All other institutions such as education, the family, manufacturing, and political parties will have only secondary significance as they seem to be designed for "living well" rather than "living" itself. As we shall discuss later, different institutions will be assigned varying levels of cruciality (centrality) as the society makes its developmental shifts.

In the agricultural sector, one can see almost invariably the practice of land reform as early as possible after the formation of a government. This phenomenon is clearly non-culture and non-ideology bound. We saw a massive land reform and "land rehabilitation" after Mao's revolution in China. Japan was not an exception as it introduced extensive land reforms following the Meiji Restoration. Most new nations of the Third World have introduced measures intended for the redistribution of land and revitalization of land use at one time or another.

Particularly when the new regime comes to power as a result of revolution, the extent of these practices will be far reaching. As these measures are intended among other things to increase agricultural productivity, there will be some attempts to induce agricultural technology but caution will be taken not to destroy the existing production mechanism. Preserving productivity is the case even with a new regime with entirely different ideologies. In China, for example, Mao and his government were determined to uproot corruptions and contradictions of the Nationalist regime and introduced land reform policies and agricultural rehabilitation measures with extreme caution. In fact, in the early phases of the new socialist regime (1949–1952), they did not introduce even the ideas of collectivization and socialization. Under the slogan of Mutual Aid, which had been the practice throughout Confucian China, they emphasized the increase of production. It was not until the mid-1950s when the Agricultural Producers Cooperatives were formed that private land ownership was gradually replaced by collective ownership. Considering the fact that an overwhelming majority of the population is likely to be farmers in this stage, the government cannot afford to disrupt the agrarian community through land confiscation and redistribution to such an extent that production capability is impaired. Farmers and peasants are basically manual laborers, and their primary need level seldom exceeds the basic need of securing physical survival; any drastic structural changes in the production mechanism could easily bring about a serious threat to their survival. They are not expected to be ideologically oriented as long as they are struggling to feed themselves, nor are they expected to enjoy much leisure.

In such an agrarian society, people will have little exposure to the world beyond their community. The community's authority structure is likely to be little more than an extension of that of the family itself, which is essentially parochial rather than contractual. The location of authority and responsibility is readily identifiable and each member of the community will know exactly where he or she belongs and will have no ambiguities as how to behave properly. This kind of life environment would force community members to develop submissive attitudes and learn the virtues of obedience. Challenges to superiors and even disagreement with them would be entirely unacceptable regardless of the issues involved. This absolute obedience is reinforced by the stoic, fate-accepting agrarianism in that farmers submit themselves to the law of nature in the practice of cultivation. Their lifestyle, even their existence itself, depends entirely upon the mercy of nature.

The police, another prevalent institution in this initial stage of regime formation, would have an extensive role in maintaining the stability of the social and authority structure. In fact, in most societies at this stage of development, an individual's only contact with political authority beyond the community would be through the police distributed widely throughout the country. More police forces would be appropriated where social unrest and political dissension are most likely. In this context, the police force would be viewed as a source of sanction and will be avoided. People would be in fear of the police and would tend to comply with orders and directives given by authority. In this way, the function of the law enforcement agency goes beyond maintaining law and order; it often includes mobilization of support for the regime.

For a cultural system in which submissive and authoritarian attitudes prevail, the police institution serves as a facilitator with its authoritative method of operation. In the absence of "due process" in societies at this formative stage, people are inclined to render blind obedience and conform to orders, as it is certain that disputes with the police will surely invite trouble.

The same can be said about the military. In the absence of any other large organization whose membership represents the whole society, the military institution enjoys an exclusive position in which it can mobilize the masses and exert absolute power and influence over the people. It is common in this case that the military and militarism enjoy a widespread reputation and prestige. It would be considered an honor to be able to enter the military academy and become an officer, and young people usually compete for such honors, particularly in times of peace.

STYLES OF POLITICS

People at this stage of political development will look to the government as the provider of their needs, and will give their absolute support for what it does in the way of guaranteeing food, shelter, and security. Support for the leadership in this case is for what it *does,* rather than what it *is:* the basis of legitimacy will have little to do with values or ideologies that the government may uphold. A bowl of rice is a bowl of rice to a hungry stomach irrespective of whether it is from a collective farm or the black market. The issue of ideological legitimacy becomes trivial and largely irrelevant. The sole consideration in politics is the effective and swift delivery of the needed resources and services. Naturally, the government will be structured in such a way that decisions can be made quickly and policies implemented without delay.

No known style of politics is more effective in this regard than a centristic totalitarian form of government with a clear position of authority and responsibility in the power structure. The government will be more paternalistic and thus rule responsibly; and obedience with reverence will characterize the political dynamics. A pluralist democracy or even a bureaucratic autocracy is not likely to develop in this initial stage. As discussed earlier, institutions adopted from more advanced societies, such as electoral systems, are likely to deviate from their original functions. Notions such as interest articulation and aggregation are almost entirely alien to this stage of regime formation and politics will not be conducted based on public opinion.

Ironically, the greatest danger to this kind of regime is its own success in raising people's perception of need by satisfying the more urgent need of physical survival. On the other hand, if such a regime is incapable of becoming an effective provider, an alternative leadership might be invited without changing the style of politics.

SUMMARY

In this chapter, we examined the mechanism by which a new regime may evolve. As most contemporary regimes have emerged as a result of regime change rather than through "primitive unification," our analytical focus has been on the dynamics of regime replacement. For this, we juxtaposed a typology of regime formation in which the inheritance of power and elections are defined as cases of legitimate succession, and the military coup and revolution are viewed as forms of illegitimate succession. While hereditary succession is rare in contemporary politics, elections have aptly been demonstrated to be inefficient means of regime change for a society in which the predominant needs are still at the level of physical survival. Consequently, most regime change at this stage of development is through a military coup or a revolution.

Attempts were made to specify the conditions that are conducive to a military coup or revolution. It was observed that a military coup is more likely to occur in a system where the regime had made sufficient progress toward satisfying the basic needs of its citizens, but was unable to adjust its policies to cope with changing needs and demands. Also observed was the fact that the conditions of civil violence are so complex that no single explanatory framework can account for the varieties of the revolutionary phenomenon. With the introduction of the "U-Curve" in this chapter, we may have enhanced our understanding of the intricacy of revolutionary dynamics.

FOOTNOTES

[1] For further discussion on this thesis, see Robert Mitchels (1949); also, Albert Pepitone and George Reichling, "Group Cohesiveness and the Expression of Hostility," *Human Relations*, VIII (Aug. 1955), pp. 327–38.

[2] References on the military in the Third World are numerous. To cite a few: Lucian W. Pye, "Armies in the Process of Modernization," in Finkle and Gable (1966); Samuel P. Huntington (1962); John J. Johnson, ed. (1962).

³Such an alternative idea of the causes of revolution is alluded to by Dahren-dolf (1952, 132) and implicit in de Tocqueville (1956, pp. 176–77).

⁴Purcell (1963) emphasizes the importance of the foreign origins of the Ch'ing dynasty as it relates to China's ability (or inability) to cope with Western intrusions. See Chapters 2 and 3.

BIBLIOGRAPHY

Brickman, Philip and Donald T. Campbell, 1971. "Hedonistic Relativism and Planning of the Good Society," in M. H. Appley, ed., *Adaptation-Level Theory*. New York: Academic Press, pp. 287–304.

Campbell, Angus, et al., 1960. *The American Voter.* New York: Wiley.

Dahrendorf, Ralf, 1959. *Class and Class Conflict in Industrial Society.* Stanford: Stanford University Press.

Davies, James C., 1959. "A Formal Interpretation of the Theory of Relative Deprivation," *Sociometry*, 22.

———, 1963. *Human Nature and Politics.* New York: John Wiley and Sons, Inc.

———, 1971. "Toward a Theory of Revolution," pp. 134–147 in *When Men Revolt and Why*, edited by James C. Davies. New York: The Free Press.

Finkle, Jason L. and Richard W. Gable, eds., 1966. *Political Development and Social Change.* New York: Wiley and Sons.

Gurr, Ted, 1968. "A Causal Model of Civil Strife: A Comparative Analysis Using New Indices," *The American Political Science Review* 62 (December), 1968, pp. 1104–1124.

———, 1970. *Why Men Rebel.* Princeton, N.J.: Princeton University Press.

Hirschman, Albert O., 1973. "The Changing Tolerance for Income Inequality in the Course of Economic Development," *Quarterly Journal of Economics*, Vol. LXXXVII.

Ho Ping-ti, 1962. *The Ladder of Success in Imperial China.* New York: Columbia Press.

Huntington, Samuel P., 1962. *Changing Patterns of Military Politics* (International Yearbook of Political Behavior Research No. 3).

Kline, Wanda, 1979. *Latin American Politics and Development.* Cambridge: MIT Press.

Johnson, John J., ed., 1962. *The Role of the Military in Underdeveloped Countries.* Princeton, N.J.: Princeton University Press.

Li, Dun J., 1971 *The Ageless Chinese*, Second Edition. New York: Charles Scribner's Sons.

McClelland, David C., 1961. *The Achieving Society.* New York: The Free Press.

Mitchels, Robert, 1949. *Political Parties: A Sociological Study of the Oligarchical Tendencies of Modern Democracies.* Trans. by Eden and Cedar Paul. Glencoe, Ill.: The Free Press.

Organski, A. F. K., 1965. *The Stages of Political Development.* New York: Alfred Knopf.

Park, Han S., "Socio-Economic Development and Democratic Performance: An Empirical Study," *International Review of Modern Sociology,* Vol. 6, No. 2, 1976.

Purcell, Victor., 1963. *The Boxer Uprising.* Cambridge: The University Press.

Teng Ssu-yu and John K. Fairbank, 1954. *China's Response to the West.* New York: Atheneum.

de Tocqueville, Alexis, 1856. *The Old Regime and the French Revolution.* Translated by John Bonner. New York: Harper.

Treadgold, Donald, 1964. *Twentieth Century Russia.* Chicago: Rand-McNally and Company.

Verba, Sidney, Norman H. Nie, and Jae-on Kim, 1971. *The Modes of Democratic Participation.* Beverly Hills, California: Sage Publications.

Chapter V

POLITICAL INTEGRATION

Once the regime attains stability and becomes capable of providing safety and security to members of the society, it will be on the track to building broad-based popular support of a diffuse nature. It will not take long for the government to generate a broad basis of legitimacy for its power, as long as people are convinced that the incumbent government is the one best prepared for assuring them physical survival. Here the government's primary tasks are to protect and strengthen the institutions designed to generate the means for people's physical survival: namely, the agricultural sector of the economy, the military, and the police. But as we pointed out earlier, people's sense of imminent needs will immediately shift to the higher level, that of belongingness, thus forcing the government to develop new policies and institutions designed to respond to this new level of needs and demands.

At this point there are three alternative courses for the nation's development. First, the regime may be replaced by another via legitimate or illegitimate means. Second, the incumbent leadership may manage to remain in power by creating a sense of emergency. This can be done either by inviting conflict with other nations or by creating life-threatening social and economic conditions within the nation. In either case people will be reduced to desire nothing more than survival and thus the regime will, at least temporarily, survive its inability to satisfy belonging needs. Third, the government can adopt or develop a political ideology under which newly emerging value orientations and the existing social groups and institutions that are designed to provide for people's belongingness needs can be used as channels for socializing the populace into pro-regime values or orientations. When the government is capable of opting for the third course, we will witness the beginning of the second stage of political integration, as spelled out in the proposed paradigm.

The state of political integration, then, is characterized by the flourishing of ideas and cultural activities on the part of the masses. Often, the government finds this state of affairs detrimental to political stability, particularly to the stability of the regime itself. As we saw in the case of the Chinese "Hundred Flowers" campaign, the unfettered expression of new ideas and political views inevitably leads to criticism of the incumbent government, sometimes to the point of necessitating a forceful crackdown on dissidents.[1] If this crackdown is sufficiently severe in its intensity and pervasive in its scope, the society may revert to a situation where people's life environment becomes unpredictable and physical survival itself may be threatened. In this case, launching into the second stage will never take place.

However, the regime can be effective in "persuading" the masses in such a way that this flowering of cultural and social expression may remain within the boundaries of acceptable diversity. For this, the leadership will feel the necessity to define the limits of such expression through its own ideographic program of political socialization or "indoctrination" of the public. This can best be achieved through the use of educational institutions and communication media as instruments of government persuasion.

To effectively socialize or indoctrinate the masses, the government will need the services of intellectuals and other cultural elite groups. The ability and willingness of the ruling government to recruit and mobilize intellectuals into the mainstream of politics and decision making is crucial to the regime's ability to survive the transitional period to political integration. If the intellectuals are not recruited, they can become so alienated as to form a counter-culture with a counter-ideology that will pose a persistent impediment to the regime's indoctrination efforts and therefore to its political integration strategy. Intellectuals mobilized by the regime will be expected to develop a new political ideology or to justify and elaborate one imposed upon them by the political leadership. An ideology will be defined and refined in such a way that the goal of national and political integration can be achieved most effectively. The goal here is to encompass and subsume conflicting values and belief systems under an integrated conception of the nature of the political community, one to which everyone can feel a positive sense of attachment. In this sense, their belongingness needs will be satisfied in the political sphere.

Thus, political ideologies may be viewed from the functional perspective as institutional means instigated by the political leadership for the purpose of the political integration of the nation and legitimation of the regime. Thus, the nature of an effective ideology will be determined by the contextual factors of the society, such as culture, social and ethnic characteristics, and level of economic development. To the extent that no societies are exactly alike in terms of their respective socio-cultural and economic characteristics, the ideologies of different countries are expected to differ from one another even if they pay homage to the same intellectual ancestors. Differences in socialist ideologies manifested in Marxism, Leninism, Maoism, and Third World socialism in Africa and Latin America can best be explained by the contextual differences to which they were applied. The same can be said with respect to capitalist democracies in Europe, Japan, and smaller Third World nations such as the Philippines and South Korea. When social and economic conditions are similar, ideologies originating from different philosophical convictions may become quite similar, as we see in the socialisms and democracies of economically underdeveloped Third World countries.

In this chapter, we shall examine the thesis that political ideologies are intended to perform the role of legitimation and political integration, first by looking at the spectrum of ideological changes as they evolved over time and then by comparing and contrasting some selected political ideologies witnessed in the post-World War II period. Later in this chapter, we shall examine the nature of mass belief systems in an effort to illuminate the process and dynamics of the integration of political culture.

IDEOLOGY AS INSTRUMENT

In the political integration stage, ideology emerges as an important mechanism by which the basis for mass support is generated and propagated. Ideology is especially useful when diverse and conflicting belief systems proliferate and political culture disintegrates, indicating a crisis of national identity and regime legitimacy. In such a context, an ideology presents the populace with a comprehensive political belief system enumerating the ultimate goals or end-states of the society and the legitimate means by which these goals can be achieved. As such, it provides the individual with a vision of his political society, his place in it, and a set of reasons why this system, and not some other, is worthy of his loyalty. It is only in this sense that we can understand why political ideologies have actually emerged at times of crisis for regime legitimacy and national identity.

In the course of evolution of political ideologies, we have seen a number of belief systems and philosophical configurations which various regimes have employed to legitimize certain power positions and to justify the suppression of others. When possession and exercise of power needed no justification in pre-modern times, philosophical ideas never coalesced into a political ideology of the regime. Throughout ancient and medieval times, power was taken for granted as the possession of a ruling elite who were regarded as superior to the ruled, thus needing no persuasion or justification for their ownership. The Platonic idea of the "philosopher king" was intended to define who should rule and who should be ruled.[2] As long as the rulers showed that they were philosophers, i.e., knowledgeable, it was taken for granted that they were qualified to rule the masses. In this situation, the ruling elite do not need to worry about the legitimacy of their power.

With the spread of philosophical individualism and the *laissez-faire* economic doctrine, however, legitimacy based on human inequality became subject to criticism. Indeed, the notion of legitimacy by the governed ascended, thus paving the way to the theory of "social contract" as advocated by John Locke. Thus, the emerging social contract theory became a powerful ideological doctrine embedded in classical liberalism, challenging the preceding capricious social and political order. In this sense, the emergence of liberalism was a response to the failure of medieval and early modern doctrines of human inequality as a means to legitimize political power. Since the introduction of the social contract, political ideologies have emerged competitively, with varying perspectives as to the proper relationship between ruler and the ruled—a question of legitimacy.

Classical liberalism, with its doctrine of civil liberties and the reinforcement of economic capitalism, advocated that the greatest collective good can be served by minimum governmental intervention in the private lives of citizens. Thus, a government that exercises the least amount of power was regarded as the best form of government. But it did not take too long for the liberalists themselves to realize that freedom from governmental constraint did not necessarily make one free: in order to exercise the right of freedom, one must have the necessary resources and values with which to obtain and maintain freedom.

The ensuing ideologies, under the rubric of socialism, were designed to remedy that situation which, to the growing number of impoverished people, the right to freedom meant only words written on a legal document. In this sense, the Marxist denunciation of capitalism can be viewed as a humanist effort to guarantee a better distribution of resources at the expense of property rights and freedom, if necessary. In fact, Leninist socialism called for maximum government intervention in creating and protecting resources and opportunities that the masses were lacking under a capitalist structure. The success of the Bolshevik revolution in Russia and the Maoist revolution in China can be attributed to the widespread disappointment at classical liberalism's failed promises in those nations. In this sense, we can say that socialism too was a means for political regimes to broaden their legitimacy. The fact that Lenin's version of socialism was not consistent with orthodox Marxism was undoubtedly due to the indigenous condition of Russian agrarian feudalism which would not have been "ripe" for a Marxist proletarian revolution.

Of all socialisms practiced in history, Maoism has affected more people and in a more profound way. Mao Ze-dong, unlike Karl Marx, was not a theoretician but a politician. What he needed was not a flawless theory but a workable doctrine for his attempt to win public support at a time when the existing liberal ideology was experiencing a serious crisis of public confidence. In the semi-feudal, agrarian, and Confucian society, Mao's forces needed a doctrine that would accommodate the salient social and cultural features of China, yet effectively challenge the Nationalist government and its attendant ideology.

Even a cursory examination of Maoism will show that Mao's socialist ideology is fundamentally different from Marxism, and the difference can be explained by the unique nature of the Chinese social and cultural milieu, as well as by the particular economic imperatives of twentieth century China. If an ideology that does not recognize the process of class polarization, and fails to take into account the centrality of class consciousness and class struggle cannot be called a Marxist ideology, then Maoism certainly is not one. Mao saw in China a diverse array of economic classes, not a simple capitalist–proletariat polarity. Consequently, he sanctified the "peaceful resolution" of societal conflicts through means of "self-criticism." In this manner he could broaden his appeal and build an effectively revolutionary class that was united not by its common relationship to the means of productions but by its shared opposition to the Nationalist regime. These un-Marxist features were intended to accommodate Chinese indigenous conditions about which Mao himself was so emphatically concerned.[3] For the same reason, socialist leaders in the Third World, such as Sengor, were never in line with orthodox Marxism due to the semi-feudal social system, colored by colonial experiences, in which they operated.[4]

Tracing the ideological spectrum in the liberal tradition will also lead us to conclude that political democracies have exhibited a variety of belief systems and policy priorities. Democracy in America today is clearly different from what the Founding Fathers had once envisioned, especially in the explosive growth of federal power and welfare politics. Smaller democracies around the world have shown a number of deviations from the classical liberal tradition, as we have witnessed in Sukarno's "guided democracy," Marcos' controlled system, South Korea's oppressive regimes, and many other systems where social and political stability is constantly threatened.

The repeated failure of non-western democracies, with political institutions originally developed in western industrial societies, has led serious students of social change to question the applicability of democratic institutions to those foreign lands. The general view is that political ideology, like any other institution, cannot be transplanted without modifications and often drastic changes. This is due to the fact that ideologies are intended to be useful for the regime in its effort to generate popular support and this effort will not be effective unless these ideologies address real needs in the indigenous social and cultural context. In this sense, we might conclude that political ideology is not a commodity that can be purchased from foreign countries if it is going to be useful to the regime as a means of legitimizing its power and control.

SOCIO-ECONOMIC CORRELATES OF IDEOLOGY: NOTES ON DEMOCRATIC CONDITIONS

Some societies are more successful with any given ideology, such as democracy, than others, implying that there might be a set of socio-economic and cultural characteristics that are more conducive to that ideology. In fact, several major studies have been done on the very question of "requisites" for democracy. If a political system is going to achieve the goal of political integration, based on the attainment of ideological consensus, it is essential for the regime to have some knowledge of the conditions and correlates of the particular ideology that will be used by the regime in its efforts to integrate the political culture.

In this section, we shall examine some empirical findings concerning the relationship between democracy as an ideology and the context in which that ideology is being implemented. Although our discussion is about liberal democracy, we can safely make inferences about conditions that are receptive to non-democratic institutional development, such as totalitarian communism, if the two ideologies indeed represent the opposite ends of the same continuum.

Socio-Economic Conditions for Democracy: Some Empirical Findings
Since Lipset's pioneering work, "Some Social Requisites of Democracy," numerous studies have inquired into the role of socio-economic development in democratic performance. While some studies, such as Neubauer's and Jackman's questioned the validity of the theory that democracy has as a prerequisite a certain level of socio-economic development, most studies appear to at least suggest a positive association between the indicators of democracy and those of socio-economic development. Some of the findings can be summarized as follows:

1. Economic Growth: Cutright, Lipset, and Fogelman, each using a different set of indicators and measures of both democracy and development, and utilizing a variety of analytical techniques, have all concluded that the development of democratic performance is strongly associated with economic growth.[5] In a comparative study of 41 countries for the period of 1946–1966, I found that there is a significant degree of correlation (.59) between the level of economic development, measured by the Gross Domestic Product, and democratic performance (Table 2). In my study, democracy was defined as the presence of a competitive form of government and was measured by an index of democratic competition.[6] However, in the same study it was observed that the level of democratic performance was negatively associated (− .18) with the *rate* of economic growth (Table 3).

This would seem to indicate that democracy is more likely to be successful in the presence of a high but stable level of economic de-

TABLE 2
Matrix of Correlations of Democratic Performance and Level of Socio-Economic Development
N = 41

	1	2	3	4	5	MR
1. Urbanization	—	.2033	.4921	.4259	.1222	.1222
2. Industrialization	(.1864)	—	.4415	.6808	.5829	.5995
3. Education	(.4791)	(.4488)	—	.6961	.7195	.8272
4. Economic Development	(.3448)	(.7650)	(.7452)	—	.5907	.8275
5. Democratic Performance	(.2392)	(.3183)	(.7380)	(.6923)	—	

(Correlations in parentheses indicate rank-order correlations—Spearman's Rho)

TABLE 3
Matrix of Correlations of Democratic Performance and Socio-Economic Change
N = 41

	1	2	3	4	5	6
1. Urbanization	—	.0405	.0429	.2572	−.2426	.1366
2. Education	(.1966)	—	−.207	−.0963	−.3785	.0896
3. Industrialization	(.3711)	(.0474)	—	.1159	−.3265	.0429
4. Economic Development	(.1827)	(−.1645)	(.2760)	—	−.1809	.2306
5. Democratic Performance	(−.2514)	(−.3323)	(−.2853)	(−.0747)	—	−.4565
6. Fluctuation in Democracy	(.4830)	(.1398)	(.1313)	(.1773)	(−.5035)	—

(Correlations in parentheses indicate rank-order correlations—Spearman's Rho)

velopment. Accordingly, we could argue that a system of democratic political institutions is not the ideal form of government for a country that is economically backward and interested primarily in rapid economic growth.

2. Industrialization: As industrialization may be assumed to be closely related to economic growth, the relationship of industrialization to democratic performance is likewise expected to be positive. Several empirical studies have indeed found such a relationship: Both Lipset and Cutright, based on their empirical assessment of democracy, have strongly suggested that industrialization is a necessary aspect of development since it facilitates the growth and maintainance of a democratic form of government. Cutright, as we see in Table 4, found a relatively high correlation (.72) between industrialization and democratic political development.[7] Reaffirming this finding, I found in the same 41-nation study a correlation of .58 between the industrial output of a nation and its democratic performance (Table 2). However, here again a negative association (−.33) was observed between the rate of industrial growth and the level of democratic performance (Table 3).

In short, these studies seem to indicate that democracy is more likely to be successful in industrial societies, but that rapid industrialization might detract from a nation's democratic performance. This would also suggest that democratic institutions might not be the ideal forms of political organization for societies desiring to achieve and working actively for rapid industrialization.

3. Education: Education, with its obvious institutional and behavioral ramifications, has consistently proven to be a powerful predictor of democracy. Virtually all studies have demonstrated that both literacy rate and school enrollment are important correlates of democracy. All three tables introduced in this chapter, and many other findings on democracy and voting behavior concur on the proposition that for all practical purposes it is necessary to have a literate populace and a high level of education in order to achieve and sustain a viable democracy. However, it is quite interesting that, as in the cases of economic growth and industrialization, there is a negative value of −.38 (Table 3) for the relationship between democracy and the pace of educational achievement, indicating that even educational development can be detrimental to democratic performance when its achievement occurs too rapidly.

4. Urbanization: As an increasingly large proportion of most popula-

TABLE 4
Cutright's Matrix of Correlations of National Measures of Political Development, and Levels of Communication,
Urbanization, Education, and Employment in Agriculture
N = 77

	2	3	4	5	Means	S.D.
1. Communication	74	88	−86	81	204.5	36.4
2. Urbanization	—	77	−75	69	49.9	8.2
3. Education		—	−78	74	105.8	16.7
4. Agriculture			—	72	53.1	10.5
5. Political Development				—	49.9	9.7

tions reside in urban areas, the process of urbanization has become an important interdisciplinary concern. While there is a rich body of literature on the processes and implications of the urbanization phenomenon, not much of a consensus has been reached on the nature of the political consequences of urbanization. Urbanization, as a form of social change necessitated by industrialization, had usually been assumed to be an element of modernization and therefore a good indicator of political development until Philip Hauser and Gerald Breeze, among other authors, came to note the possible detrimental effects for developing societies of cities that grow too rapidly for the rest of society to keep pace with: all too often the result is not development but severe urban disruptions such as high crime rates and unemployment.[8]

Due to, perhaps, the effects of "over-urbanization" in many developing societies and also the widespread urban problems in industrial societies, I found no significant degree of association (.12) between the proportion of people living in urban areas and the degree of democratic performance in that nation (Table 2). Although Cutright and Lipset would have disagreed, my findings suggest that the "over-urbanization" phenomenon in Third World nations and the common problems of urban decay in economically advanced societies offset what contributions urbanization might make toward education and economic growth, both of which are positively related to democratic performance.

5. Communication: Although not many researchers have included in their empirical analyses the variable of communication, those who have, e.g., Lipset and Cutright, have found that communication development contributes significantly to political democracy (Table 4).

In short, although Neubauer and Jackman claimed there is either little relationship or a curvilinear relationship between democracy and socio-economic development, the majority of the empirical studies on the subject seem to agree that democratic institutions are likely to be more successful when the society is blessed with a high level of economic development, education, industrialization and communication.[9] Urbanization, on the other hand, does not seem to be a strong correlate of democracy. However, when we measure socio-economic indicators in terms of their rate of growth, rather than their level of development, we find an overall negative correlation between democratic performance and socio-economic development (Table 3).

Then an important question is, how do the socio-economic indicators facilitate the growth of mutual adjustment and competitive decision-making processes? On what theoretical basis can we say that the empirical findings are meaningful with respect to the conditions of democratic performance? This issue is significant and has to be discussed because socio-economic conditions might affect democratic performance differently in different countries; and thus, this issue leads us to the more important question of what other factors need to be considered in order to comprehensively explain variations in democratic performance. And in what way are all the pertinent variables interrelated? These questions will be dealt with in the following section where we shall formulate a more comprehensive conceptual framework within which to discuss the conditions for democracy and to define the role of the socio-economic development in democratization.

What Makes Democracy Work?
In order to deal with the question of what makes democracy work, we need to be reminded of our definition of democracy. We defined democracy in terms of "government-by-the-people" and the mutual adjustment policy-making mechanism. Thus, democracy is conceptualized in terms of certain behavioral attributes: i.e., participation, competition, and bargaining. To the extent that behavior is explainable by environmental factors, we could see some validity in the relationship between socio-economic conditions and the behaviorally-defined concept of democracy. As a way of establishing the analytical context in which socio-economic conditions may be assessed, we will formulate a conceptual framework within which we can account for the phenomenon of participatory democracy. With some modifications and changes in the frameworks discussed by Milbrath, Dahl and Verba, we demonstrate in Figure 7 how the socio-economic variable is only indirectly related to democracy, through the intervening variables of the political setting and the attitudinal attributes of the people.[10]

Figure 7 implies that political participation may be viewed as a direct consequence of citizens' attitudes and the "behavioral context," both of which are in turn affected by the environmental conditions subsumed by the socio-economic variable. We shall examine these correlates of participation more carefully.

Most scholars agree that for participatory and competitive attitudes to emerge in a people's political life, the citizens need to be politically motivated and feel efficacious concerning politics. We could also argue

FIGURE 7
Contextual Correlates of Democracy

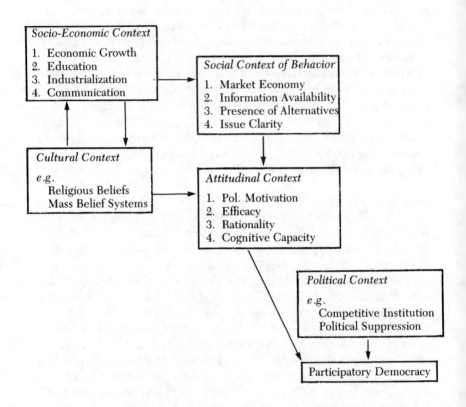

that, since we define democracy in terms of participation and mutual adjustment policy-making mechanisms, the cognitive capacity and rationality of the citizens should be included as an essential requirement for democracy.

a) "Democratic Personality":

Democracy can best be characterized by the process in which political decisions are made through the decision-making mechanism of mutual adjustment, and political legitimacy is based strictly on the contractual right by which the government is expected to represent the will of the people and to comply fully with their articulated and aggregated demands. In this, we are assuming a great deal of capability on the part of the people in that they should be capable of defining their demands and of directing such demands to the government in exchange for their support of the regime.[11] Thus, a democratic actor needs to be receptive to and provided with political information and cognizant of his position and role in the political system. In this, education contributes decisively to the formation and development of such political attitudes necessary for political participation, particularly those of political efficacy and civic responsibility. It is an established fact that persons with a high level of education are more likely to be politically efficacious than persons with less education. This has been confirmed in virtually all countries studied so far, with the exception of some cases where highly educated persons might have developed cynical attitudes about their potential for political influence and thus have become more apathetic than efficacious.[12] Persons with poor education, particularly rural residents, are believed to be politically passive. Furthermore, an educated person is believed to be open-minded and to have the ability to systematically organize his opinions, and thus is more capable of articulating his demands. A person with these characteristics of a "democratic personality" appears to be more active in group endeavors which, in turn, increases his motivation to become involved in political affairs in general.

For these reasons, it seems essential for a democratic system to have a population that is highly educated, and, as a result, imbued with the democratic personality traits needed for political participation.

Once we have met the cultural requirement of a "democratic personality," we can say that the most salient precondition for a viable democratic system has been met. However, even if you have the desire and propensity to have "democracy," other factors are necessary for the realization of such desires. Some of these factors might be identified when we define the democratic process as a choice-making process.[13]

Once we define democratic processes as participation or choice-making behavior, we need to ask the question of what it takes to make a rational choice. Choice-making of any kind has a set of requisites necessary for such behavior that include a "rational mind," the presence of alternatives, the availability of information about the alternatives, and preference ordering on the part of the choice-maker.[14] These properties or factors necessary for choice making should likewise be present for a participatory form of politics. We shall discuss the implications and significance of each of these properties as we attempt to specify the conditions conducive to the adoption of democracy.

b) Rational Mind:

This notion of rationality is derived from the field of political economy and was adopted by Anthony Downs for an analysis of choice making behavior in democracy.[15] Downs, inferring from Arrow's earlier work, *Social Choice and Individual Values,* defines rational man as one who behaves as follows: (1) he can always make a decision when confronted with a range of alternatives; (2) he ranks all the alternatives facing him in order of his preference in such a way that each is either preferable to, as desirable as, or inferior to each other alternative; (3) his preference ranking is transitive; (4) he always chooses from among the possible alternatives the one that ranks highest in his preference ordering; and (5) he always makes the same decision each time he is confronted under the same conditions with the same alternatives.[16]

As the definition clearly implies, a rational man is one who knows what is good for him and behaves in such a way as to maximize his interest. This would mean that democracy requires its citizens to be what may be called "economic men." For this, we might assume that the market economy would be conducive to the development of such an "economic mind" and rationality. In a market situation, one is expected to be a bargainer in that one wants to pay less for more. Furthermore, the purchaser is likely to be provided with alternatives from which to choose, and the very presence of alternatives will enhance his bargaining strength and the desire to make the best deal. The seller's position is exactly the same as the purchaser in that the former's bargaining strength will be enhanced when more buyers compete with each other to buy from him.

As we can assume that the market situation is characterized by a choice making mechanism, we could contend that a democracy will enhance its chances for success when a market economy prevails in the economic system of the society. Here, we must emphatically point out that it is the functioning of a market-based economic structure and the related social phenomena that is helpful for the growth of democracy and not industrialization itself, even though the latter is usually accompanied by the former. The apparent association between industrialization and democracy that we presented earlier might be attributed to the fact that industrialized societies happen to exhibit more frequently the kind of economic and social structures that might be subsumed by the concept of a market economy. If a society can retain an agricultural economy while manifesting a sound market-based economic system, it could certainly develop the type of social and cultural environment conducive to democratic development.

c) The Presence of Possible Alternatives:

When a political actor participates in the process of politics, either in the direct form of participation (election) or in an indirect way through interest group or political party activities, he is essentially expected to make choices from alternatives. The alternatives may be in the form of candidates, issues, or parties. Without the presence of alternatives for the choice maker, his decision cannot be called choice-making. Thus a clear distinction between alternatives and the presence of a wide range of alternatives are features essential to choice-making behavior.

Studies on participation have presented substantial evidence as to the facilitating role of the presence of alternatives and clear distinctions between them in increasing participatory behavior. As Milbrath and others have long held, "people are more likely to turn out for an election when clear differences are perceived than when alternatives are unclear."[17] This phenomenon may be attributed to the fact that when the alternatives are clear, the costs of collecting information and making decisions are reduced.

This phenomenon seems to suggest that the presence of alternative parties and competing candidates is needed for paticipatory democracy. Thus, discouraging the growth of a competitive party system and political competition between individuals and groups would be detrimental to democratic development.

d) Information Availability:

As alluded to earlier, for one to make rational decisions, the choice maker should have all possible information about the available alternatives in order to make a comparative assessment of them.[18] Political parties should fully communicate their policy positions and candidates should provide the citizens with information concerning their positions on policy areas as well as other pertinent issues. This would suggest that a fully functional mass communication system might be essential to a democratic society. It is in this sense that we could rationalize the empirical studies in which a high degree of association was established between democratic performance and communications development. It also suggests that freedom of communication needs to be maximized.

e) Cognitive Capacity of the Citizens:

Even if there is a widespread mass communication network and guaranteed freedom of communication, participatory democracy will not be facilitated by this if the people are not capable of comprehending political communications. The degree to which a person is capable of political communication depends on two factors: cognitive capacity and the complexity of political issues. A person's cognitive capacity is believed to be enhanced by education. Education, here, is expected to provide him with not only new information but also the ability to evaluate issues and events and to think logically.[19] The high association between educational attainment and political democracy that was found by the empirical studies discussed in this chapter is naturally to be expected when we conceive of the function of education in this way.

f) Complexity of Issues:

Perhaps one of the gravest problems with contemporary democracy is the fact that all societies are facing increasingly complex social and political issues. Furthermore, most of these issues can have a multiplicity of alleged solutions, and the public is likely to be either deceived or blindfolded with respect to which solution is best. It is in terms of this complexity of issues and problems that politics everywhere is becoming more and more centralized and the public gradually more alienated. Some critics of contemporary society have even coined an alternative concept to democracy which they cynically refer to as "technocracy."[20] Thus, for the public to comprehend political issues, the issues need to be clearly interpreted by the government as well as by the mass media.

g) Allocation of Values versus Production of Values:

As is widely subscribed to, the democratic process is not a very efficient political process. Furthermore, it is a process designed to produce an optimal level of popular satisfaction in which every individual is reasonably content rather than to produce the maximum outputs on the part of the total community. As such, democracy is expected to be more functional in a society where there are sufficient values and resources to be made available to its members. However, in a society marked by scarcity, the expectations of maximum production tend to generate public support for the efficiencies of centralized control, and some sort of socialist form of economic structure is likely to emerge. As Kautsky has concisely noted, socialism is believed to be a preferable ideology for planning and implementing developmental programs in economically underdeveloped nations.[21]

However, as a society attains sufficient resources for its citizens to maintain leisurely living, socialist arrangements will have to experience serious setbacks due to the increasing desire of the public to own private property and maintain an unconstrained (by government) lifestyle. We may be witnessing such a process of the breakdown of socialist institutions in the Soviet Union.[22] Indeed, this idea is at the core of the so-called "convergence" theories of future U.S.-Soviet relations.

SOCIO-CULTURAL CONDITIONS FOR DEMOCRACY

We have presented various factors that have been claimed to be related to the development of democracy. These factors may be summarized as follows:

1. The public needs to be politically motivated and interested in political affairs. Political apathy of the people certainly impedes democratic development.

2. Political and public decisions should be made through the mechanism of mutual adjustment, rather than central coordination. A centrally coordinated system of decision-making discourages public participation in governmental processes. It also facilitates submissive attitudes rather than efficacious attitudes on the part of the citizens.

3. The public must be rational, particularly in the sense that interest maximization becomes the primary goal of their behavior.

4. As political behavior may be defined as choice-making action, there have to be alternatives from which a choice can be made. It may be candidates, issues, or parties that constitute the alternatives, but there would have to be some form of political alternatives present for the citizens.

5. The public needs to be informed about the alternatives. Therefore the public should be provided with information about alternative choices.

6. The citizens need to be cognitively capable of comprehending information about their alternative choices and of predicting the expected benefits they should receive from them.
7. Political and social issues need to be clarified enough for the mass public to comprehend.
8. The stage of economic growth and the state of resource availability need to be such that modes of allocation of existing resources are the primary concern for the citizens and their government rather than the question of how to maximize production.

Based on these requirements for democracy we can assess the state and prospect of democracy in a particular country in the Third World. The present discussion is not intended to make an evaluation of the state of democracy in any specific country. However, we find it pertinent to the purpose of this chapter to examine one of the most widely proposed assumptions: that economic growth and industrialization are the necessary prerequisites for democratic development. Leaders of Third World democracies including Sukarno, Senghor, Touré, and Nkrumah have all sought justification for their versions of democratic processes in terms of this assumption. In light of the requirements for democracy presented in this chapter we might suggest that economic growth and industrialization will be conducive to democratic development only to the extent that they contribute to the aforementioned requirements spelled out here, particularly the development of rational attitude among the people. An affluent society also is one which most likely will emphasize redistribution or distribution of already sufficiently available resources rather than continuously relying on the growth of the production sector. But there is no reason to believe that economic growth itself constitutes the causal condition for developing the mutual adjustment mechanism in the policy-making process, nor does it provide the citizens with the cognitive capacity needed for participatory behavior. Furthermore, economic growth will be meaningless unless the consequences of growth (affluence) are shared widely by the populace; economic growth indicated by statistical averages does not mean anything insofar as its role in democratic development.

Industrialization has often been claimed to be necessary for participatory democracy but this is one of the least convincing arguments concerning the requisites of democracy. Perhaps industrialization may be said to be more productive than agriculture, and it contributes to a more rapid economic development. This does not mean, however, that industrialization is inherently conducive to the development of democratic performance.

As we suggested in Figure 7, there are clusters of correlates of democracy; some are more intimately related and others are only indirectly related to the eventual outcome of democratic performance. It is the elements of the attitudinal context which affect directly the level of democracy. All other correlates will work for democracy only by creating the kind of attitudes in the populace necessary for participatory political behavior. Our diagram suggests that even if we have all the attitudinal conditions, they will not be reflected in politics (democracy) when the political setting is not conducive; that is, when the government coercively discourages competitive political dynamics and free participation, democracy will not work. The socio-economic factors— economic growth, education, communication, industrialization—that have been discussed in this chapter are the elements most remotely related to the development of democracy: they will be helpful only when they contribute to the kind of social context in which the attitudinal requirements—political motivation, efficacy, rationality, and cognitive capacity—are created.

We have discussed in this chapter some of the conditions for democratic political development from a comprehensive conceptual perspective in which the relevant role of socio-economic development is assessed. In this assessment, we observed not only empirical research findings but more importantly, the logical and theoretical linkage between such socio-economic factors and the outcome of democratic performance level. Based on our discussion, we can conclude that a more careful theoretical study is needed before we can infer the role of socio-economic development in democracy.

IDEOLOGY AND MASS BELIEF SYSTEMS

We have discussed that political ideologies have been the convenient instrumental means for the ruling elite to legitimize political power. This utilitarian function can be effective when the ideology is coupled with socio-economic and cultural characteristics that are conducive to that ideology. At the same time, when an ideological doctrine with which the government attempts to socialize the masses is contrary to existing norms and values prevalent at the time, such an ideology will not help the regime to attain mass support. Therefore, it is imperative for the regime not only to have sufficient knowledge about the indigenous social and cultural context but to also be able to grasp the nature of mass belief systems themselves if the regime is going to avoid the political turmoil which usually results from cultural and organizational diversities in the beginning of the second stage.

As a guide to the analysis of mass belief systems, we shall now develop a typology of belief systems by which we might systematically compare and contrast political cultures in different societies as well as the dynamics of changes in belief systems over time. Before delving into the question of the philosophical nature of a belief system, we might note that political integration, the task inherent in the second stage, is a process in which various norms and values are subsumed under a common national belief system, thus, achieving an opinion consensus on the style of politics and on policy priorities.

While the concept of "ideology" has been variously used to denote philosophical dogmas, *Weltanschauungs*, lifestyles, socio-economic structures, and even institutional strategies, recent works on ideology (Lane, 1973; Converse, 1964; Satori, 1969; Merelman, 1971) frequently define the concept in terms of "belief systems," where the individuals' norms, values, and beliefs are singled out as the primary units of analysis. For the sake of analysis here it would be prudent to examine ideology in terms of belief systems because, among other things, such a conceptualization would be universally applicable in the sense that any "ideologized" person retains some sort of belief system; and thus, a belief system may provide a common basis of comparative analysis. At the same time, belief systems can be an important element with which to formulate explanatory-predictive (i.e., scientific) studies in the sense that behavior may be explicable, at least in part, by the actor's belief system.

Although some recent students of political socialization and political cognition have documented some empirical studies on belief systems, most such studies focus their analyses upon the behavioral manifestations of belief systems or upon the formal political doctrines that incorporate various beliefs, rather than investigating the structure of the belief systems itself. Converse (1964), for example, focuses his inquiry on the beliefs (politically and behaviorally manifested) of liberalism versus conservatism.

A belief system may be considered as a cognitive system pertaining to the relationship of the individual and his awareness of his environ-

FIGURE 8
Types of Belief Systems by Structure

	OPEN	CLOSED
ABSTRACT	Ideologue	Revolutionary
CONCRETE	Pragmatist	Insular Psych.

ment. In other words, a belief system concerns the role of the belief holder in his society. Consequently, political belief systems may be defined as a person's beliefs concerning his role in the political world. In this regard, we find ideology as being analogous to political belief systems because ideologies also prescribe the (legitimate) role of the individual in politics.

The Nature and Types of Belief Systems
In systematically assessing the nature and types of belief systems, we might make the analytical distinction between belief structure and belief content: the former is comparable to one's frame of mind or personality traits, and the latter to his norms or substantive beliefs. This distinction will enable us to construct a typology or political belief systems. Such a typology will not only be useful for classificatory purposes but also in explaining the role of various ideologies in the process of national integration.

a) Structure of Belief Systems:

A typology of the structure of belief systems may be constructed by combining the two dimensions that have been studied individually by Rokeach (1960) and Satori (1969), on the one hand, and by Converse (1964) and Lane (1973), on the other.[23] The first dimension has to do with whether a belief system is receptive to external stimuli (open–closed), and the second dimension contains the continuum of abstract–concrete (levels of conceptualizations, strength of "constraint" or capability of reasoning). This typology is shown in Figure 8.

Using these analytical constructs, we can discern four *structural* types of belief systems, and they may be characterized as follows:

Ideologue: An ideologue is defined as a person who is capable of abstract thinking and receptive to stimuli from the external world. Such a person sees alternative sets of concrete values as compatible with his abstract "principles" because these abstract principles, as a set, are maintained flexibly in their "openness" to change when confronted with new information. A person with high education is more likely to have this type of belief structure.

Revolutionary: A person whose belief system is "constrained" in terms of abstract principles, yet his principles, as a set, are felt to be so internally consistent that no stimuli from the external world could possibly necessitate the alteration of them or their patterns of interrelationship. Thus, while the concrete values that are pursued are justified in abstract terms, the rigidity of the system of abstract principles means that only a limited set of specific behavioral patterns and social institutions will be seen as legitimate in the sense of being compatible with the abstract principles. A revolutionary leader who has faith in a certain type of behavior as being sacred and uncompromisable might hold this type of belief structure.

Pragmatist: A person unable to give abstract or theoretical justifications for the concrete goals being pursued, yet the range of acceptable concrete values is broad and relatively flexible. The situational pragmatism of the "economic man" as he is depicted in the context of modern industrial society might be an appropriate example here. In seeking personal economic advancement, he would remain open to the possibilities of various types of economic activities as means to this end, yet without ever consciously examining *why* he wants material (economic) rewards.

Insular Psychology: This concept refers to the state of mind in which the person's range of concrete concerns is narrow and cemented, without his being able to give justification (abstract meanings) for what is being pursued. Instead, his beliefs are dogmatically rigid, and anything he believes is taken to be sacred and non-negotiable. Blind submissions of oneself to a concrete goal, as we might find, for example, in a loyal servant in feudalistic and dynastic societies, is the typical sort of behavior expected in this case.[24]

These structural types of belief systems must be filled with belief contents in order to be manifested as specific types of ideological patterns.

b) Content of Political Belief Systems:

No belief structure is without content and no belief content rests apart from belief structure. It is possible, however, that a given belief structure can store different belief contents and, conversely, a specific belief content can be housed in different belief structures.

As "political" belief systems may be seen as belief systems pertinent to the desired (or preferred) state of the political world, it is essential, in order to talk about belief contents, to define what the political world means to the perceiver. The question of defining the political world or politics is not an easy task; indeed, ultimately it is impossible to arrive at a universally acceptable definition. However, for the analytical purposes of assessing the nature and types of belief contents, we shall adhere to a definition of politics which views it in terms of *Power Conflict.*

Desirable or not (in moral terms), social conflict, especially conflict over the control of scarce resources and values, seems to have founded what is called "politics." Where there is conflict, politics (and government) is believed to be desirable as an agent for resolving such conflict; and where there is politics, conflicts are bound to arise over the control of relatively scarce resources and values. Thus, as many theories of legitimacy have alleged, politics has often been defined as the primary agent for social conflict resolution. However, in order for government (and politics) to resolve existing conflict, more often than not, it tends to generate new conflicts. But it appears to be an acceptable notion that government is designed (expected) to at least *manage* social conflict through the resolution of old conflicts and the introduction of new ones.

When we define politics as conflict management, we come to think of two issues as being pertinent to the process of conflict resolution/creation. One is the question of what the accepted *rules* are by which social conflict is managed in a given political system; and the other is the question of what the substantive *means* are of conflict resolution. A brief discussion of these two issues will perhaps clarify the distinction.

i) Means of Conflict Resolution: Throughout political history, as social conflict emerged over who controls what, there have been two fundamental courses of action available for settling the issue: one by means of the creation of new resources for distribution among those competing for currently scarce resources; and the other by means of re-distributing available resources. The former case may lead to a situation analogous to a positive-sum game in the competition over resources, and the latter to a zero-sum game.

These two means have been utilized by distinctly different political groups since the very beginning of political history. In the ancient times those who were physically capable of controlling and/or coercing others acquired food, commodities, and other resources by simply taking them away from others: thus conflict resolution for them was accomplished primarily by the re-distribution of existing resources. Those who were incapable of protecting their resources or unable to coerce others, chose the alternative of avoiding confrontation with the stronger, and satisfied their needs by generating new resources. From this, we could perhaps infer that the two different means of acquiring material resources gave birth to two distinctly different types of early societies: the hunting tribe and the cultivating tribe. Ever since, production versus re-distribution has served as an important dimension along which to classify various ideal types of society: production-oriented society has been that of the poor; and redistribution oriented society has usually been found where there are sufficient resources; hence, the developed-underdeveloped or the industrial-agricultural distinction may be seen as paralleling the production-redistribution distinction. At any rate, we propose that a society may be characterized in terms of whether it is oriented primarily toward the redistribution of existing resources or the production of more resources as the normal means of conflict resolution.[25]

ii) Rules of Conflict Management: Although I have singled out the simplistic contrast between production and redistribution as the means of conflict resolution, it is no longer the case that the stronger relies exclusively on sheer coercion to satisfy his resource needs. No matter which means one may use, the means must be seen as "legitimate" in its compliance with the accepted (authorized) rules of acquisition existing within a society at a given time. It also needs to be remembered that the available resources, whether they are cultivated or acquired from others, are always subject to reallocation. Here, too, we need some kind of ground rules for such a reallocation.

Using Lindblom's concepts of decision-making mechanisms (1965), we propose that *central coordination* and *mutual adjustment* have been the two modes by which societal conflicts in political history have been managed. These two general rules may have formed the bases of the contrasting belief systems of "authoritarianism" and "democracy."

With the variable of *production* versus *redistribution* as the substantive means of conflict management and with that of *central coordina-*

FIGURE 9
Types of Belief Systems by Content

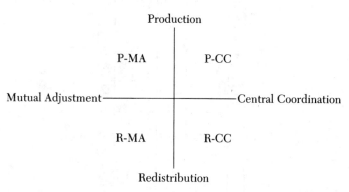

Production

P-MA   P-CC

Mutual Adjustment————————————Central Coordination

R-MA   R-CC

Redistribution

tion versus *mutual adjustment* as its rules, we can now propose a typology of political belief systems by belief content.

We see in Figure 9 that, based on the direction of one's political beliefs along each of the two content dimensions outlined above, a set of four types of political belief contents may be constructed: *production/mutual adjustment* (P/MA), *production/central coordination* (P/CC), *redistribution/mutual adjustment* (R/MA), and *redistribution/central coordination* (R/CC).

While keeping in mind the risk of inferential fallacies arising from the inference of societal characteristics from the attributes of its individual members, we can, for illustrative purposes, present examples of each of the content-types. The "P-MA" would be the kinds of beliefs found in a typically agrarian society, where one might believe that community issues should be resolved through collective discussion and shared responsibility. The "P-CC" type could be found in an agrarian society typifying an authoritarian culture and hierarchical social structure. The "R-MA" type might be characteristic of an economically affluent and consumptive (Rostow) society's mass beliefs, whereby decisions are made through negotiations and compromises. And finally, the "R-CC" type may emerge in a country that has been successful in economic development through a centrist form of political authority, while still maintaining autocratic forms of government, as the case might be in the Soviet Union.

FIGURE 10
Types of Belief Systems

	IDEOLOGUE	REVOLUTIONARY	PRAGMATIST	INSULAR PSYCHOLOGY
R-MA	Jefferson	Marx	Material-Oriented Individualist(?)	Anarchist(?)
R-CC	T. Roosevelt	Lenin	Authoritarian Individualist	Hitler Castro
P-MA	Syngman Rhee	Tito	I. Ghandi	"Japanism" (Japan since 1945)
P-CC	Brezhnev	Mao Ze-dong	Sukarno; Deng Xiao-ping	Kim Il-Sung

168

A Typology of Political Belief Systems

With the assumption that all belief systems consist of belief *content* stored in a belief *structure,* a typology of political belief systems may be constructed by associating the structural types with the content types, giving us a set of sixteen types of beliefs as shown in Figure 10.

This sixteen-fold typology may help us organize and compare systematically a number of political ideologies that we have observed throughout political history. Each of the types shows, on the dimensions of belief structure and that of belief content, the cognitive conditions indicative of that ideology. For example, the belief systems of a liberal democracy are likely to be formed when an "ideologue" (Open-Abstract) believes in the mutual adjustment mechanism as the desirable (just) means of conflict resolution while maintaining an affluent, consumption-oriented lifestyle. This we might see in a typically American upper-middle-class person. Extreme nationalism with a stable regime might be found in a belief system where an "insular psychology" structure (Closed-Concrete) houses the belief content composed of central coordination rules used in conjunction with the production of new resources as the means of conflict resolution. Such a belief system was perhaps characteristic of Meiji Japan. However, when the "insular psychology" structure is filled with the norms of the mutual adjustment system in a relatively affluent (consumptive) society, one might expect the ideology of anarchism.

In short, with this typology, we could describe, categorize and compare many different political ideologies in a more comprehensive and systematic fashion. Furthermore, we can use this typology in assessing the "environmental," economic and cultural, correlates conducive to the ideology types. If we could correlate belief system types with environmental or contextual variables, as attempts were made in the study of empirical correlates of democracy as introduced earlier in this chapter, we could not only predict the future development of mass belief systems but could attempt to control them by inducing altering contextual variables.

The Typology and Changes in Ideology

The task of community integration, when members of the community retain different sets of belief systems, will require changes in mass belief systems aimed at generating some degree of consensus. By the typology developed in this chapter, we might be able to identify the directions in which such a belief system change must proceed. In other words, we will know along which dimensions belief system must change in order for the requisite level of consensus to be achieved. For example, in the typology, Leninist socialism and liberal democracy are different in both the structure of their systems and their belief content; thus, a change toward ideological consensus (building a homogeneous ideology) would require the different task of adjusting or changing both of these components of the belief systems. By contrast, liberal democracy and welfare statism are different only with respect to their belief contents while retaining a similar belief structure. In this case, as we can foresee a rather smooth transition from liberal democracy to the welfare state in post-industrial democracies, an ideological change here would involve a relatively simple task.

When we compare the two components of belief systems—structure and content—in terms of saliency, belief content can be said to be more susceptible to change due to the fact that belief contents are by and large learned ("poured in") in the process of political socialization. On the other hand, a belief structure, which is likely to be more of a personality trait than a set of learned attitudes, might be considered a more salient factor in a belief system; thus, its structural change calls for a much more costly process, particularly in terms of the time needed for such a change. In any event, if we assume that belief structure is more difficult to change at least in comparison to belief content, we can account for ideological change more rigorously than we have ever been able to do. For instance, if we perceive an ideological disagreement in different parts of a community—say, North and South Korea—primarily in terms of belief content, then we might infer that reaching an ideological consensus here is a simpler task than a case where belief structures are also heterogeneous, as with Mainland China and Taiwan.

In short, this typology of belief systems (Figure 10), although its built-in assumptions and propositions inevitably lend themselves to re-examination, tells us what we need to change in a belief system in order to build an ideological consensus in a given community. This can be done by observing the number of different belief systems distinctly identifiable in the society and by measuring the proportions of that population adhering to each belief type. An equation may be for-mulated as:

$$H = \sum_{i=1}^{n} X_i^2$$

where homogeneity level (H) may be measured by the sum of the squares of that fraction of population adhering to each of the belief system types $(X_1^2 + X_2^2 \ldots + X_n^2)$.

THE SOCIO-CULTURAL VARIABLE AND NATIONAL INTEGRATION

Once we can empirically measure the level of ideological consensus in a given nation, the task of assessing the degree of national integration (nation building) becomes relatively simple. As was mentioned earlier, the socio-cultural variable (the other variable in Figure 7) has been rather extensively researched in comparative literature. Furthermore, this variable can be represented quantitatively by aggregate data on domestic attributes. Data on ethnic and religious attributes, as well as socio-economic indicators, have been richly documented in numerous statistical sources (Banks, 1971; Russett, et al., 1964; Banks and Textor, 1963). We believe that the level of integration (I) in a society, as measured by the various socio-cultural indicators, can be represented in a manner similar to that of belief systems: by the sum of the squares of the proportion of the population (Yi) in each of the groups $(Y_1^2 + Y_2^2 \ldots + Y_n^2)$:

$$I = \sum_{i=1}^{n} Y_i^2$$

What remains to be done is to construct a similar conceptual typology of socio-cultural homogeneity that is measurable by an index of these various indicators.

When we can measure and compare different societies in terms of levels of ideological consensus and also in terms of socio-cultural homogeneity, we should be able to measure the degree of national integration (NI) and conduct much more rigorous comparative assessments of the tasks of nation-building by simply combining the two equations:

$$NI = \sum_{i=1}^{n} X_i^2 + \sum_{i=1}^{n} Y_i^2$$

It should be noted that this equation measures only the *degree* of fragmentation in a society; it does not represent the intensity or saliency of the divisions. Therefore, a high NI value should not be automatically interpreted as implying an easier task for the nation in moving toward total integration. As alluded to earlier, ideological fragmentation along the dimension of conflicting belief *structure* should be interpreted as being a more difficult obstacle to integration than one along the dimension of belief *content*. Further, as discussed above, the presence of disagreement on both dimensions might be a more serious problem for integration than a disagreement on just one of the dimensions.

In this section, we have attempted to construct a workable typology of national integration. In devising this typology, we investigated the variable of ideology with some rigor by defining it as political belief systems and by distinguishing belief contents and belief structure as the composite elements of a belief system. However, we have not dealt with the socio-cultural variable in an equally rigorous manner because of the relative abundance of research already available in that field. Furthermore, we had only a limited discussion on the relation between the socio-cultural variable and the ideology variable. Although the decisive role of socio-cultural conditions in the formulation of belief systems and attitudes has been consistently suggested (Almond and Verba, 1963, pp. 80, 160), few universally applicable theories on this hypothesized relationship have been demonstrated to have any degree of validity. While it was not the direct intent of the present discussion, we cannot emphasize enough the significance of further studies concerning the role of various social and cultural attributes in forming specific belief systems. These further studies would increase the value and utility of the typology proposed in this chapter.

Finally, it should be pointed out clearly that the types of national integration as well as the belief system types described herein must be considered as "ideal types." Ideal types, as Max Weber (1949) maintains, are the useful tools for describing and comparing real cases, rather than being the descriptions of actual reality.[26] It is in this sense that we could expect the present study to be useful.

INSTITUTIONAL DEVELOPMENT

Once a new regime is in command and the members of the society are sufficiently certain of its institutions' capacity to provide the basic need of physical security, their need level shifts to that of belonging. This necessitates a new emphasis on social institutions such as the family, churches, local community-based group affiliations, and educational systems that function as mechanisms for the individual's gratification of these needs on a more intimate face-to-face basis.

As the initial need of physical survival might still be on the minds of many people, even if the level of urgency has subsided to the extent that they now are predisposed to the belonging need, the institutions of agriculture, police, and military remain of central importance to the community. However, these institutions will expand their functions to include activities that might promote a sense of belonging and mutual affiliation. At the same time, as pointed out above, a series of other institutions intended for generating the belonging need will attain saliency in the community. More often than not, the second stage institutions will gradually take over the functions of the first stage institutions, creating a phenomenon of institutional merging, thus changing all institutions in their functional boundaries.

The family, for example, which developed an extended family structure, as discussed in the previous chapter, for the necessity of securing household labor power, is now becoming a community social unit while still performing the same economic function of agricultural production. Thus, the meaning of the extended family system has changed from an economic unit to a social unit. There will be more cultural and social activities that the family could not afford in the initial stage. There will be more emphasis on mores, customs, and norms without which family bonds may be weakened as the old basis of economic necessity is felt as being less than imminent.

The other two institutions, the police and the military, will also modify their roles significantly and in an expected direction. When a regime seeks to prolong its power incumbency, as it usually does, the police will become an agent of the incumbent leadership in its effort to gain the support of the masses. It is well documented that voters in underdeveloped countries have often been subjected to political mobilization by agents of the regime. Often it is the police that becomes the effective "campaigner," as we can easily see in numerous autocratic democracies in Africa, Asia, and Latin America. In this stage, the military itself often becomes massively politicized and is utilized as an agent for the indoctrination of the masses. Even a cursory examination of the role of the "Red Army" in the course of socialist national integration will testify to the political role of the army, once national security is sufficiently assured.

Education is an institution whose primary function is to help people expand their knowledge, skills and social frame of reference so that they can establish a broader and richer context in which to seek out and establish their social affiliations and, hence, satisfy their belonging needs. Students meet other students and later become members of alumni groups. Furthermore, they learn ideas and beliefs with which their value positions can be defined, thus providing ideological affiliations. They also learn about other people, thinkers, philosophers, and leaders, and establish intellectual and philosophical associations which will help them promote their sense of belonging. At this stage these types of intellectual affiliations might be more salient than many other more physically proximate face-to-face associations.

In this sense, it is expected that educational curricula in pre-industrial societies will emphasize liberal arts and philosophy rather than science and technology. When we examine countries that have undergone the stage of political integration, such as the United States and Japan, we can easily observe that liberal arts and philosophical fields had their heydays in the pre-industrial times of the American post-civil war and the pre-Meiji Japan. Many Third World countries such as Mexico, Israel, the Philippines, and Korea have consistently demonstrated that liberal arts education has been given greater emphasis at times of nation building and political integration and has weakened in the process of industrialization.

The concept of compulsory citizen education will be introduced and implemented, as it presents the regime with an opportunity for political socialization. In fact, at this level of development, the government not only makes public education compulsory but it often dictates educational curricula with uniform official textbooks and other curriculum requirements. Politicization of education is seldom viewed as improper: the appearance of politicians on campuses is even fashionable and schools often compete to invite political leaders to their campuses. Students are also frequently mobilized by the goverment for political rallies and demonstrations, although anti-government demonstrations are not infrequent when the government fails to satisfy them. In any case, education in the second stage of social development becomes highly politicized and students are highly political.

The phenomenon of politicization of students leads to an active role for students in the processes of political change. In the absence of large-scale organizations and mass media in many pre-industrial societies, students as a group can be very effective in aggregating public opinion and mobilizing mass movements. We have seen many instances of student-engineered political turmoils and regime turnovers in places such as Turkey, South Korea, the Philippines, Mexico, and Iran.

As an ultimate source of psychological belonging, religious institutions will be more meaningful to the seeker of belonging. At the same time, the ruling elite will see the utility of harnessing religious institutions for the task of regime legitimation and political integration. It is for this reason that the notion of state religion as an officially approved religion has been quite prevalent in the course of nation building in virtually every country, be it in the form of Christianity, Islam, or Marxism-Leninism. This assessment of religions is not meant to undermine the theological importance of particular religions to various individuals, but rather to illuminate the commonality of the social and political functions of religion as a human institution. No one can deny the massive political and military role of the church in medieval Europe and in contemporary Middle East as well as in Japan. Perhaps more wars have been fought in the name of God and more bloodshed has been justified by the Church than for any other reason. The "military-religious complex" has often provided massive forces for a "just" destruction of political enemies, defined publicly as religious heretics. Furthermore, religion can be an integral part of education itself as the "school prayer" was a legitimate function of education in the United States. Many Third World societies at this level of development tolerate extensive interplay between education and religion.

CULTURAL CHANGE AND BEHAVIORAL DISPOSITIONS

As members of the society experience a series of institutional changes and as their behavior is altered within these changes, new value systems and behavioral predispositions will develop. We have pointed out that through the institutions of agriculture, military, and police, the regime formation stage facilitates such value orientations as authoritarianism, submission to external forces, and fate-accepting norms, as opposed to egalitarianism and self-determination. However, in the course of the second stage of development, we might expect the emergence of a new set of values and norms that may well be considered to be the antitheses of the value sets engendered in the regime formation stage.

Groupism or Collectivism

The very desire to belong implants the importance of group membership in the minds of people. They desire to identify with other people who share common views, goals, or simply achievement or ascriptive attributes. Family and ethnic groups maintain internal homogeneity in terms of the common ascriptive attributes of their members. Alumni groups and other educational organizations provide the members with common achievement attributes. Cultural groups may have common orientations and values. Religious organizations unite their members with common spiritual perspectives and world views. The belonging experience is a sharing experience; it is an experience in which one projects oneself into others. Thus, one will be inclined to be more empathetic toward other people. One will think in terms of "we versus them" rather than "I versus you," the latter having been a prevalent orientation in the survival stage.

This group orientation makes people easily susceptible to political socialization and ideological indoctrination. Ideologies that emphasize collectivism, such as socialism and communism, are usually more appealing to people at this stage of development, as newly independent nations of the Third World have demonstrated.

Altruism

Relatively speaking, the regime-formation stage marks the height of hedonistic individualism, at least in the sense that Hobbes and Machiavelli once envisioned in the context of transitional periods of turmoil that accompanied political change. By contrast, the second stage is characterized by the growth of altruism. The three main institutions—the family, school, and church—uphold the virtue of altruism. Uncalculated sacrifice within the family is always considered virtuous, regardless of structural characteristics of that institution. No religion will advocate hedonistic selfishness in the religious socialization of its members, although not every religion will sanctify nondiscriminatory love and understanding. The same can be said with respect to educational institutions.

In fact, in this stage of development, individuals become virtuous by sacrificing their personal interest, including even their lives, for the well-being of their groups. It is not unusual to place the highest respect in human sacrifice and martyrdom for religious persuasions and ideological convictions. Such acts are regarded as the ultimate manifestation of altruim. A comparative study of religious life in societies experiencing different levels of social development will most probably show the pervasiveness of sacrificial virtue at this stage.

Egalitarianism
Another norm expected to develop in this political integration stage is egalitarianism. As in the case of altruism, the egalitarian orientation also represents a sharp contrast to the submissive-authoritarianism of the first stage society.

As public education spreads, more pupils will become subjected to a new social context in which every one is presumably viewed in terms of "fellows," irrespective of their family background. Children use the same facilities, study the same material, eat the same food, and spend the same amount of time at school. This is a remarkable experience for those who have been subjected to social inequality, authoritarianism and the capriciousness of the social order in the first stage. This explains at least in part the almost fashionable phenomenon of student demonstrations against the social and political establishment in societies where such an establishment is still autocratic and authoritarian. This explains at least in part why a majority of college students in Japan are attracted to socialist ideas while they are on campus, only to become assimilated into the establishment itself after graduation. This explains at least in part why socialist movements in China, Germany, Japan, India, Pakistan, Great Britain, and the United States are started by college students. They are the ones who see the discrepancy between what they learn and experience on campus and what they see in the community. What they learn and experience is shockingly egalitarian and leads them toward socialist ideas.

Idealism
As religion provides one with transcendental experience, and education fosters abstract thinking, people in this stage become more metaphysically oriented in their thinking, especially in comparison to their cognitive orientation in the first stage. Particularly when philosophical

education and liberal arts and humanities are emphasized as much as they are in this integration stage, members of the community are expected to become idealistic in their attitudes and values. Indeed, those who are more idealistic and philosophical tend to enjoy a prestigious reputation in the cultural system, as witnessed in the relatively high social position of intellectuals in this stage. The "learned" in such a society refers to the intellectual with ideas rather than the scientist with technologies. The age-old Confucian ideas in which people who work with their minds have always been regarded as superior to those who labor with their hands should be understood in light of this perspective of the sociology of knowledge. An examination of intellectuals in the post-industrial societies of Japan and the United States will reveal the trend that the reputations of intellectuals in the humanities and philosophy have progressively diminished as the society undergoes a transformation from the integration stage to the industrial stage.

This second stage idealism, however, prompts people to be oriented toward political ideologies, and behavior is dictated by ideological persuasions rather than pragmatic interests.

Universalism
As Parsons correctly juxtaposed in his "pattern variables," value systems in more primitive societies tend to be universalistic rather than specific, indicating that people at this early stage of social development are inclined to maintain synoptic views of the world. When they assess an object or a person, they think in simple terms of "good" or "bad" rather than being able to clinically examine both good and bad aspects. This is attributable in part to the excessive ideological orientation of their value systems and attitudes in this stage. Universalism combined with idealism will lead the actor to exhibit extreme forms of behavior, seeking "all or none" without compromise.

Furthermore, people who seek belongingness are afraid of being isolated or alienated. They want to be in the mainstream of society. This tendency would discourage the development of minority group-based identity and a pluralistic style of politics, as we will discuss later. Decisions in the group setting are most likely to be made by the convention of unanimity rather than the majority rule; a unanimity that is created by the predominance of the need to conform for the purpose of gaining a sense of belonging.

With these attitudinal and behavioral dispositions, government and politics will exhibit a unique set of styles different from the initial stage of regime formation. I shall discuss some prevalent political characteristics in the following section.

RULE CHARACTERISTICS

Charismatic Leadership
Most societies experiencing the diversification of ideas and views on public issues at this stage of development tend to be unstable, as the sheer coercive capability of the first stage regime is not capable of accommodating the newly emergent need of belonging. Some societies have managed to avoid the dissolution of the regime by developing a charismatic quality for their leaders. Here, the masses will render uncalculated support and loyalty to the regime, personified in the person of the charismatic leader.

Charismatic leaders have emerged in many societies that have gone through a period of colonialism and the struggle for national independence. Most charismatic leaders were the very people who had been known as national heroes to the masses for their leadership in independence or revolutionary movements. In this sense, we can say that charisma is born in time of national crisis. Thus, efforts to generate charisma for a leader in time of peace and prosperity are doomed to fail. By the same token, we can say that charismatic leadership cannot be inherited from parent to child.

Under a charismatic leader, the leadership style is expected to be that of mass leadership, prohibiting the development of an entrenched bureaucracy or any other form of intermediary power groups. In fact, for the sake of solidifying and stabilizing his power base, a strong leader will not promote or encourage any other leadership. Indeed, a successor to a charismatic leader will not likely be designated before his death. As a result, a period of extreme turmoil will follow the death of such a leader, usually culminating in collective leadership.

Doctrines and Extremism
As expected in this stage of political integration where ideologies are extensively utilized for power consolidation, politicans will associate themselves with legitimizing doctrines. Policies with strong ideological objectives will be formulated and implemented, which sometimes may be counter-productive for practical purposes. Power conflict is to be

maintained in terms of ideological confrontations. Social and political organizations will likely be justified in terms of ideas and values. In fact, people with stronger value positions will be more likely to be leaders of various organizations and institutions.

When politics is guided by ideological considerations, it will become extremist rather than being amenable to compromise. Sometimes even violent means are employed to convey political views. Mass demonstrations are often politically mobilized by politicians and the government. Under these conditions, the presence of divergent political groups will most probably lead to social turmoil and instability, resulting in either a repressive dictatorship or continuous political instability inviting successive regime turnovers. If a charismatic leader emerges, the society is likely to have a repressive dictatorship. If not, it is headed toward the vicious cycle of military coups.

Thus, when a society has built-in social and cultural diversity and pluralism, the political task of achieving national integration is most demanding and difficult. However, when integrated social and cultural forces are already present in the indigenous society, this second stage of political integration can be expeditiously achieved. Japanese nationalism and the Shinto culture made Japan's post-war integration rather easy, even with a foreign ideology at its base. By contrast, the Indian case represents a situation where indigenous social and cultural conditions are not conducive to national integration, even with a longer period of political socialization with a similar political ideology.

Politicization of the Public

For the purpose of legitimizing leadership, the government needs to facilitate the political education of the masses through various mechanisms. For one thing, it will expand the public school system and ensure that children get the necessary ideological education, endorsing the ruling elite and their official doctrines. The government usually writes textbooks for all public schools in the country. When the regime changes, the new leadership customarily rewrites textbooks which may be pertinent to ideological education. We see this in changing societies such as China, where there were sharp contrasts in the content of public education before, during, and after the Cultural Revolution.

Also, the regime will attempt to censor and control mass media to ensure that only the "right" information is promulgated to the masses. Surveillance and intelligence activities will be stepped up, and possibly among the public widespread fear of government sanctions will become an effective instrument for maintaining order and stability. Because the role of intellectuals is vital to successful politicization, the regime will attempt to gain the support of intellectuals, particularly well-respected national spiritual leaders. If intellectuals are not readily manipulable, they can be subjected to harassment or subtle pressure.

However, mass culture at this point is more sympathetic to intellectuals, and the suppression of intellectuals can generate massive disenchantment with the regime. Thus, the government can face a serious legitimacy crisis when its policy on intellectuals fails.

Mass Participation

As a result of increasing politicization of the public, levels of political participation can be extremely high in pre-industrial societies as witnessed in Third World democracies such as the Philippines, South Korea, Mexico, and India. These Third World nations have consistently recorded high participation rates in public elections and other forms of participatory mechanisms, considerably higher than their industrial counterparts in the United States, Great Britain, Canada, and West Germany.

There may be different explanations for active political participation on the part of people in pre-industrialized societies; but the fact that they do participate more actively than industrial citizens remains undisputed. In explaining this phenomenon, some suggest that people in underdeveloped societies, especially those in the lower socio-economic stratum, are easily mobilized by the incumbent regime in its effort to generate mass support. Others maintain that there are unique social and cultural characteristics that prompt the masses to invoke greater political interest in politics. The contention being inferred here affirms both of these explanations, as we maintain that people in this second stage of development are being actively politicized and they have the predisposition to be indoctrinated readily. They become more politically oriented and thus participate more actively. At the same time, the government's efforts to mobilize their support can be effective in the context of the hyper-politicized culture.

SUMMARY

Based on the assumption of this present paradigm that people's need level will shift from survival to belongingness when they are assured of their physical subsistence, we have discussed a series of new developments in such a successful regime. Among them is the emergence of political ideology as a vital institution for the regime to legitimize its power base and establish political consolidation at a time when the masses are more inclined to seek associations with one another. Whether the regime is going to stay in power will largely depend on its ability to integrate the political community without causing serious dissatisfaction on the part of belongingness-seeking masses. In order to analyze the process of political integration, we suggested that understanding the nature of mass belief systems is essential. Further, we attempted to investigate the structure of mass belief systems when we generated a sixteen-fold typology of belief systems. With the typology we might be able to assess the extent to which a nation is culturally integrated and to be able to compare different political communities in terms of mass belief systems.

In this chapter, we also examined the likely direction in which institutional changes may occur, particularly in the form of new emphasis on socialization agents such as family, education, and religious institutions. Finally, we observed that a series of sequential cultural changes and evolutions in political styles may follow. On the whole, the process of political integration will mark a style of politics markedly different from the initial stage of regime formation.

FOOTNOTES

[1] The Hundred Flowers campaign refers to the policy of allowing the masses to express their political views through a variety of media during the period following the rather successful First Five Year Plan of 1952–57.

[2] Plato's *Republic* in which the public can be served best by the Philosopher King was an early example of such an ideology. Thomas Hobbes in his justification of Leviathan re-emphasized the necessity for governmental initiation in policy-making and its supervision of the masses. For the relatively new example of such interpretation of human nature, see Reinhold Niebuhr (1972).

[3] For a further exposition of this view, see Han S. Park, "The Ideology of Chinese Communism," in Gary K. Bertsch and Thomas W. Ganschow (1976).

[4] Refer to articles by Touré, Senghor, and Nkrumah in Paul Sigmund, ed. (1967).

[5] References include: Phillips Cutright, "National Political Development: Measurement and Analysis," *American Sociological Review*, Vol. 28 (April,

1973), pp. 253–64; Seymour M. Lipset, "Some Social Requisites of Democracy," *American Political Science Review,* Vol. 53, No. 1 (March, 1958), pp. 69–105; William H. Flanigan and Edwin Fogelman, "Patterns of Political Development and Democratization," in John V. Gillespie and Betty A. Nesvold, eds. (1979).

[6] Han S. Park, "Socio-Economic Development and Democratic Performance," in *International Review of Modern Sociology* (Vol. 6, No. 2, 1976).

[7] Although Cutright uses national development, rather than democracy, as the dependent variable, his measurements of national development are essentially the measurements of participatory democracy.

[8] Refer to Philip Hauser, "The Social, Economic, and Technological Problems of Rapid Urbanization." in B.F. Hoselitz and W.E. Moor, eds. (1963); Gerald Breeze, (1966).

[9] For Neubauer and Jackman's findings, see Deane E. Neubauer, "Some Conditions of Democracy," *American Political Science Review,* Vol. 61, No 4 (December, 1967), pp. 1002–1009; Robert W. Jackman, "On the Relation of Economic Development to Democratic Performance," *American Journal of Political Science,* Vol. XVII, No. 3 (August, 1973), pp. 611–621.

[10] For somewhat similar conceptual frameworks, see Lester W. Milbrath (1965, p. 28); Verba and Norman H. Nie (1972, pp. 125–137); Robert Dahl, (1973, p. 45).

[11] Robert Dahl discusses lucidly such a requirement when he discusses the working and problems of democracy in America. See Dahl, *op. cit.* (1973).

[12] For a discussion of such cynical attitudes among highly educated electorates, see Han S. Park, "Socio-Economic Status and Political Participation: A Comparative Study," unpublished doctoral dissertation (University of Minnesota, 1971).

[13] William C. Mitchell analyzes the process of American government as one of a choice-making process in his innovative text (1971).

[14] For a general discussion of rational calculation in choice-making, see Robert A. Dahl and Charles E. Lindblom (1953); also, James Buchanan and Gordon Tullock (1967).

[15] For an excellent statement of this notion of rationality, see Milton Friedman, "The Methodology of Positive Economics," *Essays in Positive Economics* (Chicago: University of Chicago Press, 1953).

[16] Anthony Downs (1957, p. 7).

[17] Milbrath, *Op. Cit.,* p. 105.

[18] William Riker urges the need for "systematically complete information" for a rational decision-making in a game situation. See William H. Riker (1962).

[19] The element of logical thinking is discussed as an important function of political education by Warren Miller, "The Political Behavior of the Electorate," in Earl Latham, et al. eds., *American Government Annual, 1960–1961.* (New York: Holt, Rinehart and Wilson, 1960), pp. 40–48.

[20] The term technocracy has been used frequently by critics of the post-industrial society. For an early exponent of this term, see Daniel Bell (1969).

[21] For a concise discussion on this thesis, refer to John H. Kautsky, "The

Appeal of Communist Models in Underdeveloped Countries," in his book (1968).

[22] For the changing style of politics in the Soviet Union, see Frederick J. Fleron, Jr., "Co-optation as a Mechanism of Adaptation to Change: The Soviet Political Leadership System," *Polity* II (1969), pp. 176–201; Milton Lodge, "Soviet Elite Participatory Attitudes in the Post-Stalin Period," *The American Political Science Review*, LXII (1968), pp. 827–839; also F. Fleron, "Toward a Reconceptualization of Political Change in the Soviet Union," *Comparative Politics*, I, 2 (1969), pp. 228–244.

[23] This typology would house all six of Kohlberg's categories (Kohlberg, 1969; Kohlberg and Tapp, 1971) which would not be subsumed under any of the other major classifications of ideology or cognition.

[24] The term "insular psychology" was adopted from C. Yanaga (1956, pp. 47–49).

[25] Growth theories by Rostow (1952) and Organski (1965) appear to confirm this analogy between production/redistribution and underdeveloped/developed.

[26] For a concise, yet lucid description of "ideal types," see Don Martindale (1963, pp. 33–67).

REFERENCES

Almond, G. and S. Verba
      1963   *The Civil Culture.* Princeton, N.J.: Princeton University Press.
Banks, Arthur S.
      1971   *Cross Polity Time Series Data.* Cambridge, Massachusetts: The MIT Press.
Banks, Arthur S. and Robert B. Textor
      1963   A *Cross-Polity Survey.* Cambridge, Massachusetts: The MIT Press.
Bell, Daniel
      1969   *End of Ideology.* New York: Collier Books.
Bertsch, Gary K. and Thomas W. Ganschow, eds.
      1976   *Comparative Communism.* San Francisco: W.H. Freeman and Company.
Breeze, Gerald
      1966   *Urbanization in Newly Developing Countries.* Englewood Cliffs, N.J.: Prentice Hall
Buchanan, James M. and Gordon Tullock
      1967   *The Calculus of Consent.* Michigan: University of Michigan Press.
Converse, Philip E.
      1967   "The Nature of Belief Systems in Mass Public," in David E. Apter, ed., *Ideology and Discontent.* New York: The Free Press.

Dahl, Robert
1973 *Democracy in America*. Chicago: Rand McNally.
Dahl, Robert and Charles Lindblom
1958 *Politics, Economics and Welfare*. New York: Harper and Row.
Deutsch, K.W.
1957 *Political Community and the North Atlantic Area: International Organization in the Light of Historical Experience*. Princeton, N.J.: Princeton University Press.
Downs, Anthony
1957 *An Economic Theory of Democracy*. New York: Harper and Row.
Hoselitz, B.F. and W.E. Moor, eds.
1963 *Industrialization and Society*. Paris: UNESCD and Mouton.
Kautsky, John H.
1968 *Communism and the Politics of Development*. New York: John Wiley and Sons.
Kohlberg, Lawrence
1971 (with June L. Tapp) "Developing Senses of Law and Legal Justice." *Journal of Social Issues*, 27, No. 2, pp. 66–91.
1969 "State and Sequence: The Cognitive Developmental Approach to Socialization," in D. Goslin, ed., *Handbook of Socialization Theory and Research*. Chicago: Rand McNally.
Lane, Robert E.
1973 "Political Belief Systems," in Jeanne D. Knutson, ed., *Handbook of Political Psychology*. San Francisco: Jossey-Bass.
Lindblom, Charles E.
1965 *The Intelligence of Democracy*. New York: The Free Press.
Martindale, Don
1963 *Community, Character, and Civilization*. New York: The Free Press.
Merelman, Richard
1971 "The Development of Policy Thinking," *American Political Science Review*, Vol. LXV (December), pp. 1033–47.
Milbrath, Lester W.
1965 *Political Participation*. Chicago: Rand McNally and Co.
Mitchell, William C.
1971 *Public Choice in America*. Chicago: Markham Publishing Co.
Nesvold, B. and J. Gillespie, eds.
1970 *Marco Quantitative Analysis*. Beverly Hills, Calif.: Sage Publications.
Neibuhr, Reinhold, *Moral Man and Immoral Society*. New York: Charles Scribner's Sons. 1932.
Organski, A.F.K.
1965 *The Stages of Political Development*. New York: Alfred A. Knopf.
Riker, William H.
1962 *The Theory of Political Coalition*. New Haven: Yale University Press.
Rokeach, Milton
1960 *The Open and Closed Mind*. New York: Basic Books.

Rostow, W.W.
    1952   *The Process of Economic Growth.* Cambridge: Cambridge University
            Press.
Russett, Bruce M., et al.
    1964   *World Handbook of Political and Social Indicators.* New Haven: Yale
            University Press.
Satori, Giovanni
    1969   "Politics, Ideology, and Belief Systems," *American Political Science
            Review,* Vol. LXII (June), pp. 398–411.
Sigmund, Paul, ed.
    1967   *The Ideologies of the Developing Nations.* New York: Praeger Pub-
            lishers.
Verba, Sidney and Norman H. Nie
    1972   *Participation in America.* New York: Harper and Row.
Weber, Max
    1949   *The Methodology of Social Sciences.* New York: The Free Press.
Weiner, Myron, "Political Integration and Political Development," *Annals of
    the American Academy of Political and Social Science* 358 (March, 1965),
    pp. 53–64.
Yanaga, Chitoshi
    1956   *Japanese People and Politics.* New York: John Wiley and Sons, Inc.

Chapter VI

RESOURCE EXPANSION

As we saw in Chapter III, the structure of human needs is such that when people are assured of physical survival and of sufficient levels of psychological and social belonging, the need for leisure will emerge as the most urgent and imminent need determining their behavior patterns. In this chapter, I shall examine the structure of leisure itself as a psychological and sociological concept. Subsequently, I shall elaborate on the thesis that industrialization was initially instigated and has since been advanced because of the human desire for leisure. Finally, the impact of industrialization on cultural and social change will be examined, as I discuss the ill-symptoms of industrial society.

LEISURE AND SOCIAL CHANGE

The Psychology and Sociology of Leisure

"I never met a blacksmith who loved his anvil."
                                        Kurt Vonnegut

Though perplexity may characterize the question of whether man has the inherent desire to work, human history tells us that his more consistent desire has been to avoid work rather than to look for more.[1] Worker demands for longer vacations and fewer working hours in all societies are unmistakable indicators of the human desire for more leisure time. This is not to suggest that a person without work is in an ideal situation. What is being suggested here is that it is not work itself

187

that one desires when and if one does work; rather it is what work brings to the individual by way of securing survival and social belonging that is the source of his work motivation. The needs for physical survival and social belonging in this context may be considered to be more urgent and basic than the leisure need; thus the former are expected to be pursued at the expense of the latter if necessary. In any event, the present analysis is based on the assumption that man pursues leisure as soon as he is assured of more basic needs, and that this characteristic in human beings may well be universal, unrestricted by cultural norms, ideologies, or social differences.

In line with the definition offered by Weis (1964, p. 21), leisure time is defined as "that portion of the day not used for meeting the exigencies of existence." Those who just manage to live on a subsistence level or those who are seriously ill, thus devoting all their energies to the task of staying alive, cannot be said to have leisure time. As Weis clarifies, leisure time is time made available by work, not time in which work is made possible. It is, therefore, different from time for relaxation or rest to recover from work and for more work. In this sense, leisure involves the consumption of time, energy and other resources. Leisure is a commodity whose value is measured by the amount of free time available and the amount of non-essential commodities available for enjoyment during that time.[2]

Man's desire for a more leisurely lifestyle has been an important driving force in the invention of tools. Tools help one finish one's work in a shorter period of time and with less energy. The more efficient use of both time and energy is vital for leisure as well as increased productivity. As the agricultural sector's share of total employment decreases (or the share of the work force engaged in industrial and service activities increases), the average or typical number of work hours will be reduced. This trend is expected to be the case in all industrializing societies, as labor-intensive agriculture is replaced by capital-intensive industry.[3] According to one study, leisure time for Americans has increased steadily since 1900, whereas their work hours declined over the same period of time, indicating a close link between industrial development and the amount of leisure time (Table 5). In Table 5, a grand total time of 1,329 billion hours for 1950 was computed based on a total population of 151.7 million people in the United States, each of whom had twenty-four hours a day for 365 days a year. Based on numbers of people in each age and occupation group and on the typical pattern of daily activity, a total budget of time was prepared for 1900 and 1950, and estimates were made for 2000. The amount of leisure time increased from about 27 percent in 1900 to 34 percent in 1950, whereas work time decreased from 13 percent to 10 percent during the same period.

At the same time, as industry expands, there will be a greater demand for new laborers, enabling previously employed, or seasonably unemployed workers, to find more secure and better paying jobs. As a result, family income will increase, and the additional income will help them use available leisure time in more "efficient" and enjoyable ways. In order to expand leisure activities, workers will demand material consumption beyond the level of basic needs, and industry will respond with the production of goods designed to enhance a leisurely lifestyle. For example, in a farm family in a non-industrial society, one or more members of the family may spend an entire day out of each week washing by hand the family's laundry. This is activity that is highly labor-intensive and time-consumptive, yet produces virtually no increase in the family's wealth. By contrast, a factory worker in an industrial society may buy a washing machine that will do the family's laundry but with less human labor and in less time. Thus, the family members whose time and energy were once consumed in washing clothes now can invest that time and energy in other activities, some of which may well be leisure activities such as playing tennis or watching television. Automobiles perform the same function: they reduce the amount of time and energy consumed in various activities, thus creating additional time and energy to be invested in productive or leisure activities. The growth in the proportion of women in the work force and of two-income families has been made possible in part by the proliferation of such products of the industrial society. The same can be said of the growth of the "leisure industry" which produces such things as televisions, sports equipment, movies, video games and a myriad of other non-essential leisure goods.

The shift from an agrarian economy to an industrial one will eventually lead the society to a more complex class structure organized along the line of achievers and non-achievers in the command of skills and technology.[4] Those who have skills and technological know-how will enjoy more leisure time, and those who do not will continue to be engaged in labor-intensive occupations, thus having less leisure time. It is expected that unskilled laborers in industrializing societies will

TABLE 5
National Time Budget and Time Division of Leisure, 1900, 1950, and 2000
(Billions of Hours Annually)

Use of Time	1900	(%)	1950	(%)	2000	(%)
Total time for entire population	667	(100)	1,329	(100)	2,907	(100)
Sleep	265	(39.7)	514	(38.7)	1,131	(38.9)
Work	86	(12.9)	132	(9.9)	206	(7.1)
School	11	(1.6)	32	(2.4)	90	(3.1)
Housekeeping	61	(9.1)	68	(5.1)	93	(3.2)
Preschool population, nonsleeping hours	30	(4.5)	56	(4.2)	110	(3.8)
Personal care	37	(5.5)	74	(5.6)	164	(5.6)
Total, accounted for above	490	(73.5)	876	(65.9)	1,794	(61.7)
Remaining hours, largely leisure	177	(26.5)	453	(34.1)	1,113	(38.3)
Daily leisure hours	72	(10.8)	189	(14.2)	375	(12.9)
Weekend leisure hours	50	(7.5)	179	(13.5)	483	(16.6)
Vacation	17	(2.5)	35	(2.6)	182	(6.3)
Retired	6	(.9)	24	(1.8)	56	(1.9)
Other, including unaccounted	32	(4.8)	26	(2.0)	16	(.6)

Source: James C. Charlesworth, ed., *Leisure in America* (Philadelphia, Pennsylvania: The American Academy of Political and Social Science, Monograph 4, 1964), p. 10.

struggle at the bottom of the social strata for little more than physical subsistence, whereas skilled technicians and white collar workers will develop the kind of culture and lifestyle that are suitable for satisfying the leisure desire, as they attempt to ensure what Lenski refers to as "creative comfort" (Lenski, 1966, p. 38). They would promote the value of privacy and freedom in order to gain uninterrupted blocks of time for leisure. When a society consists of a larger leisure class, or at least, leisure-seeking class, the production of commodities in the areas of labor-saving appliances, hobbies, and recreation will increase.[5] At the same time, technological innovations and modifications will be designed to make them even more convenient and less time and labor consumptive. The "industrial man" will eventually become totally dependent on machines, and by this time the age of "push buttons" and "disposables" will be imminent.

Leisure and Division of Labor
As Durkheim observes, "an industry can exist only if it answers some need. A function can become specialized only if this specialization corresponds to some need of the society." The emerging imperative for the industrializing society is in the expansion of commodities designed to make more leisure time available for the consumer. Thus new specialization is aimed at increasing and improving productivity so that more goods can be made with fewer man-hours (Durkheim, 1933, p. 272).

Division of labor in a sense can be viewed as a social expression of "simplifying work" when work is unavoidable. By engaging in only limited segments of production, one expects to make the work routinized and easy to perform. As a result, the division of labor facilitates role specialization and professionalization. Acquiring role expertise is viewed as highly desirable in a society where its members are appraised by the *performance* of their functions. This is especially true in a new urban community where its members are assigned their relative status not on the basis of their ascriptive characteristics but by virtue of their achieved positions.

In short, the desire for leisure inherent in human nature may have been a powerful facilitator for the invention of tools, technological development, and industrialization. Industrial growth in turn led to extensive social and cultural change, directly in the forms of role differentiation and functional specialization, and indirectly in a number of other, more profound ways.

INDUSTRIALIZATION AND SOCIAL CHANGE

The kind of social change induced by industrialization tends to be most drastic and profound, for this change is likely to unravel the very fabric of the conventional social and cultural structure. It is a common historical experience that industrialization is inevitably accompanied by urbanization and the expansion of a market culture, and eventually the growth of a middle class. Furthermore, as the industrial economy crosses national boundaries and penetrates into the world market, a global community will emerge with a patterned network of economic interaction. The much referred to North-South nexus replacing the ideological polarization of East-West hostility is indicative of this development.[6] In this process, world cultures will become increasingly similar and mutually integrated as traditionally different peoples on this planet come to experience similar problems and generate homogeneous aspirations for industrialization and material prosperity. In this process, the "rational man" will be born, and he will become the model personality type. We shall discuss some dynamics and implications of these aspects of social change, since they are ultimately responsible for many of the emerging global problems.

Mass Consumption and Marketing

The desire for leisure and "conspicuous consumption" (Veblen, 1931) on the part of the consumer is an effective impetus for continuous industrialization. The industrial economy is fundamentally different from the agricultural economy in that it possesses the capability for virtually unlimited production of consumer goods, and these goods, unlike most agricultural products, are usually not essential for physical survival. Rather, industrial goods are intended for the more leisurely living desired by the consumer who has already secured the basic needs for survival.

For the survival of industry itself, the economy will be compelled to sell new products to the leisure-minded "conspicuous" consumer. This would require advertisement and marketing. At this stage of social change, a huge amount of resources is invested in this relatively new sector for market expansion. The survival of an industry will depend on its ability to sell what is already produced, and to make "better" products continuously so that "old" products can be replaced and mass consumption maintained. The automobile industry in America, for example, will not survive unless the consumer is after new models coming out every year. It is not in the industry's interest to encourage the consumer to retain his present automobile for a prolonged period of time by making them durable and keeping the same style year after year. The same logic is applied to a number of other consumer goods, ranging from appliances to clothing fashions.

In an attempt to induce the masses to consume, a variety of marketing strategies will be devised. In the United States we could point to coupons toward the purchase of goods, rebates, trading stamps, discount sales, catalogue sales, allowance on trade-ins, and using price tags deceptively marked $9.99 instead of $10. Advertising techniques are extremely sophisticated in all industrial societies where marketing is an integral part of economic and social life.

Since mass consumption necessitates advertisement in such a way that the public can be reached, mass media will become powerful instruments for the expansion of demand for industrial products. Commercials dominate newspaper pages. Radio broadcasts programs with a multitude of sponsors. Television commercials alone in the United States reportedly cost some $30 billion annually. Indeed, the mass media themselves are completely reliant upon advertising sponsors. Although the mass media have always carried advertisement, the extent to which the advertising of consumer goods overwhelms the media is a relatively recent phenomenon, expected only in mature industrial societies.

I have made a comparative examination of the Sears Roebuck Catalogue in selected years of 1900, 1920, 1940, 1960, and 1980 in an effort to observe the pattern of emphasis on consumer goods. In the 1900 catalogue, there was virtually no item that we might identify as being leisure oriented. The closest thing was fishing equipment, which might not have been for leisurely fishing alone. In 1920, however, some sporting items such as baseball equipment and archery appeared, but only in a few pages of the catalogue. By 1940 we see consumer emphasis on domestic commodities such as furniture, rugs, refrigerators, stoves, washing machines, and kitchen accessories, but in limited variety. A major change in consumer goods was observed in the 1960 catalogue where a variety of sporting goods are listed, including golf, billiards, weight lifting, croquet, tennis, badminton, basketball, baseball, and of course fishing. There was even a variety of children's toys. In addition, there were, for the first time, fourteen pages of camping equipment, indicating that an increasing number of people by then had the time and resources to enjoy leisurely camp-outs. Commodities geared for convenience and saving time were prevalent in the 1960 book, such as vacuum cleaners, rug shampooers, washer/dryers, freezer/refrigerators, electric kitchen appliances, dishwashers, electric stoves, and even adding machines. Some eight pages were concerned with pools and accessories. The 1980 book is distinctly characterized by electronic and computerized consumer goods. The appearance of the microwave oven in this book dramatizes the importance of time-saving. It might be noted that these commodity items have new looks and more sophisticated features in each of the subsequent volumes.

Credit and the "Precarious Consumer"

By the time society is deeply into the process of industrialization, the masses are likely to have jobs with limited and fixed incomes. Here emerges a social dilemma: the masses are attracted to consume a wide variety and larger quantities of goods, yet their income may not warrant such consumption. At the same time, the industry needs to sell commodities in volumes that the consumer cannot afford.

To ease this dilemma, banking and credit systems develop to allow the consumer to spend with credit and loans of all types. Due to the relative stability of this stage of society, the creditor can extend loans to be repaid over an extended period of time. Buying a house on a thirty-year loan, which is a common practice in the United States and other industrial nations, is something unheard of in many countries, particularly those in the Third World.

The magic of credit buying induces the consumer to seek newer commodities and more convenient items. Consumer debt in the United States, and probably in all industrial countries, has been steadily rising in the aftermath of the "buy now, pay later" syndrome.[7] By making credit easily available in large amounts, banks and other lenders offer additional purchasing power with which one can buy and enjoy now. To the fashion-minded consumer, it is difficult to refuse such an offer, for among other things people prefer to have goods now rather than later. Their propensities are, of course, to go the quick route, the easy route to consumption. Coincidentally, government policies at this stage of social development encourage credit use as a way of stimulating buying power and higher levels of economic activity.

Bank credit cards, "plastic money," offer safety and convenience for consumers who are attracted to the temptations offered by credit companies. To the business world, the simple fact is that debt is profitable—an end in itself for businessmen and bankers. Indeed, in a mature economic situation such as post-industrial society, merchandise and service sales are becoming a means to sell debt. In this credit economy, one can live rather comfortably, even consuming far more than one's income or social status warrants.

However, when the commodities one uses are acquired through credit buying, and thus not truly "owned" by the consumer, one's state of mind must be different. At the end of each month when the consumer is forced to pay his bills, he must be reminded of the fact that his possessions are not entirely his. This could have profound psychological implications for the credit buyer in that he might feel uneasy and uncomfortable, although his physical comfort may appear to be secure. Thus, as the consumer becomes addicted to convenience and to the relaxed use of credit that lenders are eager to offer, he will become a psychologically uneasy yet conspicuously comfortable looking consumer. This kind of consumer may be called a "precarious consumer" because his state of mind would be precarious with the fear of default and with the burden of debt.

Money Addiction
With the expansion of the market culture, in which every commodity and every form of service are translated into a single yardstick of money, people's overwhelming aspirations center around enriching themselves. Unlike smoking or drug addiction where health warnings and social sanctions work as prohibitive forces, money addiction is virtually unchecked. In fact, a unique feature of money addiction is the fact that more money is always looked at as something to be desired, whereas the other forms of addiction are not usually admired or desired by the non-addict.

People get addicted to drugs because it does "wonders" which only the addict knows. But one does not have to be an addict to know what wonders money can do in the industrial market society. It is hard to think of anything that money cannot buy.

In this third stage of resource expansion, however, money is not earned for accumulation but for the consumption of industrial commodities that are designed to appeal to the leisure-seeking consumer. Indeed, the consumer rarely makes enough money to accommodate his desire for the conspicuous goods that are constantly being replaced by newer patterns and more convenient models.

I once asked college students to make a list of consumer goods that they think are designed primarily for convenience and for the expansion of leisure time. The following are some of the most frequently mentioned items:

electric garage door
hair appliances: blow dryer, curling iron, rollers
hot shaving machine
sun lamp
electric can opener
dishwasher, dryer, washing machine
garbage disposal
automatic nail buffer
drive-through window (banks, restaurants)
microwave oven
automatic ice maker
electric toothbrush
"inside-the-egg" egg scrambler
automatic telephone dial
home computer
remote control television
electric knife
moving sidewalk
escalator
cruise controlled car; power windows; electric trunk opener
riding lawn mower
digital watch
golf cart
super glue
electric hand dryer in bathroom
jogging board
tennis machine
shower massager
giant screen television

In light of the fact that the sample consumer goods are subject to constant refinement and "improvement," keeping up with the current fashions requires an enormous amount of money. Furthermore, as alluded to earlier, the industry has by now acquired a lifestyle of its own, where its survival depends on its ability to innovate styles and more appealing products, thus continually promoting sales. In addition, the leisure-seeking consumer is attracted to time-saving and convenient commodities such as a variety of disposables. The list of disposable household items has been expanding steadily in industrial societies. To name a few: cups, dishes, utensils, diapers, razors, hats, umbrellas, lighters, pens, towels, filters, tissues, bottles, thermometers, and vacuum cleaner bags. These consumer items are intended primarily for convenience and efficiency, rather than for "showing off" one's economic status. Thus, these items are not to be confused with the "conspicuous consumption" that we will be discussing in the next chapter.

Bureaucratization and Alienation

The process of industrial production, with its foundation in the division of labor, forces social institutions to transform their organizational structure from a hierarchical structure, which is typical of agrarian communities, to a pyramidal structure. In the pyramidal structure, as typified by bureaucracy, social interaction is compartmentalized and peer interaction is restricted.[8]

Such an industrial bureaucracy will spread to all other social organizations and political institutions where roles become specialized and performed by line experts. This phenomenon of role specialization will contribute to the development of a "diffracted" society, to use Riggs' metaphor, as the previously "diffused" society will undergo a structural and functional transition analogous to the "prismatic" effect whereby a ray of light breaks up into a series of discernably different rays as it passes through a prism (Riggs, 1964). In this kind of organizational structure, we would expect an incremental process of decision-making in which synoptic or innovative decisions on the part of the organization as a whole will be unlikely. This would affect the practice of government bureaucracy in such a way that its role can be limited to care-taking and maintenance. Any kind of drastic change is likely to provoke serious dissent and turmoil, as witnessed in the industrial societies where sweeping government organizational changes are highly impractical and improbable. Government authority at this stage will experience a transformation of its basis of legitimacy from traditional or charismatic persuasion to "rational" persuasion.[9]

In the operation of a bureaucratic organization, work performance will be rewarded on the basis of *efficiency* in terms of tasks defined in a narrow job description, rather than on the basis of *effectiveness* in meeting broader objectives of the organization as a whole. By working on an assembly line, one is not expected to comprehend the entire process of production or to appreciate its final output. On the contrary, the assembly line worker tends to dig a small hole in which he finds peace and privacy, although boredom may prevail. "Industrial man" thus becomes gradually alienated from other members of his own organization as well as from his product. As Berger (1962) suggests, alienation would seem almost complete when one can say with honesty and moral conviction, "I am not what I do; do not judge me by what I do for a living," and when one turns to a non-working life for values and identity. If workers in industrial and commercial bureaucracies are indeed psychologically alienated, the Marxist indictment of capitalism as being an alienating agent of humans from things is indeed applicable to all bureaucracies.

Tyranny of Technology and New Victims
Schumacher (1963, pp. 146–147) in his seminal work *Small is Beautiful* laments that "technology, although of course the product of man, tends to develop by its own laws and principles . . . [It] recognizes no self-limiting principle." As individuals become helpless cogs in a machine, they lose control over the machinery. Furthermore, when the machine gets more sophisticated, workers are compelled to adapt themselves to it by obtaining new skills and technical know-how, or they will lose their jobs. Thus, as ironical as it may sound, man becomes subject to machines, and technology controls man rather than the converse.

Technological sophistication is assumed to be unlimited because without it no industry can survive. Unlike agriculture, industry came only to expand, and industrial expansion is made possible by an increasing demand for industrial products. As discussed earlier, technological innovations on a continuing basis are necessary for producing commodities which will appeal to the eyes of the leisure-minded masses and the "precarious consumer." The growth of technology itself is virtually unlimited and, more importantly, it is unchecked. Technology transcends national boundaries or ideological differences. There is no such thing as capitalist technology as opposed to socialist technology. For that matter, there is no American technology which will be repudiated in the Soviet Union simply because of its origin. In this sense, as Boorstin (1978) observes, we may be drifting into the "republic of technology," where civilization will become increasingly homogeneous and humankind will experience common problems of a common life environment. In the triumphant march of technological growth, all humans will end up as the victims, as they will be subservient to machines.

In a society where technocrats prevail, and new technical innovations are so swift that no one can acquire sufficient skills to enjoy competence throughout his life, the elderly will be sure victims because they are not as able and motivated as younger people to retrain themselves. As a result, older people will easily be eliminated from the work force and those who remain will be discriminated against.

In the United States in 1976, there were 22 million adults who were 65 or older; one out of every ten persons in America belongs to this group, which is rapidly growing due to the prolonging of life and the declining birth rate.[10] A predominant view is that not only will the elderly population keep growing, but it will become more concentrated in the upper ages of that segment, exacerbating the problem further.

Historically, the elderly were dependent on the family for survival. But the spread of industrialization and urbanization changed the institution of the family so that the place of work and home were separated, leaving fewer roles for the elderly. The extended family system was replaced by the nuclear family. Houses became smaller, women worked, mobility increased and family care for the elderly became more of a burden.

In a typical society, the increase of the aging population leads to a transfer of functions from family to government. Over the last 50 years or so there has been a profound development in the transfer of functions from the family to the government in the United States and Europe. This period corresponds to the time of active industrial development in the western world.

As Sussman (1977) correctly observes, for some tasks primary groups such as the family can be more effective than bureaucracy. These include: (1) the acquisition of general knowledge and communication with respect to one's physical needs—e.g. eating, dressing, etc.; (2) personal problems and issues that bureaucracy cannot meet, such as human relations, emotional issues, and the values a person should pursue; (3) idiosyncratic events such as dealing with car accidents. These functions are to be performed by family members and more intimate friends, rather than institutions and government bureaucracies.

As a result, the elderly maintain a precarious lifestyle: one fourth of American senior citizens fall below the federal poverty level and more than 10 percent of them are as vulnerable and defenseless as children.[11] Furthermore, the elderly suffer psychological and social alienation, with many of them turning helplessly to the crutch of drugs and alcohol.

Over-Urbanization

While urbanization is a natural outcome of industrialization, some cities increase their population without the accompanying increase in industrial development, exerting a parasitic effect on social stability.

Hauser (1964) characterizes "over-urbanization" as a situation in which "a larger population of people lives in urban places than their degree of economic development justified." As implied here by Hauser, the concept of over-urbanization is defined only in relation to the level of economic development, rather than the sheer number of people residing in a city. Breeze (1966, p. 6) directly relates "over-urbanization" to the gap between urbanization and industrialization that makes it possible to provide employment to all persons coming to urban areas.

Many other authors advanced the notion that over-urbanization can occur when the size of a city is unrealistically large, as though there is an optimality in city size. According to this view, the relation between the efficiency of a city and the size of its population is curvilinear; in other words, a growing city is expected to contribute to economic development and social stability only up to a certain point. An overly grown city would have an adverse effect on its socio-economic and political development. Estall and Buchanan (1961, p. 107) assert that:

> At some time or other most of the world's great industrial complexes have been thought to be beyond the point where economics are offset by the extra cost incurred in various ways.

Still others maintain that the phenomenon of a primate distribution of cities will be harmful to the society. The primate distribution phenomenon will occur when one or a few core cities grow rapidly, thus slowing down the growth of smaller and middle sized cities. This will accelerate the core cities' modernization at the expense of the rest of the country. It is believed that a tendency toward the primate distribution of cities is not only destructive for the balanced growth of the cities themselves but also harmful to the political stability of the nation. Conversely, this would mean that a "rank distribution" of cities of varying sizes present simultaneously is conducive to the nation's development.

In any case, mechanization of agriculture, combined with the apparent promises shown by new industrial jobs, facilitates the process of over-urbanization of one sort or another, contributing to urban unemployment and other social dislocations. The influx of incoming population by the thousands would make it difficult for the government to control effectively and such cities would become subject to increasing urban crime and violence as one can easily see in large cities everywhere.

The Middle Class
As a direct consequence of industrial development and urbanization, one should never forget the emergence of the middle class, a class that was not foreseen by Karl Marx when he so penetratingly evaluated the process of social change accompanying the market economy. What made the middle class different from the proletariat was its ability to influence the mechanism of production as both producers and consumers. Industrial workers managed to develop their expertise and claim their fair share through collective bargaining and strikes. Thus, the blind exploitation on the part of the capitalist was not naturally resultant as Marx predicted.

The middle class person is by and large a self-supporting person with job security and constant income, usually as a salaried worker. As such, he is a typical consumer in an industrial society, without much control over his income or production. The volume of consumption on the part of the middle class, however, could be so large that the industrial sector becomes completely dependent upon it. It is by its collective purchasing power that the middle class gets appropriate recognition which will help it improve its social and economic position. We discussed earlier how dependent the industry would be upon the continuous consumption of the masses, and it is the middle class who have the purchasing power and develop the tendency of mass consumption.

Such a middle class person, as discussed earlier, is likely to be socially and psychologically alienated from others, as we see in a typical urban worker residing in an apartment cell. Such a middle class may have prevented a proletarian revolution which Marx would have loved to see, but it could be blind to the emergence of ill symptoms that the industrial society has to deal with if it is going to survive. Some of these symptoms include the absence of public regard, selfishness, alienation, and laziness. We shall discuss some of these problems later in this chapter.

So far, we have discussed the idea that the human desire for leisure may have paved the way for technological development and industrialization, and subsequently for behavioral and social change. We shall now examine the impact of such development on societal institutions.

INSTITUTIONAL CHANGES

It has been maintained that industrialization is a comprehensive process of social change in which the traditional community is rapidly dismantled. In this process, some farm land will be destroyed and converted into industrial parks, highways and parking lots, resulting in a sharp decline in farm population although not in agricultural productivity.[12] The military will undergo a process of declining relative importance as it becomes subservient to industrial pressures, and yields to the broader "military-industrial complex." The family as a primary institution will experience a profound transformation endangering the very foundation of its existence. Education would have to adapt itself to the new cultural and societal demands. And even religious organizations will become more secular and commercialized. We shall examine some of these changes in more detail.

Agriculture: A Perennial Loser

It seems almost as though farmers are the perennial losers in all societies. Since what the farmer can do is limited to the production of food and basic necessities, his function will be appreciated less and less in societies where people's imminent needs are beyond those necessities. Furthermore, as agricultural productivity is restricted in part by the amount of arable land and other natural conditions, agriculture can offer competition to industry in generating an expanding national product for a society which is geared to the expansion of leisure production. On the other hand, industrial output is relatively free from national boundaries so long as market expansion accompanies this process.

As the farmer's function becomes more peripheral to the nation's economy, agriculture also suffers in its relative importance in the changing culture. Many farmers in agrarian societies enjoy their prestigious position in a culture where farming is regarded a sacred job, only to find that the wave of industrialization overwhelms them with social change.

Unlike urban industrial workers, farmers are tied to their land and have little mobility. They lack bargaining power because they seldom have alternative employment. Work boycotts are not realistic tools for bargaining because farmers cannot afford to lose a whole year's crops, since most of them are already impoverished or at least deeply in debt. Furthermore, since farmers are more individualistic than group oriented, they are not motivated to organize collective bargaining. Thus, they eventually are absorbed by industrial expansion.

The Military-Industrial Complex

Once industrialization gets under way, it is difficult to contain its expansion because industry has its inherent dilemma of "growth or death." Industrial economy is such that firms cannot accommodate any reduction in their operation. As such, the forces of industrial expansion are fierce and they will spill over into every other aspect of the society. The military can hardly be an exception.

The institution of the military, despite its sacred and exclusively assigned function of territorial defense, will be impaired by industrial intrusion.[13] Realizing the fact that the military is a unique institution for which there can be no economic recession, industry will be eager to benefit economically by penetrating into the operation of the defense apparatus.

The phenomenon of the military-industrial merger is more apparent in capitalist industrial societies where weapons are manufactured by industry upon terms of contracts. In this case, the parties in the contract represent two different behavioral entities: while the government is a publicly funded organization that does not have to be "rational" or profit motivated, the industry is a profit maximizing institution. This would lead to terms of contract favoring the industry without personally costing the government personnel who have a virtually unlimited source of funds in taxes. Given the magnitude of the cost for building aircraft, tanks, and other weapons for the military, we can easily imagine the volume of economic interest on the part of the industry.

In the case of the U.S., there are, as of the 1960s, some 22,000 prime contractors who do business with the Department of Defense, and all are advocates of the free enterprise system. However, 90 percent of all weapons procurement is now done without competitive bidding. The contractor will make a low estimate, but go on and spend two or three times as much as estimated, without worrying about the Pentagon cancelling the order. This is a form of "private socialism" in which the public takes the risk and the companies profit. At least 68 weapon systems, worth $9 billion, had to be abandoned as unworkable, including the nuclear-powered plane on which $514 million was lost, the B-70 superbomber (a loss of $1.5 billion), the Snark robot bomber ($678 million) and numerous others. Such cases of wasteful spending and inefficiency would stagger any normal business or government agency, but when it comes to defense spending, the nation has become accustomed to such waste.

In the fiscal year of 1968, the hundred companies that did more than two thirds of the prime military work, held on their payrolls 2,072 retired military officers. Many of the same men who negotiated the deals with private business had worked for the Pentagon. After they retired, they used their influence and knowledge to land a profitable job working with defense companies. As an example, Litton Industries had 49 retired high ranking officers on its payroll. With all these opening doors into the right Pentagon office, it is little wonder that Litton jumped from thirty-sixth largest prime defense contractor in 1967 to fourteenth in 1968.[14]

Due in part to the syndrome of ever-expanding industry, military buildup, in collaboration with industry, can also be unlimited, as we witness in the unending process of the arms race between industrial giants. As a way of promoting the endless process of military build-up, military super powers are often compelled to become merchants themselves when they cannot consume all the hardware the industry wishes to produce. This would involve selling arms to surrogate countries and even enemies of the surrogates. Indeed, it often appears that it is in the interest of the super powers to facilitate conflicts and wars around the world so as to meet domestic industrial demand. We should not be misled into believing that the arms race toward the alleged balance of power has necessarily contributed to global security. In fact, many wars and regional conflicts during the Cold War era have been "sponsored" by the super powers themselves, and many of them for the domestic reasons of the military-industrial complex. One need not be a critic of the United States to be able to see the formidable role of the industry in shaping American military policy.

The Family: A Last Resort Threatened
The extended family system was commonplace in agrarian communities, for it was conducive to organizing and mobilizing the labor force, and the practice of uncalculated mutual aid within the family was beneficial to labor-intensive farming. But as the community opened up its door to industrialization and urbanization, the institution of the extended family system was the first to be affected. As youthful members of the family were attracted to urban centers, their allegiance and loyalty to the extended family came to a gradual end. At the same time, the new young members of the city were left with the awesome responsibility of forming a new family without the close guidance and protection of the more experienced members of the extended family. As Mead observes in the American context, "thousands of young couples are living together in some arrangement and are wholly dependent on their private, personal commitment to each other for the survival of the relationship."[15]

In the urban setting, where there would be little social interaction and communal congeniality, the nuclear family becomes the sole source of psychological comfort for individuals who seldom find a sense of attachment to their work environment. Thus, the socially isolated and emotionally lonesome "industrial man" seeks and expects the psychological comfort of belonging in the small nuclear family. But in the industrial society, both spouses are likely to be providers, though often failing to become mutual providers. This and other complications contribute to the endemic popularization of divorce epitomizing a crisis in the institution of the family in industrial society.[16]

Additionally, families that manage to avoid breaking up through divorce are not necessarily performing their proper functions in protecting the children and providing their belonging need. It is no longer shocking news that children are breaking away from homes. What is shocking is the fact that a majority of these children are from relatively well-off families, by economic and social standards. The soaring suicide rate among the young people in relatively affluent societies may be attributed in part to the breakdown of the family.[17]

Industrial development has changed the nature of the family institution in a number of ways. Among others, the relative roles of men, women, and children have undergone a profound transition. In the pre-industrial society, many men worked at crafts and farming in or near the home. They were nearby to eat all meals with the family and share their workload with other members. This contrasts with industrial men who are expected to work away from home and whose work is in isolation from the family.

The role of women has changed perhaps more than that of men. In the past, housewives' tasks included the manufacturing of clothing, soap, bread, and other staples. Additionally, they were expected to educate children when public education was limited. These types of work required creative efforts on the part of women. In the industrial society, women's jobs at home became somewhat easier and less time-consuming thanks to automated appliances and ready-made food. As a result, they could go out and become wage earners.

The role of children has also changed drastically. Instead of being babysitters and helpers around the house, they now spend long hours away from their families, and often become wage-earners themselves. Indeed, in the early expansion of industrial work demand, children became a part of the labor force, as we witnessed in the United States and Great Britain, where the government had to intervene with child labor laws to curtail the unjust exploitation of children.

As the industrial society penetrates the family in such a way that its members become wage earners, relations among members are likely to be defined in terms of "give-and-take" which is essentially a contractual relationship. In industrial and post-industrial societies, compensating children for their daily chores and other household work is hardly perceived as unusual. Keeping separate banking accounts and legally defining property shares between husband and wife are no longer considered unusual. In fact, the family has ceased to be a natural social and human group. It is a contractual and legal association which is readily subjected to the intervention of the court.

Education: An End to the Total Person
With the necessity to respond to industrial demand, educational curricula will gradually do away with liberal arts and philosophy and incorporate technical and scientific training. This trend is rapidly reinforced by the ascent of the technocrat in the community power structure. As Bell (1973, p. 78) observes, "with the rise of the technician has come the belief that advanced industrial society would be ruled by the technocrat." In response to the changing status of the technocrat, education as training for the total person will be replaced by technical training,

and education will be viewed as a tool for obtaining more attractive (better paying) jobs, which tend to be in the technical area. Whereas fields such as philosophy and ethics lose popularity and in some cases vanish for lack of students, new fields and disciplines will emerge for areas dealing with technology and management.

Traditionally, in societies of the second stage of development, education's primary function used to be one in which children learned norms and beliefs predominant in the society, so that they could join the mainstream of the cultural system. But industrialization has completely altered the meaning of education; education here is little more than vocational training intended to prepare the student for a particular job. Indeed, technical schools and vocational junior colleges will draw more students, and only a small number of "deviant" people will still take liberal arts and humanities courses. A layman's observation of educational institutions in developing Third World countries will convincingly testify to the shift to technocratic training.

Religion: Secularization

As with all organizations, religious organizations are expected to have the social function of providing a sense of belonging to their members. In this respect, religion has secular functions. Nevertheless, the religious organization is different from all others in that its primary *raison d'être* lies in its pursuit of visions beyond worldly affairs. Yet, churches in the industrial and post-industrial society become profit-seeking enterprises themselves, and many members profess to be "believers" on utilitarian grounds.

Furthermore, thanks to the failure of the family institution and problems with education in the industrial society, the masses are easily attracted to religious sects that appear to be more paternal and intimate in human relations among the members. These sects have proven to be as much business organizations as religious entities as we have seen in many recent cases such as Jim Jones and the Unification Church of Rev. Sun Myung Moon.

The story of Reverend Moon is a truly unbelievable one. With a limited education, Rev. Moon tried to establish a Christian denomination of sorts in his own country, Korea, but never succeeded. His church was merely one of many frequently emerging religious sects. Unlike most of his competitors, Moon had a strong nationalist appeal to the Koreans, in that he proclaimed them to be a chosen people. This aspect of his religion helped him gain lukewarm political support from President Park, who was himself an ardent anti-foreignist.

Rev. Moon's success in the United States, Japan, and Western Europe was indeed an unexpected surprise, even to the church leaders themselves. The fact that young people, many of whom were of a rather affluent social background, were helplessly and passionately absorbed into the Family of Rev. Moon remains a mystery. One most plausible explanation is that the social context of the industrial societies is such that many young people develop a deep sense of alienation, especially from their family. The Unification Church, with its doctrine that all members are brothers and sisters and belong to the same Family, is quickly appreciated by the lonely youth. They find the rare opportunity to show their devotion to altruism by living together, working and sharing. Altruistic and brotherly living is much discussed in conventional churches, but idealistic and naively innocent youth may never find the preaching convincing. Thus, they become highly suspicious of the religious associations that the industrialized and "rationalized" Church offers. In this sense, we might even say that if someone is responsible for the religious sect, it is the society, the broken family institution, and the inhumane industrial culture that is liable, more than anyone else.

This analysis is not to condone and sanctify the religious sects we have witnessed in recent years. In fact, churches themselves are failing. Of all conceivable deceptions, deceptions in the Church may be most grave. Despite the acclaimed brotherhood and equality before God, how many churches in the United States are making serious efforts to have a racially integrated membership? Indeed, few social groups are as segregated and closed as churches. In order to belong to a certain church, you have to belong to a certain secular status group in the first place. How can you justify this in the name of God?

CULTURAL CHANGE AND BEHAVIORAL DISPOSITIONS

When people are swept by the wave of industrialization and urbanization and the accompanying social changes, they are forced to alter their attitudes, values, beliefs and even behavioral patterns. In the previous chapter, we identified a cultural system indicative of the second stage of political integration as having values such as collective orientation, altruism, egalitarianism, universalism, and idealism. These values and beliefs will undergo a profound transformation in the resource expansion stage, in that nearly all the norms observed in the process of political integration will be replaced by a set of antithetical values.

Individualism
With the breakdown of traditional social systems such as the extended family and the rural community, members of the newly forming urban society will lose a sense of communal bonding and experience social and psychological alienation. The new life environment will eventually force them to develop a reverence for privacy and individualism.

Furthermore, the worker's job environment is such that reward is in proportion to individual achievement, and his work relationship is limited essentially to the employer, curtailing his group orientation and collective behavior. When the worker participates in some sort of collective bargaining or strike, he does so not for the purpose of promoting collective interest but for calculated self-interest. Thus, mass movements are not expected to succeed when such movements involve a high degree of risk to the participant, and the payoff is not readily translated into tangible individual gains for the present. This may be a partial explanation for the lack of mass political organizations and revolutionary social movements in industrial societies. The group oriented phenomena of mass movements are most prevalent in the political integration stage where individuals in sufficient numbers are willing to sacrifice their individual interests for the collective good.

Rationality: The Birth of Economic Man
The concept of human rationality has evolved in a most intriguing way. Following the dark ages of the medieval times when legitimacy of power had little to do with "people's consent," and with the introduction of "Social Contract" along with the concurrent development of philosophical individualism and *laissez-faire* economics in the ensuing decades, philosophers and political thinkers raised the issue of the state of human nature as an ultimate source of justification for different types of politics. Machiavelli, Hobbes, Locke, and Rousseau, to name only a few, had varying perceptions as to the state of human nature,

and hence, different views of legitimate forms of government.[18] Nevertheless, they all agreed that "rationality" is virtuous and desirable, although they interpreted the degree of human rationality differently. Further, they had a consensus on the meaning of "rational man" in that he is benevolent and altruistic. Selfishness was regarded as "irrational," and it laid the foundation for tyrannical theories of political order as espoused in *The Prince* by Machiavelli and *The Leviathan* by Hobbes.

As the industrial economy with its market culture swept western civilization, the economic conception of "rational man" overpowered the traditional philosophical version of human rationality. The economic "rational man" was ironically the very "irrational man" in the traditional sense. A man who is motivated to maximize benefit by minimizing cost is defined as "rational," and this very man would have been regarded as being "irrational" for his selfish motivation. In the mature industrial society, "selfishness" disguised as "rationality" is hardly considered a vice. Thus, hedonistic utilitarianism is accepted as a norm and anything unselfish is typically viewed as being "irrational" and abnormal.[19]

In short, the industrial society made man not only selfish but justified his selfishness as being moral and natural.

Particularistic Values
In contrast to the value orientation of universalism in the previous stage of political integration, for reasons germane to the phenomenon of industrial-urban development, people will gradually become oriented toward particularistic values. Here, man will develop an evaluative form of mind analogous to the clinical assessment in which an object is sliced into various parts for examination and treatment. The society is viewed as a system of parts, and it is the parts that make the whole system meaningful, thus rejecting holistic views as well as universalistic values. Accordingly, as every object in the market has a separate price tag, every part of the society has its own value and meaning irrespective of its relationship to the whole.

An individual's ability to evaluate issues and people will be greatly enhanced by a particularistic value orientation. Thus, public opinion can be articulated on the grounds of greater rationality and careful deliberations. Perhaps it is for this reason that participatory democracy is commonly regarded as being more suitable for industrial societies than agrarian societies.

Realism

Unlike the idealistic cultural norms and values that were prevalent in the political integration stage, people will now become preoccupied with realistic values and tangible accomplishments. The age of ideology, as Bell (1960) observes, may be coming to an end as the society enjoys the fruits of industrial advancement. As we discussed earlier, educational programs and the commercialized mass media will promote realism and pragmatic behavior to the extent that men with ideas will be put in the hands, and at the mercy, of men with matter.

STYLES OF POLITICS

The extensive social and cultural change expected in the process of industrialization and urbanization will profoundly affect the nature of politics and style of government. I shall point out some major characteristics of politics one might expect in this stage of resource expansion.

Technocrats and Managerial Leadership

The autocratic leadership of the first-stage society and the charismatic leadership of the second-stage society will no longer maintain their popularity in the stage where "money does the talking." In the industrial and post-industrial societies, leadership groups will center around industrial elites such as capitalists and managers. In addition, government bureaucracy will become stabilized and professional bureaucrats will be established just as technocrats are finding their stable positions in the industry.

An essential requirement for any aspiring politician is the ability to ally himself with business and secure its support. As such, there will be an intimate functional interaction between the business circle and politics. Just as in the case of the military-industrial complex, business will spill over the entire spectrum of politics. In fact, it is highly likely that many political posts will be occupied by business executives, and many politicians will take business posts after retirement from political life. This phenomenon is quite evident in post-war Japan where government retirees have usually been invited by big businesses.

When business personnel become an integral part of politics, the leadership style will be patterned after the managerial and technocratic mode of industrial operation.

Economic Priority

With the imminent need for resource expansion, governments of all ideological hues will place top priority on strategies for economic growth. Quite often, they install development plans with specific growth targets, and their implementations are engineered by government initiation. Some governments exercise greater amounts of control than others but government intervention in the economic sector tends to be quite extensive in all cases. Government monopoly of major industries are affected by tight regulations, sometimes with quotas imposed by the government.

All major industrial countries such as the United States, Great Britain, and Japan had a period of growing governmental intervention in the nation's economy. After the Civil War, American government expanded its power over the industry with new fiscal policies and regulatory measures intended to control business, as well as direct intervention in the areas of railroad construction, metal and mining industry, and transportation.[20] Japan was not an exception. Since the Meiji restoration in 1868, concerted efforts have been made by the government to formulate policies to encourage capital investment in industrial production. The extent of government involvement in resource allocation is demonstrated by Rosovsky's study which points out that the mean government share of gross domestic fixed capital formation from 1887 to 1896 was 42.5 percent.[21] It is hardly overstated when Allen (1946, p. 30) points out that "there was scarcely any important Japanese industry of the Western type during the later decades of the nineteenth century which did not owe its establishment to state initiative." A similar pattern is found in the experience of British economic growth where the government initiated economic programs and policies intended to protect and expand the industry.[22]

Industrialization for the "late comer" has shown a unique pattern in that it benefits from technology available in advanced societies and the international market in which it can compete favorably with industries of the labor-scarce advanced economy. Thus, a large number of countries managed to achieve economic growth in relatively short periods of time.

A comparative observation of Tables 6 and 7 shows that it is the Third World nations that have accomplished the greatest economic growth during the decade of 1965–1974 when the number of nations categorized as middle-income or rich was increased from 11 to 32, while the First and Second World remained unchanged.

TABLE 6

Distribution of GNP Among the First, Second, and Third Worlds, 1965

Per Capita GNP	First World	Second World	Third World	Total
Poor nations <$500	None	4 nations $258 mean GNP/capita 780.6 million population	66 nations $209 mean GNP/capita 1405.3 million population	70 nations $226 mean GNP/capita 2185.9 million population
Middle-income nations $501–$1000	2 nations $684 mean 9.3 million population	3 nations $695 mean GNP/capita 28.4 million population	14 nations $709 mean GNP/capita 98.6 million population	19 nations $704 mean GNP/capita 136.3 million population
Rich nations $1001<	23 nations $3142 mean GNP/capita 642.8 million population	7 nations $1636 mean GNP/capita 330.7 million population	4 nations $3090 mean GNP/capita 33.7 million population	34 nations $2646 mean GNP/capita 1007.2 million population
Total	25 nations $3107 mean GNP/capita 652.1 million population	14 nations $669 mean GNP/capita 1,139.7 million population	84 nations $304 mean GNP/capita 1537.6 million population	123 nations $978 mean GNP/capita 3329.4 million population

Source: U.S. Arms Control and Disarmament Agency, *World Military Expenditures and Arms Transfers 1965–1974* (Washington: USGPO, 1976). Table includes only those countries for which data are available.

Note: First World = Western industrial countries; Second World = authoritarian Marxist countries; Third World = all Latin American, Middle Eastern, Asian, and African countries not in above categories.

TABLE 7

Distribution of GNP Among the First, Second, and Third Worlds, 1974

Per Capita GNP	First World	Second World	Third World	Total
Poor nations <$500	None	4 nations $209 mean GNP/capita 962.1 million population	65 nations $223 mean GNP/capita 1840.8 million population	69 nations $218 mean GNP/capita 2802.9 million population
Middle-income nations $501–$1000	None	2 nations $561 mean GNP/capita 10.5 million population	20 nations $730 mean GNP/capita 341.9 million population	22 nations $725 mean GNP/capita 352.4 million population
Rich nations $1001<	25 nations $4035 mean GNP/capita 707 million population	8 nations $2274 mean GNP/capita 379 million population	12 nations $3004 mean GNP/capita 76.6 million population	45 nations $3393 mean GNP/capita 1162.6 million population
Total	25 nations $4035 mean GNP/capita 707 million population	16 nations $791 mean GNP/capita 1351.6 million population	95 nations $394 mean GNP/capita 2259.3 million population	136 nations $1114 mean GNP/capita 4317.9 million population

Source: U.S. Arms Control and Disarmament Agency, World Military Expenditures and Arms Transfers 1965–1974 (Washington: USGPO, 1976). Table includes only those countries for which data are available.

Note: First World = Western industrial countries; Second World = authoritarian Marxist countries; Third World = all Latin American, Middle Eastern, Asian, and African countries not in above categories.

Growth over Distribution

As alluded to earlier, many Third World countries are making rather effective efforts to industrialize the economy due to technology transfer and the international market. However, industrialization is often marked by seriously inequitable distributions of income, to the extent that the masses come far short of enjoying the leisure mode of life. It is not until the process of industrialization reaches its optimal point where the purchasing power of the masses becomes imperative for continuous industrial prosperity that the mode of income distribution will shift toward a more equitable form. Even then, if the domestic market is not vital for industrial growth due to the vast reservoir of the international market, domestic income distribution could be unaffected, leading the political system to become even more repressive and protective of the establishment. This perpetuation of gross inequality and the capricious control by the ruling elite have paved the way in many potentially stable countries to mass revolts and political turmoil, as might be the case in Iran, South Korea, and El Salvador in the late 1970s and early 1980s. Table 8 shows income distribution in selected Third World countries where the top quintile of the population control a vast proportion of income.

The government will attempt to justify the inequitable distribution of income in the name of economic growth, and there are a good number of theories to rationalize such an attempt. However, the public to whom leisure is a most imminent need will not tolerate a situation where their needs are continuously and indefinitely denied in the name of the nation's economic growth. A nation's growth may mean much to a person who is desperately demanding the need of belonging, but it may mean little to the leisure-seeking consumer.

SUMMARY

In this chapter, we observed various aspects of social and political changes that are likely to result in the process of industrialization and urban development. We maintained that the invention of tools and the subsequent development of technological growth and industrialization were all expected as they were necessitated by emergent human needs and wants: in this case, leisure and comfort-seeking human nature.

In all the changes characteristic of the resource expansion stage, one common element is the fact that what was achieved and developed in the previous stage has been altered or replaced by something antithet-

TABLE 8
Income Distribution in Selected Third World Countries
(Percent of Total to Each Quintile)

	Bottom Quintile	Second Quintile	Third Quintile	Fourth Quintile	Top Quintile
Mexico (1963–1964)	3.6	6.9	10.9	20.1	58.5
Brazil (1966)	6.0	8.4	11.8	17.5	56.3
Argentina (1966)	7.0	10.3	13.2	17.6	52.0
Lebanon (1960)		25.0		15.0	60.0
India (1956)	18.7		14.8	19.7	46.8
Thailand (urban, 1970)	6.5	10.5	15.0	22.5	45.5
Thailand (rural, 1970)	5.5	8.5	14.0	21.0	51.0

Sources: Celso Furtado, *Economic Development of Latin America* (Cambridge, England: Cambridge University Press, 1970), p. 61.

Elias Gannage, "The Distribution of Income in Underdeveloped Countries," in Jean Marchal and Bernard Ducros, eds., *The Distribution of National Income* (London: Macmillan, 1968), p. 330.

Brewster Grace, *Population Growth in Thailand, Part I: Population and Social Structure*. American Universities Field Staff *Reports* (Asia), *XXII, 1* (1974), p. 8.

ical to what was. This is particularly the case with changes in cultural and behavioral characteristics, as an emphasis on "matter" takes over one on "mind" in a manner that a dialectical theoretician would love to see for his logic.

At any rate, in this stage of resource expansion, the society has begun a journey that, once embarked upon, is irreversible. Industrialization and market expansion are here only to expand; and as the globe offers limited resource availability that can satisfy everyone's want, the post-industrial era seems to signal warnings that can no longer be ignored as we will discuss more fully in the next chapter.

FOOTNOTES

[1] To the Greeks, leisure was concerned with those activities that were worthy of a free man, activities we might today call "culture." Work, on the other hand, as an instrumental and productive activity, was regarded as below the

dignity of free man. Since then, the work ethic may have changed significantly but the unmistakable fact is that it is leisure, not work, that man has sought and largely earned in the course of human history. For a concise discussion on this thesis, see Bennett M. Berger, "The Sociology of Leisure," in *Industrial Relations*, Vol. 1, No. 2, February, 1962.

[2] For a further analysis on the measurement of time allocation, refer to Gary S. Becker, "A Theory of the Allocation of Time," *Economic Journal*, Sept. 1965.

[3] In this respect, I challenge the Marxist overture that human effort to eliminate labor is not to increase leisure but to maximize profits and the opulence of the capitalists.

[4] Michael Young, in order to depict this aspect of class structure, discusses the emergence of "technocracy" in industrial societies (Young, 1965); see also A. Rahman, "Science and Technology for a New Social Order," in *Alternatives*, Vol. IV, No. 3, January, 1979.

[5] As Lenski specifically points out, leisure not only requires free time but, equally important, "the production of various kinds of nonessential goods" (Lenski, 1966, p. 121).

[6] For a landmark study on this proposition, see Brandt (1980); on the formation of a homogeneous culture, Mazrui in Mendlovitz (1975).

[7] Consumer debt outstanding including mortgage debt in the United States was $1.6 trillion as 1978 ended, representing 13 percent over the previous year. Repayments needed to service debt required 23 cents of each dollar of after-tax disposable income.

[8] David Apter utilizes the concept of pyramidal/hierarchical authority structure in building a typology of society, where the pyramidal structure is implied as being in industrial market systems (Apter, 1965).

[9] For the three bases of legitimacy, I am using Max Weber's authority types. See his work (Weber, 1947, chapter 3).

[10] Jones, Rockwell, *The Other Generation* (1977), p. 3

[11] For these and other data, see George Madox; and Louis Harris (1975).

[12] According to a report by a presidential advisory commission in 1982, some 12 square miles of farm land are being converted into highways and parking lots every day in the United States. The same report warns that if this trend continues, we will have serious food shortages by the year 2000.

[13] A long list of books taking this position could be cited. Among them: Richard J. Barnet (1969); William Domhoff (1970); Anthony Sampson (1973).

[14] For these and other facts of the military-industrial complex, see Lens (1970). Also, Pursell (1972); Cooling (1977); Kennedy.(1975).

[15] Smelser (1963) in his analysis of industrial impact on the family summarizes: "As the family ceases to be an economic unit of production, one or more members leave the household to seek employment in the labor market. The family's activities become more centered on emotional gratification and socialization." This observation reinforces the contention that the family has become an organization from which its members seek belonging more than

from any other social group. The quotation of Mead is from *U.S. News and World Report*, October 27, 1975.

[16] In the United States, there were 26 divorces for every 100 marriages in 1960, 48 in 1975, and 63 are expected by 1990 (*U.S. News and World Report*, Oct. 27, 1975).

[17] For suicide statistics for America and selected European countries, refer to Walter A. Lunden (1978).

[18] For an excellent introduction of Hobbes, Locke, and Rousseau in this regard, refer to John Plamenatz (1963), chapters 4, 6, and 10.

[19] For a classical exposition of this thesis, see Milton Friedman (1958).

[20] For government regulations and development subsidies in the process of economic expansion in the United States, see John M. Peterson and Ralph Gray (1969), especially chapter 10.

[21] Henry Rosovsky, *Capital Formation in Japan*, (1868–1940), pp. 23–24 and Table 9 on pp. 25–26. These figures include relevant military expenditures. Excluding military expenditures, the figure still is 33.5 percent.

[22] For a further discussion on the role of government in economic development in Japan and Britain, see Holt and Turner (1966).

REFERENCES

Allen, George C.
   1946   *A Short Economic History of Modern Japan*, 1867–1937 (London).
Apter, David E.
   1966   *The Politics of Modernization* (Chicago: University of Chicago Press).
Barnet, Richard J.
   1969   *The Economy of Death* (New York: Atheneum).
Barnet, Richard J. and Ronald E. Muller
   1974   *Global Reach: The Power of the Multinational Corporations* (New York: Simon and Schuster).
Bell, Daniel
   1960   *The End of Ideology* (Glencoe, Ill.).
   1973   *The Coming of Post-Industrial Society* (New York: Basic Books).
Berger, Bennett M.
   1963   "The Sociology of Leisure," in Erwin O. Smigel, ed., *Work and Leisure* (New Haven, Conn: College and University Press).
Boorstin, Daniel J.
   1978   *The Republic of Technology* (New York: Harper and Row).
Brandt, Willy
   1980   *North-South: A Program for Survival* (Cambridge, Mass.).
Breeze, Gerald
   1966   *Urbanization in Newly Developing Countries* (Englewood Cliffs, N.J.: Prentice Hall).

Charlesworth, James C., ed.
1964 *Leisure in America: Blessing or Cure?* (Monograph by The Academy of Political and Social Science).
Cooling, Benjamin F., ed.
1977 *War, Business, and American Society* (New York: Kennikat Press).
Domhoff, William
1970 *The Higher Circles* (New York: Random House).
Durkheim, Emile
1933 *The Division of Labor in Society* (New York: Macmillan Co.).
Estall, R. C. and R. Ogilive Buchanan
1961 *Industrial Activity and Economic Geography* (London).
Friedman, Milton
1953 *Essays in Positive Economics* (Chicago: University of Chicago Press).
Hauser, Philip
1964 "The Analysis of 'Over-Urbanization'," *Economic Development and Cultural Change*, 12 (January, 1964), pp. 113–22.
Holt, Robert T. and John E. Turner
1966 *The Political Basis of Economic Development* (Princeton, N.J.: D. Van Nostrand Co., Inc.).
Kennedy, Gavin
1975 *The Economics of Defense* (Great Britain: Western Printing Service).
Lens, Sidney
1970 *The Military-Industrial Complex* (Pilgrim Press).
Lenski, Gerhard E.
1966 *Power and Privilege* (New York: McGraw-Hill Book Co.).
Lunden, Walter A.
1977 *The Suicide Cycle* (Montezuma, Iowa: The Sutherland Printing Co.).
Owen, John D.
1969 *The Price of Leisure* (The Netherlands: Rotterdam University Press).
Peterson, John M. and Ralph Gray
1969 *Economic Development of the United States* (Homewood, Ill.: Richard D. Irwin, Inc.).
Plamenatz, John
1963 *Man and Society* (New York: McGraw-Hill Book Co.).
Pursell, Carol W.,
1972 *The Military-Industrial Complex* (New York: Harper and Row).
Sampson, Anthony
1973 *The Sovereign State of ITT* (New York: Stein and Day).
Schumacher, E. F.
1973 *Small Is Beautiful* (New York: Harper and Row).
Smelser, Neil J.
1963 "Mechanisms of Change and Adjustment to Change" in Bert F. Hoselitz and Wilbert E. Moor, eds., *Industrialization and Society* (The Hague: UNESCO and Mouton).
Sussman, Marvin B. and Ethel Shanas, eds.

1977   *Family, Bureaucracy, and the Elderly* (Durham, N.C.: Duke University Press).
Veblen, Thorstein
1931   *The Theory of the Leisure Class* (New York: The Modern Library).
Vosburgh, William
1960   *Social Class and Leisure Time* (unpublished dissertation, Yale University).
Weber, Max
1947   *The Theory of Social and Economic Organization* (New York: The Free Press).
1958   From Max Weber (New York: Oxford University Press).
Weis, Paul
1964   "A Philosophical Definition of Leisure," in James C. Charlesworth, ed., *Leisure in America* (Monograph by the American Academy of Political and Social Science).
Young, Michael
1958   *The Rise of Meritocracy* (New York: Penguin Books).

Chapter VII
CONFLICT MANAGEMENT

Man is never content with what he has, at least not in the political arena. Human desire knows no limit. With all the fruits of mature industrial society and the material prosperity of an affluent society, we find that man's political desires still are not satisfied. He remains unhappy because once he has achieved the material comfort of a leisurely lifestyle, he must have "more," not just of these same goods and other resources but, more critically, more than other people. The desire for status, prestige, power, and control over others—all manifestations of this desire to have "more" of social values than other people—gives rise to the central political dilemma facing regimes in this stage: How to satisfy the demands for control by one group without alienating, and thus losing the support of, those groups that must inevitably lose control in this reallocation of such fixed-sum social values. The ultimate political manifestation of this basic human need is the desire to have some measure of control over the decision-making process by which all social values—including control, prestige, and power—are allocated.

Thus, the very search for satisfaction of this need will inevitably lead to social competition and conflict, conflict of a type that cannot be totally resolved. After all, to satisfy one person or group's demands for control over the decision-making process necessarily means reducing some other individual, group or groups' control over that same critical process. As conflict in the technologically advanced stages of social and political development could have devastating effects (after all, there is so much to be lost at this point in a society's development), it becomes vital for the regime to develop the capacity to *manage* such conflict in order that its scope and intensity not grow to the point that it represents a threat to the continued stability of the society and, thus, the continued existence of the regime itself.

CONTROL NEEDS AND THE ZERO-SUM SOCIETY

In a society where a substantial proportion of the people have attained an effective and reliable means for satisfying their survival, belonging, and leisure needs, they will begin to pursue the need for "social control," where its satisfaction is determined by their position along certain dimensions of achievement, *relative to the position of their significant others*. Of course, there are other bases of comparison in addition to the social basis (i.e., comparing oneself with others). These alternative modes of comparison include temporal comparison, where one compares his present position with his position at a previous time. Even here, however, I would maintain that one's *rate* of improvement is assessed by comparison to the rate of achievement others have attained over the same time period. Thus, even the temporal comparison can become a type of social comparison. Similarly, the spatial mode of comparison—where one compares one's achievements along one dimension to one's achievements along other dimensions—also involves some social comparison in that one determines whether there is a greater discrepancy between dimensions of achievement by comparison to the amount of discrepancy (or lack thereof) between dimensions of achievement attained by others.

When people are formulating their demands by comparing what they have with what others have, government must serve as a "peacekeeper" of sorts in that it must concentrate its efforts on maintaining social equilibrium through facilitating a "just" distributive system. It must provide the mechanisms by which people can take steps to remedy what they see as an unjust distribution of social values and at the same time provide mechanisms by which those who lose in the reallocation of relative amount of social control can be persuaded not to withdraw their support from the regime. In short, a successful political regime at this stage must be capable of managing conflictual social relations of a zero-sum character. In this sense, this stage of political development involves aspects of what Daniel Bell has described as the politics of "post-industrial society," where increased production is no longer the central goal of society or of government policy. We shall elaborate on this point later.

In order to clarify the zero-sum character of politics in this stage, we can compare the nature of the needs characteristic of this stage of development (and the valued objects which serve for their satisfaction) with those characteristic of the earlier stages of development. In an agrarian society, where popular needs center around the need for survival and are met through the production of food and other necessities of human existence, social conflict is not necessarily of a zero-sum character. People can, under some circumstances, increase the amount of food and other goods available for consumption. More generally, the supply of the goods that serve for the satisfaction of survival needs is not necessarily fixed in either the short term, or more importantly, the long term. Increased food production combined with control of population growth would mean that over the long term, and even in the short term, one person's satisfaction of their own survival needs does not necessarily reduce significantly the ability of others to satisfy their survival needs. Similar arguments can be made for the subsequent two levels of needs and stages of development: The satisfaction of one person or group's belongingness needs does not necessarily reduce the ability of others to satisfy the same needs. Indeed, it may even enhance the ability of others to satisfy such needs, since the larger the group to which one wants to belong, the more easily that individual can be absorbed into the group without posing any threat to existing patterns of relationships within the group. Similarly, the satisfaction of one person's leisure need need not reduce the ability of others to satisfy their leisure needs. In an expansionary economy, such things as wage increases, shorter working hours, the availability of leisure goods (both time-saving devices such as cars and washing machines, as well as leisure "consumption" goods such as baseballs, televisions, and public parks) are not necessarily of a fixed-sum variety. Thus, one person's satisfaction of these needs need not necessitate some other person's dissatisfaction with respect to the same needs.

Where people compete for the sake of "winning," such a competition cannot be resolved without the loser's loss; thus, the winner's satisfaction will be offset by the loser's suffering. Social and political competition in the mature industrial societies is generally of this kind, namely, a zero-sum game.[1] It is for this reason that societies that may have reached a mature stage of industrialization tend to shift their policy emphasis from production to redistribution.

In this regard, it is not surprising that definitions of politics offered

by scholars of western post-industrial origin tend to focus on the function of redistribution as we witness in the instances of Easton's "authoritative allocation of values" (Easton, 1953), and Lasswell's "who
gets what, when, and how" (Lasswell, 1958). These definitions of politics presuppose the existence and availability of "values" to be allocated
and resources to be acquired by someone in the first place.

Post-Industrialism: A Threshold to the Fourth Stage
Daniel Bell in his seminal work, *The Coming of Post-Industrial Society*, defines the post-industrial society as one that emphasizes "the
centrality of theoretical knowledge as the axis around which new technology, economic growth, and the stratification of society will be organized" (Bell, 1973, p. 112). With the presentation of a comprehensive
schema of social change, Bell contrasts the post-industrial society with
the industrial and pre-industrial societies in terms of various dimensions of social life (see Table 9). Here, using the United States as a sole
example of such a post-industrial society, he maintains that "the concept of a post-industrial society is not a picture of a complete social
order; it is an attempt to describe and explain an axial change in the
social structure . . ." (1973, p. 119). Thus, the central criterion for a
society to be called "post-industrial" is the central importance of
"theoretical knowledge" as the axis around which patterns of social life
revolve. While much of his analysis coincides with the empirical reality
of America, the question of what makes post-industrial development
necessary does not seem to be sufficiently addressed by Bell. It seems
to be true, however, that the role of theoretical knowledge has a far
greater potential and actual impact in human lives than the mere technical skills that the industrial society once revered so highly, as is
exemplified by the development of nuclear science. At the same time,
I find it difficult to follow Bell's contention that the primary institutions
in such a post-industrial society are universities, academic institutions,
and research corporations, although it had appeared to be when the
Americans waged an all-out campaign to catch up and surpass the
Soviets in scientific research in the decade following the Sputnik shock
of 1957. This is not to undermine the pioneering work that Bell has
made in defining post-industriality as being uniquely different from the
industrial society.

    As an alternative conception of the post-industrialism, the present
paradigm suggests that a society enters the threshold of post-industrial

TABLE 9
General Schema of Social Change

	Pre-industrial	Industrial	Post-industrial	
Regions:	Asia Africa Latin America	Western Europe Soviet Union Japan	United States	
Economic sector:	Primary Extractive: Agriculture Mining Fishing Timber	Secondary Goods producing: Manufacturing Processing	Tertiary Transportation Utilities Quinary Health Education Research Government Recreation	Quaternary Trade Finance Insurance Real estate
Occupational slope:	Farmer Miner Fisherman Unskilled worker	Semi-skilled worker Engineer	Professional and technical Scientists	
Technology:	Raw materials	Energy	Information	
Design:	Game against nature	Game against fabri- cated nature	Game between persons	
Methodology:	Common sense experience	Empiricism Experimentation	Abstract theory: models, simulation, decision theory, systems analysis	
Time perspective:	Orientation to the past Ad hoc re- sponses	Ad hoc adaptiveness Projections	Future orientation Forecasting	
Axial principle:	Traditionalism: Land/resource limitation	Economic growth: State or private control of investment decisions	Centrality of and codification of theoretical knowledge	

Source: Daniel Bell (1973), p. 117

society when its primary social and political issue shifts from the task of resource expansion to that of "just" distribution. A society in this stage will force the government to shift its policy orientations toward distributive justice issues, which can no longer be obscured by the existence of further economic growth and development. Following a period of industrialization and resource expansion in which the masses are told by the political and economic establishment to wait for the arrival of the more affluent society that industrialization will bring, the consumer will reach a point where he can no longer tolerate the inequitable structure of social and economic life, particularly when further growth is not seen as necessary for him to claim a comfortable share of the existing resources. When the political system is insensitive to this rising expectation of the consumer, social and political unrest may result.

In the course of industrial development, the economic structure will reach a point where industrial expansion will become stabilized, as the United States and European nations have experienced invariably in recent decades. As Table 10 shows, most industrial societies have already passed the peak point where the percentage of the work force employed in industrial sectors starts to decline. Interestingly enough, no society has reached the point where a majority of the population has ever engaged in work in the industrial sector. Table 11 also indicates the fact that the industrial societies have generally passed the threshold point some time in the early 1970s when "economically active population" declined, while such a population continued to grow in the less developed countries.

Concurrently, the post-industrial society will see the expansion of the service sector with a dramatic surge of white-collar workers such as brokers, lawyers, accountants, and managers. Furthermore, service oriented institutions will become prominent in controlling more resources and social values than the industrial sector itself. This sector may be seen as centered more around allocating resources than producing resources. The newly surfacing service sector includes banking institutions, insurance companies, trade firms, real estate, transportation and communications. Just as the industrial sector was the axis locus of social structure in the resource expansion stage, the service sector will now become the primary force in the management of class stratification and social change.

The Discontent of the Middle Class: A New Source of Social Conflict

In the previous stage of resource expansion, industrialization and urbanization reshaped not only the demographic composition of the society but the structure of social class. Throughout the resource expansion stage, with the emergence of skilled workers and technocrats, social class structure underwent a profound change in which the traditional aristocracy had to yield their preeminent social position, and the new industrial middle-class gained social and political leverage.

But as industrial maturity reaches a "peak point," thus stabilizing social and class mobility, lower-class people become no longer capable of moving themselves upward on the ladder of social success by simply

TABLE 10
"Postindustrial" Labor Structure
(Percentage of the work force employed in industrial sectors)

	1950	1960	1970	1974	1978	1990*	2000*
United States	33.9	35.0	32.4	31.0	27.9	24.0	20.0
Japan	21.0	28.5	34.3	37.0	34.5	29.0	25.0
Germany	42.3	48.6	48.0	47.3	45.1	40.0	35.0
France	33.2	37.6	36.9	39.6	37.1	32.0	27.0
U.K.	49.0	46.0	42.3	42.3	39.7	35.0	30.0
Canada	33.7	31.2	30.0	31.1	28.5	24.0	20.0
Italy	31.5	40.4	42.2	39.4	38.3	34.0	30.0
Netherlands	33.2	42.2	36.3	35.6	32.5	28.0	25.0
Sweden	40.8	45.1	40.2	36.3	32.9	28.0	24.0
Belgium	48.8	45.7	42.3	41.2	36.7	32.0	28.0
Switzerland	46.6	50.4	48.2	47.0	41.7	37.0	32.0
Austria	37.1	41.0	41.8	40.9	40.4	37.0	34.0
Denmark	33.3	36.5	35.7	32.3	30.3	26.0	22.0
Norway	36.6	36.6	37.3	34.5	31.5	28.0	26.0
Average	37.2	40.3	38.9	38.2	35.5	29.5	27.0

Sources: International Labor Office, Yearbook of Labor Statistics (Geneva, various years) and OECD, Economic Surveys (Paris, 1979).
*Estimates based on OECD & ILO projections

TABLE 11
Employment in Manufacturing (1970 = 100)

Postindustrial Countries	EconActive Population	1968	1969	1970	1971	1972	1973	1974	1975	1976	1977	1978
United States	94,645	102.2	104.2	100.0	96.0	98.7	103.7	103.6	94.8	98.0	101.1	105.7
Japan	57,261	95.3	97.6	100.0	101.0	101.0	105.2	105.0	99.5	99.0	98.4	98.4
W. Germany	27,972	93.2	97.5	100.0	99.3	97.7	97.7	96.2	90.6	90.3	89.8	—
United Kingdom	26,053	98.8	100.1	100.0	96.6	93.3	93.9	94.4	89.8	86.9	88.2	87.7
France	22,336	96.5	98.3	100.0	100.5	101.2	103.0	103.4	100.4	99.9	98.7	97.0
Italy	20,527	93.5	96.6	100.0	102.0	101.1	102.8	107.0	107.2	107.5	112.9	110.8
Canada	9,539	99.4	102.0	100.0	99.0	100.7	105.8	109.0	107.8	104.3	102.9	—
Netherlands	5,149	99	100	100	99	94	93	92	88	86	84	82
Belgium	3,774	—	—	100.0	100.1	98.9	100.1	101.2	95.0	91.2	87.6	—
Sweden	3,671	95.8	98.0	100.0	97.3	95.7	97.9	100.5	100.8	100.0	101.2	97.8
Switzerland	3,180	100.8	100.6	100.0	98.6	96.1	94.7	94.4	85.9	79.8	79.6	80.2
Denmark	2,379	94.3	98.4	100.0	96.7	98.4	101.4	98.4	89.4	89.9	88.0	87.3
Less Developed Countries												
India	240,285	95.2	97.0	100.0	102.2	106.5	109.1	111.9	110.7	113.4	117.3	
Nigeria	24,666	63.6	80.7	100.0	114.5	131.8	131.3	138.0	—	—	—	
Turkey	17,052	94.2	95.7	100.0	107.7	119.8	130.9	124.7	136.6	154.1	162.1	
Philippines	15,699	86.5	105.5	100.0	104.4	100.0	110.6	118.5	122.3	126.1	132.1	
Rep of Korea	12,686	92.7	96.7	100.0	96.4	115.8	145.3	173.1	194.1	233.5	247.7	

Sources: same as Table 10

obtaining industrial and urban jobs, because such jobs no longer provide the kind of rewards sufficient to improve one's social position in a post-industrial environment. Instead, people engaged in the service sector—as opposed to the production sector of either agriculture or industry—will acquire the power to influence decisions on the social distributive system. Here, without government protection, people of lower socio-economic status can easily fall victim to their lack of influence over the distributive process, the new "axis" of social development. While they are likely to receive government protection (for reasons that we will discuss later when we examine the nature of the welfare system) these allocations are of a maintenance level at best, and do little to alter their relative lack of influence over the allocation process itself.

The middle class that emerged with the expansion of urban industrial jobs will now become most vulnerable to manipulations of the social and economic establishment. In the process of industrial maturity, the middle class, who were basically wage earners, surfaced as the mainstream of the society with their distinct psychological and behavioral characteristics. They were the people who were more rational, consumption oriented, "private-regarding," and politically apathetic. With the expansion of the market economy, these wage earners with a fixed income are faced with no other alternatives but to maximize their share of resource allocation by being rational in their spending. They all become bargainers and bargain hunters, a behavioral pattern that persists in the post-industrial era. As was discussed in the previous chapter, industry, for its continuous survival and growth, will make its products more appealing to the mass-consuming middle class. In this course of development, the middle class becomes exceedingly selfish and private regarding.

One consequence of this is that they will be unwilling to pay for the expansion or maintenance of public goods. They will be private-regarding because they are rational. Since they are rational, they will be unwilling to pay for public goods because so long as these goods are provided, they will enjoy their benefits regardless of whether they assume part of the goods' cost. As a result, public institutions and services will face an inevitable deterioration of public support so long as the government fails to intervene. Services such as defense, maintaining law and order, upgrading public parks, highways, and other public facilities will become totally dependent upon the government because, to the rational private sector, they are "none of its business."

However, it is not the middle class who avoid paying for the public goods. Ironically, it is the very rational middle class on whom the government will dump the burden without facing much resistance. A cursory observation of the American taxation structure, for example, will confirm the fact that it is indeed the middle class, especially the lower middle class, who assume heavier tax burdens, while upper class Americans escape the tax burdens.[2]

Realizing their unavoidably shrinking economic status, the more affluent middle class who were property owners in California decided to cry out by calling for a referendum intended to lower property tax, and they succeeded with their campaign known as *Proposition 13*.[3] This event in an affluent state of America epitomizes the middle class's response to what it perceived as an intolerable deprivation. As we discussed in the previous chapter, these people are by and large salaried workers who were so isolated and unorganized politically as to make any organized collective bargaining movement against the government extremely difficult. However, as their lifestyle has become threatened by allocation decisions that shift social costs on them as a group, we have witnessed the proliferation of organized political activity by the middle class aimed precisely at avoiding these costs and shifting the burden to other groups.

As Parker observes, it was as early as in the 1950s that the United States experienced a transition from the primacy of blue-collar work to white-collar work. Such a transition was considered "the harbinger of a great social revolution, the movement to the 'postindustrial society'" (Parker, p. 9). As automation increases, the number of blue-collar jobs will continue to decline, and the service sector will continue to grow. Today there are approximately thirty-five million blue-collar workers in America. As a group, observes Parker, "they have made significant gains since the beginning of this century." But he questions the durability of such gains.

With the precarious state of the middle class, women are forced to work to supplement their husbands' incomes in order to provide a more leisurely lifestyle for their families. In 1975, 46 percent of all American women 16 years of age and over were in the labor force. Fifty-eight percent of them were married and living with their husbands. Approaching the mid to late-1960s, it was almost impossible for a family to live as freely and as comfortably as they wished on a single income; salaries were not rising as quickly as prices in the late sixties and were almost at a standstill compared to the spiraling, double-digit inflation of the 1970s. Wives and mothers were freed from the home by the many innovations that accompany the later stages of industrial development. Convenient and time-saving devices such as frozen food prepared in minutes by microwave ovens have liberated women from the kitchen, just as washing machines and permanent press clothes have freed them from the laundry. The liberation of the woman from the home and many of its domestic responsibilities, coupled with the expansion of the service sector and new job opportunities open to women through new policies such as the Equal Opportunity programs, leaves but one logical alternative: a job outside the home.

The fact that women are forced to work contributes directly to the social and psychological dislocation of family members in such a way that the very foundation of that institution itself becomes unstable, which is another prime source of frustration and discontent on the part of the middle class.

THE RULE OF LAW AND SOCIAL JUSTICE

As the fixed-sum conflict is prevalent in a society, survival of the society will depend on the extent to which it is maintained by the rule of law, quite analogous to the playing of an actual game such as chess, where the functional stability is managed by the players' observance of the law. When there is disagreement or conflict, the ultimate reservoir of settlement lies in legal authority. The court as the interpreter of laws will intrude into all spheres of life including the very primary institution of the family. It is perceived to be quite natural in the context of the American society that family disputes are brought to court to decide who will get what and how. Perhaps it is no exaggeration to say that the majority of families in America end up in court over some matter, as we are reminded by the statistical fact that six out of ten marriages end in divorce.

The absolute sanctification of laws in some cases paralyzes the function of secondary social institutions such as schools. When teachers are preoccupied with lawsuits that might be brought against them by their students, education is invariably hampered. Educators in America are competitively challenging the school administration for a larger share of resources and values, a challenge for which an optimal solution is rarely found in any redistributive model due to the zero-sum nature of the competition. Here, again, the court is the authority and the ultimate peace-keeping agent.

For a society at the stage of conflict management, a bad law is still better than no law, and a bad interpretation of laws is more desirable than no interpretation at all.

The Advent of the Advocate

In a society in which winning is all that matters, there must be arbitrators. It is in this context that post-industrial societies come to depend on lawyers and managers to resolve conflicts. As the locus of the social interaction moves to legal solutions for social and human problems, the social status and prestige of the profession that is authorized to interpret the law will become more respectable than its counterpart in other societies. It should not be viewed as a historical accident that judges and lawyers in the United States enjoy relatively higher prestige and social status as studies on American social stratification have consistently revealed. In fact, the American political arena—and, for that matter, its business arena—today seems to be dominated by lawyers, a condition which is quite unique even compared to industrialized societies in Europe. An examination of the 97th U.S. Congress that convened in 1981 indicates that 202 of its 535 members were holders of law degrees (JD or LLB).[4] This is due to the simple fact that lawyers are the champions of advocacy. Indeed, a good lawyer can demonstrate the intellectual ability to overrule common sense decisions concerning controversial issues and justify the unjustifiable.

Virtually every public issue in the United States maintains two sides at the same time, the *pro* and the *con:* abortion, the ERA, nuclear proliferation, school busing, school prayers, the military build-up, and affirmative action programs, to name only a few that characterize the controversial nature of the American political system.[5] It should also be noted that these issues, involving the allocation of wealth and of opportunities, are zero-sum conflicts in nature.

What Is Legal Is Also Just

Corresponding to the society's increased reliance upon and, indeed, reverence for the legal profession is the preeminence of the laws themselves. As laws come to govern people's lives and fortunes, it is people who eventually "worship" laws. Because laws have the power of enforcement embedded in them, it does not take much for people to forget about morality as a means of regulating behavior; they come to think that what is legally safe is also morally correct. This confusion of legality with morality is further facilitated by the lack of a consistently propounded ideology. In the age of advocacies and confusion, the concept of justice is constantly defined and redefined by conflicting interests and by masters of advocacy. Thus, social justice to any degree of objectivity is inexistent at least in the mind of the post-industrial mass public. What is just is what was last affirmed by the courts. Since the time of Plato laws have always been only the minimum device for maintaining orderly interaction in the society. Laws, as such, are intended to draw a boundary between what is allowable and what is not, rather than what is morally desirable or undesirable. As the question of what is just and desirable becomes an issue subject to interpretation and determined by hired advocates, the society at this stage of development is not likely to have the benefit of an objective (or even intersubjective) notion of social justice. Thus, legality remains the only tangible yardstick by which to evaluate behavior. The rule of law is indeed the only insurance for the precarious maintenance of social stability and communal integration. If this last resort is threatened, the society itself will break down as unwritten morals and ethics, even if there are such things, are no longer the effective means of conflict management.

Social justice as a concept stems from a philosophical conviction as exemplified by such norms as equality and individual autonomy as the guiding principles for human relations. As such, the concept of social justice should precede legality in that its appeal is toward specific normative prescriptions. Obedience to laws cannot be a value in itself, although it could be an instrument to safeguard other normative values. Even in the case of safeguarding other values, however, the rule of law is implemented through the negative means of punishing the violator rather than the positive means of rewarding the promoter. Thus, members of the society will be preoccupied with what they should *not* do, rather than what they should do for their behavioral parameters.

Equitable Versus Equal Distribution
Human equality as an ideal is hardly challenged. But as a practical policy guideline, equality is seriously hampered in this advanced stage of conflict management. As each member of the society is inclined to

think he is more valuable than his rewards indicate, devising a formula for the allocation of values and resources will always be problematic. Furthermore, in the mature industrial society where its members are socially evaluated for what they do and not for what they are, diversities in social functions by different members of the society will have to be rewarded differently. This is true even in socialist systems where the Marxist formula of "from each according to his ability, to each according to his need" is practically unrealizable.

To rationalize a distributive justice which is not egalitarian, the notion of equity is introduced. An equitable distribution could be any or any combination of the following: (a) according to their needs; (b) according to their ability; (c) according to their efforts; (d) according to their accomplishments; (e) according to the supply and demand of the market place; (f) according to the requirements of the common good; (g) so that none falls below a specified minimum; (h) according to their legitimate claims; and (i) so that they have equal opportunity to compete without external favoritism and discrimination. As such, an equitable distribution could be practically any mode of allocation as long as it can claim to be just. In an age of advocates, any allocation will indeed be advocated as being legitimate.

Under these circumstances, social distribution will be commenced and maintained for the advantage of the elite because they have the most influence over the political process by which such distributions are mandated. Thus, we find a peculiar situation where the upper class will subsidize the lower class at the expense of the middle class, as alluded to previously.

MINORITY RIGHTS

With the expansion of the service sector in the post-industrial society, the composition of the middle class will become more complex. White-collar workers will be the predominant body of the class, while its lower segment will be further detached from the middle class itself. The lower middle class, including blue-collar workers, will become a class in itself with the precariously maintained incongruence between their middle-class expectations and their limited actual achievement. This very gap between their expectations and achievements will lead to what Davies terms a "revolutionary state of mind." When these lower middle class people are stigmatized, as are American blacks, they become a serious source of social unrest, as was sufficiently demonstrated by civil violence in the 1960s.

The Silent Majority and the Noisy Minority

As discussed earlier, the middle class is the product of industrialization. With the division of labor and professionalization involved in the process of industrial maturity, middle-class people become rationally indifferent to public affairs. Even when they are deprived, they tend to maintain silence as the reality reminds them that there is little they can do by way of restructuring the social order.

The most deprived minority, on the other hand, tends to develop intense opinions and attitudes protesting their deprived status. The extent of their frustration is such that many of them will employ such means as demonstrations and civil violence. With the help of the mass media, which is another unique aspect of the post-industrial society, minorities effectively claim their rights through techniques that the establishment cannot afford to ignore. To be able to demonstrate that the regime is determined to help the "underdog" is always beneficial to the leadership, as it can draw widespread sympathy for the loser in the mass public

It is in this context that we shall look at the origin of the "equal opportunity" program in the United States and the ever-expanding welfare state throughout the post-industrial world.

Equal Opportunity

> You do not take a person who for years has been hobbled by chains and liberate him, bring him up to the starting line of a race then say, 'you are free to compete with others' and still justly believe that you have been completely fair.
>
> LBJ

The above statement by Lyndon B. Johnson represents the principle of *equalization* in order to ensure equal opportunity in the future by taking "compensatory" measures to correct past discrimination. Affirmative action programs intended to restore equal opportunities grew with the civil rights movement in the 1960s. The civil rights movement of the sixties focused American consciousness on the severe deprivations that minorities suffered as a result of centuries of discrimination and neglect. But no sooner had the programs challenged the establishment than severe counterforces struck back with the argument of "reverse discrimination."

The affirmative action program in education is more vigorously challenged because its consequences are expected to be more profound in the long run. The case of the Regents of the University of California versus Allan Bakke was one of the landmark cases concerning affirmative action programs in education. In this case, the Davis medical school set aside sixteen of one hundred student slots each year for "disadvantaged" applicants. Every person admitted through this special admissions program during the years of 1970–74 was a minority group member. Bakke was rejected by Davis and twelve other medical schools. Bakke filed suit claiming reverse discrimination because he felt "less-qualified" applicants were admitted. After the ruling on the Bakke case, it was stated that quotas are unconstitutional but that minority status can be considered as one criterion in admissions policies. Many institutions became divided as to what to do with affirmative action programs, leaving them in a virtual state of limbo.

This experience clearly demonstrates the difficulty in introducing any measure that might challenge the established order of society. People in the upper echelon will allow the deprived to be helped on the grounds of their own idealism but when that idealism gets promoted to the extent of threatening their own status, they can be merciless.

The Welfare State

With the twin phenomena of (1) "losers" coming out in the process of social and economic competition and (2) the losing minority tending to be more vocal and expressive of its discontent, the government is forced to develop policies to quiet the minority. Concurrently, the main body of the middle class, comprised mostly of salaried workers, makes it easier for the government to extract taxes from their paychecks which will be needed to finance skyrocketing government expenditures in the areas of welfare and social security.

Throughout the industrial societies, provisions have been made for the payment of benefits to the aged, widows, young children, the disabled, the unemployed, and low income persons. In the United States, Congress passed a bill establishing such provisions for these groups, known as the Social Security Act of 1935. This legislation was a vital component of President Franklin D. Roosevelt's "New Deal." This

Act established a system of benefits for elderly workers, a federal/state system for unemployment insurance payments, and a source of funds with which the federal government can provide financial assistance to the states. Since its inception, the Social Security program has increased with a snowball effect. And there is no turning point in sight (Table 12).

In 1977, one out of every five Americans received some sort of public assistance amounting to $160 billion, five times more than what it was in 1965. The welfare rolls are constantly increasing. From 1967 to 1976, less than 25 percent of those receiving welfare benefits worked their way permanently off the rolls.[6]

There are many other problems with the welfare policies and programs in the United States, and perhaps other societies as well. For

TABLE 12
Estimated Aggregate Cost of Major Social Security Programs
and Veterans' Benefits 1960–2000
(In billions of dollars)

I. Low-Cost Estimates

Program	1960	1970	1980	1990	2000
All benefits under H.R. 2893 except					
Temporary Disability	4.65	7.54	10.07	12.15	13.24
Temporary Disability	1.45	1.56	1.65	1.75	1.87
Compulsory Health Insurance	6.60	6.90	7.20	7.30	7.40
Unemployment Compensation	2.95	3.12	3.30	3.50	3.74
Total major insurance programs..	15.65	19.12	22.22	24.70	26.25
Public assistance	.90	.80	.70	.60	.50
Veterans' benefits	5.00	6.00	7.00	6.00	6.00
Total low cost....................	21.55	25.92	29.92	31.30	32.75

II. High-Cost Estimates

Program	1960	1970	1980	1990	2000
All benefits under H.R. 2893 except					
Temporary Disability	7.16	10.91	14.69	18.27	20.60
Temporary Disability	2.18	2.34	2.48	2.63	2.81
Compulsory Health Insurance	15.50	16.30	17.00	17.20	17.30
Unemployment Compensation	4.43	4.68	4.95	5.25	5.64
Total major insurance programs..	29.27	34.23	39.12	43.35	46.35
Public assistance	1.50	1.20	1.00	.80	.60
Veterans' benefits	5.00	6.00	10.00	9.00	8.00
Total high cost	35.77	41.43	50.12	53.15	54.95

one thing, the system provides few or no incentives to work for those who earn an income around the minimum wage, since they realize their income is no better than welfare. For instance, in a family of four where no one works, the total assistance available in 1978 was $739.33 per month. If someone were to work earning $100 a month, the total family income, including the welfare check, will increase by only $31.54. If $500 in wages were earned, the total income would rise by $65.77; for $700 in earned wages, family income would rise even less, by $65.28; if $1000 in wages, one's family income rises by only $167.98.[7] Being rational human beings, as they are expected to be in the post-industrial society, welfare recipients find little profit in working while under a system such as the American system. Compounding this problem, the expansion of government bureaucracy that is accompanied by the welfare explosion contributes to corruption, inefficiency, and waste.

Efforts at alleviating problems with the welfare system cannot be effective because the idea of helping the needy has always been associated with the system, and any effort to undermine it can be condemned for being inhumane. Here lies the dilemma: the political system cannot prolong its snowballing game of providing welfare benefits, yet at the same time no government can afford to lose the basis of mass support by curtailing the welfare system. This dilemma is not necessarily limited to the U.S. but is fundamentally inherent in all societies experiencing post-industrial economy.

MASS MEDIA AND POLITICS

In the previous chapter, we discussed that the mass media were promoted by industrial expansion in that industry needed their services for exploring markets and advertising its products. As the development of technology knows no limit, the mass media grew in such a way that commercial messages can reach the consumer more easily and more widely. We saw the growing circulation of newspapers and the diversification of radio and television programs in the process of industrial expansion. Those media influences feed the spirit of American competition. Americans identify with politicians, sports figures, and Hollywood celebrities. They also compete in political discussions and in their ability to reflect current trends through clothes, activities, and personality. The media help in shaping their thoughts, and they readily adapt to media trends. In this Fourth Stage, the government tries to survive via the process of conflict management. It tries to ensure the maintenance of a high level of support, yet simultaneously must prevent any institution from becoming so powerful that it threatens the government's security.

The government has an especially touchy situation in its interaction with the press. It needs the media desperately yet fears it. All elected representatives depend, in varying degrees, on the support of the media. In addition, they must be certain that they keep the media satisfied enough so that they do not incite a popular revolt against them at the voting booth or anywhere else.

Politicians can never make the mistake of thinking themselves beyond the scope of the press. After his landslide re-election in 1972, Richard Nixon felt secure enough to launch a series of assaults on selected journalists and news networks. The press reacted with bitter editorial comment, especially during the subsequent Watergate scandal. A more forgiving media response to the scandal might have kept Nixon in office.

As the consumer is already leisure oriented, it is the more convenient video medium of television that has recently grown uncontested at the expense of newspapers and radio. It is no accident that major papers such as the *Washington Star* are forced to shut down. Radio is no longer a viable communication medium in this advanced stage where virtually every family can own at least one television set.

Leaning on a comfortable couch in the living room, one can watch colorful programs at a minimal cost, far less than a subscription to a newspaper. What is truly intriguing here is the fact that the television viewer in this post-industrial stage looks more for competitive games as a form of entertainment where he can identify himself with a player or team in an effort to seek the psychological glorification that is expected from winning a competition. An average person in this stage of social change has the psychological propensity to participate in competitions, and desires to emerge as a winner. However, such a desire is most likely to be blocked off due to the increasingly rigidified social structure and class mobility. Thus, this frustrated person seeks vicarious "winning" through his player or team. To understand the game-loving masses, one only needs to thumb through TV programs in the United States, Japan, and other mature industrial societies.

Game players on television will, in turn, satisfy their own ego for promoting self-esteem since television exposure makes them instant "celebrities." Such celebrated players are valued so highly that they are actually paid what are viewed as outrageous salaries, salaries which will be paid ultimately by the viewer himself in the form of higher consumer prices. A careful observer will notice that it is the idea of promoting celebrated players that guides TV sports and other game-oriented programs. The business of sports has become an enterprise in every sense of the word.

For this matter, politicians are also actors seeking media exposures. The media not only promote but can easily damage politicians as they attempt to manipulate or at least manage public opinion. The success of politicians and politics is so profoundly dependent on the mass media that what rules America is certainly not limited to the three traditional branches of government. Some authors realistically characterize the media as the fourth branch of government.

The mass media's impact on society is widely recognized as crucial in forming public attitudes and behavior. Through agenda setting, the mass media assert that audiences learn salient issues from their report which may well represent biases on the part of the journalist. As a result, our knowledge of political affairs may be based on a small sample of the real world. That world shrinks as the news media decide what to cover and which aspects to report. As Lippmann pointed out, our political responses are made to that tiny replica of the real world, the "pseudoenvironment," which we have fabricated and assembled almost wholly from mass media materials.

Furthermore, the common viewing, listening and reading patterns of a large portion of the public tend to set for the entire society some common foci of attention, some common agenda of discussion. The tendency of the media to homogenize the contents of information will eventually develop similar "mind sets" including common preferences, values and behavioral orientations. This, coupled with the commercialization of the media industry, will stimulate the public in such a way that they will become motivated to compete for commonly sought values, and, as a result, social competition will become more intensified. Concurrently, as the horizons of one's world expand as the world comes to the viewer at home, especially through the visual medium of television, the field of competition expands, putting social competition on a national and international scale.

Actor Leadership and the End of Ideology

If the typical leadership type for the initial stage of regime formation is the military, for the political integration stage the charismatic leadership, and for the industrial stage of resource expansion the corporate leadership, then for the post-industrial stage of conflict management it is a celebrity type of leadership. In this stage members of the society tend to be issue oriented and are expected to be hedonistically rational and competitive. Studies of American voters have found that issues rather than party membership have become important considerations for voting decisions (Figure 11).

However, issues are presented to them by professional advocates in such a way that the public becomes thoroughly confused as to which course of action will be more beneficial. In such confusion, the voter is open to no alternative but to make his decision based on affective considerations, in which politicians with personal appeal have the advantage. In fact, as Figure 11 suggests, personal attributes have been the primary factor in American voting behavior of the post-war period.

Furthermore, when issues concerning the allocation of social and economic values are such that not everyone can come out as a winner, a politician who has a superior ability to "show many faces" in order to attract people of conflicting interests will be more successful. Such a politician must be a superb actor; even professional acting experience will often prove helpful. In a mature industrial society such as the U.S., Japan and some European nations, celebrities of various types including sports stars are gaining positions in elected offices. This trend is obviously due to the fact that the government would have a hard time maintaining a comfortable level of public support since conventional politicians who deliver "straight talks" can hardly attract the losing half of the population in zero-sum political dynamics.

In an effort to avoid alienating any more people than is absolutely necessary, politicians learn to avoid controversial issues while campaigning. Instead, they focus on such topics as leadership, spirit, and integrity. In general, they run on their images. At some point there arises a generation of politicians who has not only abandoned ideology in the interests of attracting votes, but who has never internalized any coherent ideology in the first place. These politicians are the end product of the breakdown of social institutions and alienation in the industrial stage. Furthermore, these actors are encouraged not to for-

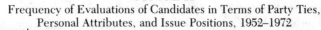

FIGURE 11
Frequency of Evaluations of Candidates in Terms of Party Ties,
Personal Attributes, and Issue Positions, 1952–1972

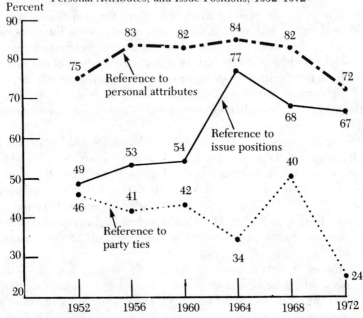

Source: Norman H. Nie, Sidney Verba, and John R. Petrocik, *The Changing
American Voter* (Cambridge, Mass., Harvard University Press, 1976),
p. 167

mulate policy on any ideological base because constituents are more
concerned with results than deontological considerations.

War Technology and Political Terrorism

The concept of terrorism is not new; what is relatively new is the
profound destructive potential of technology and the extent of publicity guaranteed by the mass media.

The uncontrollable technological innovations that have already attained their autonomous course of development made mass destruction and mass killing possible without having to employ large
manpower. For example, much has been written about the availability
of nuclear-device design data in the publicly available literature (Willrich and Taylor, 1974, McPhee, 1974), and it appears to be true that

there is sufficient material available in unclassified literature to provide a potential bomb-maker with enough information to produce such a weapon.

Furthermore, utilizing such a mass-killing weapon will not inflict the sense of guilt usually expected of a killer whose aggression is directed at specific individuals, since mass killing is ultimately carried out by technologically advanced weapons which will separate the killer from the killed. Apel observes (Dallmayer, p. 83):

> Neither aggression nor aggression restraints play an essential role in [the act of killing], because the nature and dimensions of modern weapon technology completely shield [the killer] from a human encounter with the so-called enemy. He merely presses the button as ordered; the result of his bombing, however, are so immense that he can no longer experience them on a concrete, emotional level.

With the readily available destructive technology and the moral neutrality concerning killing, contemporary politics is marred by political terrorism. As an immediate motivation of terrorism, publicity through media is considered to be most important. Bard O'Neill (1978), in a discussion of the Palestinian resistance movement, attributes terrorism to publicity more than anything else. In this sense, we might conclude that the mass media may be the chief facilitator of political terrorism.

In short, the growth of the mass media as an inevitable outcome of industrial maturity has indeed revolutionized politics and society. With the arrival of the computer age and the certain perpetuation of industrial expansion, we foresee an even greater sophistication and universal distribution of the mass media which will make the life world ever more precarious and unpredictable.

SOCIAL DETERIORATIONS

The Affluent Economy and the Poor Society

As one observer put it succinctly, "Future historians will likely characterize the twenty-five years from 1945 to 1970 in American society as a period of foolish affluence fueled by borrowed money" (Gappert, p. ix). Noted economist John K. Galbraith concluded, "If people are hungry, ill-clad, unsheltered or diseased, nothing is so important as to remedy their condition. Higher income is the basic remedy; their problem is thus an economic problem." But "with higher income, questions beyond the reach of economics obtrude."

Gappert (x–xi) observes:

> The struggle for subsistence is not the issue for the United States. No. The questions that obtrude beyond the reach of economics are social and personal in nature. The problem of post-affluence is a social problem. . . . The isolation and needs of the urban and rural underclasses provide evidence that the United States now faces the end of the myth that "more will be better." There isn't much more to be had, and some say that there will be less, but there will be enough. That is to say, there will be enough if we redefine what "enough" is.

Just as the nation loses control over its economy, individual members of the society will lose control over their own lifestyles. Their lives are lived in fascination of consumerism and the myth of affluence. The poor consumer is passively overwhelmed by a sense of alienation, loneliness, and above all, helplessness. The traditional institutions of family, school, and religion, which have experienced a process of deterioration, have now become incapacitated as agents of "rehabilitating" the post-affluent loser.

It is in this context that the emergent debate over the "quality" of life should be understood. Until recently, it was indicators such as the Gross National Product, GNP per capita, industrial output, and urbanization that measured social and political development. But these measurements have proven to be fallacious as barometers of "human" development, a concept that is looming large in these days' discussion of social change. As alternative measurements, some authors suggest a series of more intimately human factors for measuring the condition of the world's life situations.[8]

The Decline of Social Systems

A social system is a network of human interactions with an established pattern of relationships among members of the society. In such a system, one maintains his social position by performing a role that is appreciated by other members of the community. It is appreciated because its place in the perpetuation of the self-subsistence of the community is recognized, and thus, perceived to be essential. Industrial and post-industrial social change, however, deprives the community of its self-subsistence in exchange of the alleged gains in economy and efficiency. No town or city is self-subsistent any more. Indeed, no nation is self-sufficient in the wake of the formation of a global system.

The society ceases to be a social system because its members are unaware of their relative social positions or of the pattern of social interaction in which they take part. As discussed in the previous chapter, the urban center has ceased to be a place for communal interaction. Social relations in the city are managed by a system of material transactions and through a network of information, rather than by its patterned *human* interactions. The global system makes its individual members mutually interdependent, and thus, incapable of self-subsistence. Just as in the case of urban life, the global system is managed in its equilibrium through information systems and functional relationships among groups of functional entities, instead of individual members. With the help of sophisticated information storage and processing facilities made available by the computer technology, the global system has become ever more structured, and this process is made even more efficient by virtue of its alienation from human attributes. As they say, we are all numbers; if one lacks a number, one is nonexistent!

As we discussed earlier, the family system has responded to industrial change by reducing its structural size from the extended system to the nuclear family unit. When the post-industrial cultural system prevails upon the family, it simply breaks up. The ultra-rational personality of the post-industrial man directs the family relationship into a convenient bond maintained by the rule of cost-benefit calculations. It is mutual utility that ties a husband and wife together, and the relationship will last so long as such a utility remains. When people fail to see the usefulness of family, they are willing to stay out of the institution of marriage as is amply demonstrated by the critical state of the family in many industrial societies such as the United States and the Scandinavian countries. The no-longer highly controversial issues of "living together outside of marriage" and homosexual relationships in the United States indicate the intensity of the problem of the traditional family system. These developments could have been easily predicted if we had examined carefully the social ramifications of the post-industrial society.

When an overwhelming majority of the people reside in urban areas and are engaged in the industrial and service sectors and occupations, and at the same time live in or out of the troubled family, we can safely conclude that they are on the verge of being eliminated from social systems as social systems themselves crumble away.

When there is no society with a pattern of interaction and with human bonds maintained by mores and norms that members of the society will be inculcated with in their socialization process, the socialization of children into patterns of behavior that are supportive of the system will begin to erode. Indeed, children in post-industrial America appear to be removed from the experience of socialization, a process in which they learn the norms and values predominant in the society and become functionally integrated members. With all the consumerism and promotion of consumer goods throughout the mass media and even in schools, American children seem to be preoccupied with ideas and desires for conspicuous consumer goods. If a child fails to go with the tide, and is serious about "human" growth and social norms, he is likely to become alienated from his cohorts, a severe social sanction which could be a fatal blow to the tender mind of the child.

SUMMARY

In this chapter, I have discussed some aspects of post-industrial development in an effort to demonstrate the fact that the development process does not cease after the attainment of the industrial stage. Indeed, the social and cultural implications of post-industrial change are likely to be detrimental to the maintenance of a social and cultural system, the same system that helped members of the society seek their belonging needs. It is intriguing to observe that just as the third stage of development—the resource expansion stage—destroyed the institutions of the first stage through the perversion of agriculture and the military-industrial complex, this fourth stage has adverse impacts on the social institutions of the second stage, hinting at the irony that we tend to neglect what we have and we pursue what we don't have.

FOOTNOTES

[1] For an excellent discussion of the nature of a zero-sum society, refer to Lester C. Thurow (1980).

[2] For a further examination, see Richard Parker (1972) and Michael Parenti (1977).

[3] For a description of the event, see *TIME*, June 19, 1978.

[4] Source: Congressional Directory, 97th Congress (U.S. Government Printing Office).

[5] For an excellent exposition of this issue, see *Taking Sides: Clashing Views on Controversial Issues*, edited by George McKenna and Stanley Feigold (Guildord, Connecticut: The Dushkin Publishing Group, Inc., 1982).

[6] See "Welfare Reforms," *Newsweek*, August 29, 1977, pp. 19–24.

[7] See "The Disincentive Factor," *TIME*, October 2, 1978, p. 55.

[8] Morris (1979), for example, proposed an index consisting of life expectancy, infant mortality, and literacy rate as a more meaningful comparative yardstick.

BIBLIOGRAPHY

Bell, Daniel, *The Coming of Post-Industrial Society* (New York: Basic Books, 1973).

Dallmayer, Fred R., ed., *From Contract to Community* (New York: Marcel Dekker, Inc., 1978).

Eston, David, *The Political System* (New York: Alfred A. Knopf., Inc., 1953).

Gappert, Gary, *Post-Affluent America: The Social Economy of the Future* (New York: New Viewpoints, 1979).

Lasswell, Harold, *Politics: Who Gets What, When, How* (New York: Meridian Books, 1958).

McPhee, John, *The Curve of Binding Energy* (New York: Ballantine, 1974).

O'Neill, Bard, "Towards a Typology of Political Terrorism: The Palestinian Resistance Movement," in *Journal of International Affairs*, Vol. 32, No. 1, 1978.

Parenti, Michael, *Democracy for the Few* (New York: St. Martins, 1977).

Parker, Richard, *The Myth of the Middle Class* (New York: Harper and Row, 1972).

Thurow, Lester C., *The Zero-Sum Society* (New York: Basic Books, 1980).

Willrich, Mason and Theodore B. Taylor, *Nuclear Theft: Risks and Safeguards* (Cambridge, Mass.: Ballinger Publishing Co., 1974).

Morris, David Morris, *Measuring the Condition of the World's Poor: The Physical Quality of Life Index* (New York: Pergamon Press, 1979).

Chapter VIII

DEVELOPMENT AND GLOBAL CONSEQUENCES

The post-industrial society cannot be contained within a nation, for industrial expansion defies national boundaries. Industries in the developed societies will find it increasingly difficult to exist within their national boundaries due, among other things, to expensive labor costs, scarce resources, and public pressure from environmentalists which causes ever demanding government restrictions. Also consumer products can no longer find a sufficient market within the post-industrial society itself, forcing businesses to explore foreign markets. It is in this context of the spilling-over of the post-industrial economy that we should discuss more current topics such as the multi-national corporations, technology transfer, and the New International Economic Order.

ECONOMIC INTERDEPENDENCE: A NEW SOURCE OF CONFLICT

A firm drilling an oil well in the Persian Gulf, using American technology, Japanese machines, Chinese labor, and an energy supply from Saudi Arabia is no longer a company under the influence of a single nation. For the single objective of economizing, industrial firms are becoming multi-national and, to that extent, depend on the international economic system.

The international economic system is a relatively new concept. In the conventional world, there was no system of order among the nation states. As Raymond Aron observed, the international system "has always been anarchical and oligarchical: anarchical because of the absence of a monopoly of legitimate violence, oligarchical in that, without civil society, rights depend largely on might" (Aron, p. 160). But with the increasingly predictable functional system of the international community, one might see the birth of an international order. Yet, we can hardly infer from this that this new order will facilitate peace among nations. On the contrary, as nations interact with one another from a position of functional utility for one another, they are more likely to expect a greater share of value distributions which could possibly accentuate competition and conflictual interactions.

Unlike the conventional international order where *might* prevailed, the developing nations are raising their voices of resentment against the role of developed economy even in the area of technology transfer. The Third World nations do not hesitate to criticize the fact that sophisticated technology transferred from the industrial world has not achieved what their governments expected of it at the time that they initiated industrialization programs. It did not help create employment, cater to the basic needs of the population, build up the indigenous technological ability, or create the necessary infrastructure for the indigenous technological development of developing nations.

The so called North-South global system is bound to be one of confrontation rather than cooperation. The North tends to perceive its development as a privilege, while the South is determined to claim its development as a right.

In the North-South dispute, what is evident is the notion held by the South that poor countries are forced to remain poor as a result of continuous exploitation by the North, dating to the beginning of colonialism. This suggests that the political independence that new nations have gained simply amounts to a transition from political colonialism to economic colonialism. Nyerere of Tanzania put it unambiguously:

> In one world, as in one nation, when I am rich because you are poor, and I am poor because you are rich, the transfer of wealth from the rich to the poor is a matter of rights; it is not an appropriate matter for charity . . .[1]

According to this view, the development of the North has been achieved at the expense of the South, and it is now the rich countries who have the moral obligation to return some of the wealth they took away from the poor. It is being widely contended that much of the large-scale aid provided by the West in the past under the "trickle down" theory of growth has failed to reach the poorest people in Third World countries, thus, failing to enhance the conditions of their life world. This situation has led some authors in the "dependence" school of thought to claim that foreign aid actually serves the interests of the developed countries, while further incapacitating the LDCs.

Johnson (1972, p. 100) summarizes this contention:

> United States private investment, and programs, foreign policy, military assistance, military interventions, and international agencies, . . . are interwoven and oriented toward the promotion and maintenance of influence and control in other countries.

The LDCs argue further that the sophisticated technology that has been made available to the "latecomer" has not achieved what was expected of it. As Graham put it:

> [Sophisticated technology] did not help in creating employment, catering to the basic needs of the population or building up the indigenous technological ability of the countries concerned. This was partly because industrialization took the form of import-substitution which in effect often meant that the transfer of technology was geared not to meeting the basic needs of the population but rather to the satisfaction of a demand for modern sophisticated consumer goods by a small but prosperous upper and upper-middle class.[2]

If, as they contend, the LDCs have been exploited for the prosperity of the developed world, and if the DCs alone have created dependency on the part of the LDCs, then one might conclude that the DCs may have the moral responsibility to help the LDCs overcome developmental difficulties.

The DCs, however, seem to be determined to undermine such accusations and to maintain that national poverty is self-inflicted, in that the LDCs lack the cultural and historical prerequisites for economic development. In addition, political corruption, mismanagement, the absence of the infra-structure needed for economic development, and ideological commitment to redistribution as opposed to reinvestment are frequently cited as the prime sources of fault on the part of poor countries.[3]

In response to the exploitation charge, Bauer and Yamey (1977) point to the fact that those Fourth World (the least developed) countries are the ones that have had little economic contact with the West, and the extreme backwardness of countries such as Chad, Burundi, Lesotho, Rwanda, Afghanistan, Yemen, and Sikkim can hardly be due to exploitation by international economic powers. Indeed, it has been richly documented for the record that the latecomers to the development process, particularly the "newly industrialized countries" (NICs) of the Third World, have benefited from advanced technology, international markets, and foreign capital provided by the already industrialized societies. Thus, in the view of the DCs, the development of the LDCs is in no way within the purview of their moral responsibility. According to this position, poor countries have no right to demand anything but should appreciate with gratitude any humanitarian assistance if and when it comes.

In short, there appears to be no common ground upon which the issue of obligatory relations among nations for international development is being understood. Each side seems to have sufficient reasons to rationalize its own contentions but not enough to persuade the other. This lack of consensus has become a new source of international conflict in the post-cold-war era.

THE HEALTH OF THE PLANET

The Trauma of the Ecosystem

During the early stage of political development, man lived in close harmony with the physical environment. In a time when man was trying to survive, all he had to do was to live *with* nature. One of man's early advantages was he was not able to disturb the environment permanently due to a small population. Some disturbance was seen in the burning of fields and forests for agriculture. However, it was not total devastation by any means. The ecosystem survived, and so did man. When food gathering turned to food planting, it was a step toward regime formation but it was a step away for man from the ecological harmony that he had enjoyed for centuries.

The building of walled cities in ancient history in which surplus grain was stored is a good example of how man began to manipulate his household at the expense of the environment. This in itself was not bad, but when the nation-building occurred and population increased, man became more exploitative. The history of man from the early river valley civilization to the modern super powers has been an avalanche of political integration at the expense of the environment. The nature of the nation requires that it be built on something, and the people erroneously believe they can live off the land.

Since populations increased and the need to belong grew with the expansion of people, there was a need for greater agricultural production to support the population. As the cities and nation states outgrew their boundaries, the need for new frontiers was great. Man found new frontiers and was, for a while, satisfied. But one of the major events for the ecologist occurred with the discovery around the end of the nineteenth century that there was no more frontier land for man to conquer. Frederick Jackson Turner not only shocked historians at the turn of the century but also inadvertently aroused the environmentalist. He reminded us that: We had reached our limit-border of our ecosystem. We now have to look back at our environment and see what we have missed in the years of pillage. It is interesting to note that man spent the first 15,000 years surviving; the last 5,000 trying to belong in human communities. Only within the last century and a half has our lust for leisure and control put all of our accomplishments in jeopardy.

Man was fairly safe with his ecosystem up until the Industrial Revolution. The attempt by man at resource expansion has never been effectively controlled. The need for leisure, easier lives, drove man into an industrial boom. Man had to turn on his heels and review what resources of the frontier he had missed.

The answer to much of the competitive resource expansion came with the marriage of science and technology. Science had opened the door for technology to expand. The urbanization that followed on the heels of invention of heavy industry was formidable. There developed from this an even more dangerous feeling that, with time, technology and science could solve any problem man has created. This human self-confidence has proved to be an absolute fallacy. The idea of controlling the excesses of industry in the environment are alien to man. Even the great economist Adam Smith who advanced the optimistic notion that the "invisible hand" would eventually do what is good to most people failed to foresee the environmental threat. Even theology encouraged environmental exploitation. The Judeo-Christian doctrine teaches that man should have domain over nature, rule over it, and subdue the environment. The exploitative nature between these two views, one of easy going economics and the other of misguided Christian dominion, both of which facilitated gross materialism, show that the environment did not warrant much consideration in man's vision of his future.

As the life environment becomes unhealthy, people look for a better environment by deserting cities as residential areas and moving to the suburbs. The phenomenon of suburbanization in post-industrial societies is indeed interesting in the sense that people are "pushed" away from the city just as they were "pushed" away from the rural areas in the process of industrialization. Suburbanization as a common phenomenon of post-industrial societies leaves behind the urban ghetto and all the problems associated with it. As no one is equipped with the desire and resources to deal with urban problems in social, economic, and political arenas, only the government is looked upon as the agent that will take care of these problems, thus, forcing a rapid expansion of welfare programs.

In an effort to avoid the deterioration of the environment, industry searches for a "pollution-free haven" abroad. As affluent countries enact stricter environmental regulations, their businesses find themselves becoming increasingly less profitable. They look to less developed countries as factory sites, and find an attractive "haven" in poor countries. As Enloe observes (1975, p. 131):

> The dilemma of underdevelopment is choosing between two unwanted and uncompromising conditions. A government that wants economic growth may feel that it must accept foreign intervention and potential environmental hazards. The very opportunity for attracting overseas capital may come from an affluent nation protecting its own environment.

Countries that are considered successful developing systems, such as Brazil, Singapore, Nigeria, South Korea, and Malaysia, have achieved their economic growth at the expense of environmental pollution. They are the countries that have opted for economic industrialization over environmental quality, and have readily offered their lands to foreign investors who need pollution-free havens.

The underdeveloped countries are selling their "havens" not only to foreign investors but to tourists. People of the industrialized societies find their own territories eaten up by industrial and commercial exploitations but they are the ones who possess more time and funds for leisure. They look around the world for "unspoiled" areas where air and land are still pollution-free and life is reminiscent of their own "good old days," and go on foreign tours. The notorious Japanese tourist reflects not only the country's economic affluence but more directly the deteriorated environment from which he has the urge to get away.

In short, when industrial development deteriorates the environment, rational citizens of the affluent society seek to *avoid* the polluted environment rather than seeking solutions to the problem itself.

Who Will Pay?

The matter of ecosystem, with the pressing issue of environmental quality, is of a "public" nature. A public issue, as discussed earlier, is one that benefits or hurts everyone regardless of one's contribution to its creation or solution. In this regard, the heart of the issue lies in the fact that a rational individual will be unwilling to make sacrifices for the "public" benefit since this is exactly what he is not supposed to do as a "rational" man. Here we should be reminded of the fact that citizens of the mature industrial society have already acquired a rational personality and calculating attitudes in the process of industrial development as espoused in Chapter VI. In the case of air pollution, for example, clean air is a commodity that does not distinguish those who have contributed to its creation or preservation from those who have not, as long as it benefits people who breathe. It would be perfectly rational for any individual to avoid paying the cost of clean air if he expects someone who needs clean air more desperately to pay for it; for the benefit will reach him no matter who pays for it.

In an effort to fight energy shortages in recent years in the United States, drivers have been sufficiently informed of the bleak energy future and asked to drive less. But the public did not respond effectively until gasoline prices went up. This price response behavior indicates that rational individuals will only behave "rationally" and they cannot be persuaded by the noble idea of public regard or altruism. As long as citizens of the industrial society remain rational, social problems of a public nature will need the merciful hand of the government, no matter how wasteful and inefficient its operations may be. The expansion of the welfare state is not a public choice but the inevitable result of industrial development.

Maldevelopment

When nations of the pre-industrial stage come to interact with societies of mature industrial stages, the former can be easily induced to maldevelopment due to the premature absorption of foreign institutions and behavior styles. In a society where the predominant public needs remain at the level pf physical survival with hunger and starvation as chronic problems, policies aimed at industrialization will bear little direct relevance to the masses. Such policies will only facilitate social disintegration and economic imbalance, thus leading to the abnormal development of social and political institutions and behavior styles of its members. As we discussed in Chapter IV, electoral institutions and voting behaviors in Third World countries often show deviant characteristics, and such a deviance could be attributed to the fact that these institutions have been transplanted under the influence of foreign nations when the indigenous society was unprepared to receive them. Likewise, when a person in a Third World country is uncertain about the more urgent needs such as food and shelter, and yet imitates the conspicuous lifestyle of an affluent society, he could exert a parasitic effect on his society and its institutions.

As discussed earlier, the post-industrial necessity to explore new markets often reaches the remotest corners of the world where the society is unprepared for industrial fruits. Being in contact with foreign commodities and new ways of life is likely to stimulate the people to generate new demand in addition to the more urgent old needs. The presence of diverse demands placed upon the society will make it more difficult for the government to respond effectively, and ultimately make the society more vulnerable to political unrest.

When consumer items produced for leisure are transmitted to a society where the vast majority of its members are still seeking survival and belonging, they are often used for other purposes than convenience and time-saving. In this case, consumer goods such as refrigerators, color television sets, and automobiles can be used for the purpose of displaying a certain lifestyle reserved for a certain social class. Thus, class differences are more concretely demonstrated in material terms, and as a result, the underprivileged could develop a class consciousness of sorts, eventually leading to social and political unrest.

A balanced development, as opposed to maldevelopment, is one where all areas of the society—such as human needs, institutions, behavioral dispositions, policy preferences, and leadership characteristics—are making simultaneous and mutually reinforcing progress toward a higher stage. This balanced development is often disrupted by the intrusion of more advanced societies. In view of this, we might evaluate the role of advanced societies in the development of the Third and Fourth World countries with greater caution.

Food: The Ultimate Crisis

While industrial development tends to curtail agricultural productivity, science and technology, which accompany industrialization, contribute to a prolonged life expectancy and a reduction in infant mortality, thus causing a population increase, especially in the nonproductive age groups such as the elderly and children.[4] This phenomenon, as discussed earlier, encourages the expansion of welfare policies and the growth of the governmental sector in the postindustrial society. Globally speaking, the transfer of science and technology contributes to the population explosion in such a way that the kinds of attitudes and government policies needed for effective population control will only lag behind. As we see in Figure 11, the population imbalance between the poor countries and the affluent nations will only be intensified, indicating the certain future of mass food problems in the less developed countries. Food import requirements of all less developed countries in 1970 were 25 million tons of cereal grains. In 1974 they were 37 million tons. The United Nations Food and Agricultural Organization estimates that by 1985 import requirements could increase to 100 million tons. Whatever surplus food the world may be able to raise to meet these requirements will be produced primarily in the United States and Canada. It will be well beyond the financial ability of the developing countries to purchase this vast quantity of food and it will probably exceed its capacity to transport it from North America even if the needy countries have the ability to develop the necessary infrastructure for distribution to the needy people.

Beyond these practical problems, there are a number of unavoidable value issues. A most important and controversial value question is the issue of the moral obligation of the haves to feed the needy. Supposedly, the developing countries are unable to pay for food imports. Can the developed countries withhold food shipment when people die of hunger and malnutrition? In these days of discussions on human rights, a predominant view seems to be that humans have the inherent right to life; thus basic needs such as food are within the purview of natural human rights. Food that the earth produces is to be consumed by its inhabitants. This humanist sentiment may not be acceptable to

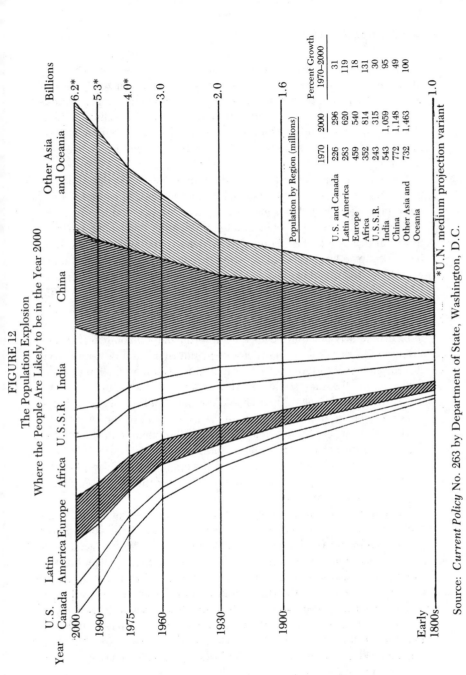

FIGURE 12

The Population Explosion

Where the People Are Likely to be in the Year 2000

Population by Region (millions)		
	1970	2000
U.S. and Canada	226	296
Latin America	283	620
Europe	459	540
Africa	352	814
U.S.S.R.	243	315
India	543	1,059
China	772	1,148
Other Asia and Oceania	732	1,463

Percent Growth 1970–2000
31
119
18
131
30
95
49
100

*U.N. medium projection variant

Source: *Current Policy* No. 263 by Department of State, Washington, D.C.

257

the producers of the developed countries. Global inequities in food distribution are indeed scandalous. The most industrialized countries feed more cereal to their livestock than is consumed by the populations of the developing countries put together. What are the ethical dimensions of this inequality? Does such an unequal distribution of food constitute a human injustice in and by itself, thus requiring corrective measures?

There are also policy issues regarding food. New agricultural equipment such as the rice-threshing machines in the underdeveloped countries often replaces laborers, posing a dilemma: Which is more important, jobs for farmers or greater production efficiency? Furthermore, in places like the Philippines, Okinawa, and South Korea, U.S. bases occupy a large acreage of prime productive land. Which is more important, the use of land for food production or for strategic interests? If U.S. grain reserves are to help feed the world's hungry, should American farmers receive special subsidies for growing wheat?

The issue of food aid is further complicated by the fact that the world food problem is not limited to the underdeveloped countries. As we discussed in this and previous chapters, industrial and post-industrial development deteriorates the agricultural sector and alienates the farmer from the mainstream of the society. At the same time, the increasing polarization of the rich and the poor leads to an expansion of a segment of the population that suffers from malnutrition. According to the 1975 census, there are at least 26 million people in the United States who do not have the means to ingest a nutritionally adequate diet. This being the case, American public opinion would not allow the government to feed people abroad when some of their own people are suffering from malnutrition.

In short, industrial development and the transfer of science and technology have contributed to the exponential growth of world population, while the production and distribution of food are faced with almost insurmountable dilemmas. Thus, the problem of feeding the hungry has become a focal issue in a world where increasing numbers of people are entering the threshhold to industrial and post-industrial stages. Humans huddled together to cultivate crops when survival was the ultimate goal for primitive man. But ironic as it may sound, the long journey of "development" has left us with the same task of feeding humans. What have we accomplished when getting food has once again become a focal concern?

SUMMARY

Once propelled, the momentum of development is almost unstoppable. There is no known boundary within which the drive toward industrialization and the human search for supremacy can be contained. In this chapter we examined the global consequences of national development, which are both unavoidable and undesirable.

Intense competition for the control of more resources has led to the depletion of energy sources, the deterioration of the environment, and the decline of social systems and institutions. If this course of development continues unchecked, the human species will be left with no destiny but self-inflicted extinction. Thus, in this final chapter, I portrayed a pessimistic view of the prospect of continuous development.

FOOTNOTES

[1] *African Affairs*, April, 1976, p. 242.

[2] *Transfer of Technology: Its Implications for Development and Environment* (United Nations, Sales No. E. 78. II. D. 10).

[3] See Irving Kristol, "The New Cold War," *The Wall Street Journal*, July 17, 1975, p. 18.

[4] For comparative data on life expectancy and other social indicators, see Morris (1978).

REFERENCES

Aron, R., *Progress and Disillusion: The Dialectics of Modern Society* (N.Y.: Praeger, 1978).

Blaney, Harry C., III, *Global Challenges* (New York: New Viewpoints, 1979).

Johnson, Dale L., "Dependency and the International System," in James D. Cockcroft et al., *Dependence and Underdevelopment* (N.Y: Anchor Books, 1972).

Bauer, P.T. and B.S. Yamey, "Against the New Economic Order," Commentary, Vol. 63, No. 4 (April 1977).

Enloe, Cynthia H., *The Politics of Pollution in a Comparative Perspective* (New York: David McKay Co., Inc. 1975).

Morris, David Morris, *Measuring the Condition of the World's Poor* (New York: Pergamon Press, 1979).

POSTSCRIPT

I have depicted a rather gloomy picture for the future of social development which tempts us to question the desirability of development itself. In the process of development, we saw a systematic and predictable deterioration of human life situations, ranging from the moral decay of human society and the breakdown of social institutions to the erosion of the physical quality of the planet itself. As long as human nature remains as characterized in the present paradigm, the prospect for human survival, let alone human development, is indeed bleak, perhaps hopeless. Post-industrial development may really mark the threshold to self-inflicted human extinction.

I have suggested that the absence of human development beyond the primitive level of basic needs and innate desires is the ultimate source of developmental problems. It was maintained that the structure of human nature is such that the desires for survival, belongingness, leisure, and social control are universally observable in all forms of societies, and, further, that human nature as such is as manifest in adults as it is in children. With this, I asserted that human development is arrested by the recurrence and perpetuation of the same needs and desires, indicating the termination of human growth at that level and in that vicious cycle. In closing this book, my sincere hope is that my interpretation of human nature in this regard will prove to be false. The paradigm itself needs to be wrong for the future of my children and many more generations thereafter. If, however, the paradigm carries any degree of empirical validity, we must search at all costs for remedial and preventive solutions. It is in this spirit that I shall sketch a few thoughts in this postscript.

Serious efforts should be made at exploring new normative visions and institutional blueprints for human social and political development. Development ought to refer to human growth above and beyond the simple attainment of basic needs and innate desires. Human success must mean more than the achievement of material possessions and social position. Social relations ought to be managed by mutual *respect*, not solely by calculations of self-interest. The concept of virtue should be revived in society, and a person of virtue should be given respect and proper recognition. The control of emotions and the overcoming of innate desires ought to be encouraged not prevented. The reverence that such values were accorded was explicit and unchallenged in the Greek, Islamic, and Confucian civilizations until they were systematically and decisively overpowered by the arrogance and alleged pragmatism of the Christian civilization and the accompanying material aspirations of the West.

The paradigm proposed in this book was based on an *empirical* definition of development, although as an "ideal type" it was not an isomorphic description of an arbitrarily chosen society. The incremental progression of human wants was not meant to be a normative imperative. It was rather an "ideal" construct inferred from historical experience. If there were to be a normative concept of development, it would be anything but the definition offered in this book.

A normative course of development should entail *human* development. No matter how development may be defined, its primary beneficiary should be the development of humans themselves, not those instrumental means by which life may be made more enjoyable. I, for one, would define development in terms of *communicative* capability among members of the community. A person becomes more capable of communication by acquiring more information and being more knowledgeable about the life world. But more importantly, human communication begins with compassionate feelings toward others and empathy for divergent life situations. In the process of industrial development, humans have voluntarily restricted their understanding of the life world in the name of efficiency; institutions have effectively curtailed human contacts and education has mercilessly sliced human minds into isolated pieces in the name of specialization. Humans have devotedly built walls around themselves in the name of social progress. And in the end, society has become little more than a network of functions devoid of any overriding sense of community to guide the further evolution of those functional matrices. A penetrating reassessment of the process of social change and political development in a way that we have attempted in this book will urge us to reconceptualize development in such a way that social maturity supercedes the manifestation of material transactions or the fulfillment of contractual obligations.

We are told that a developed society is one in which people are more achievement oriented and social mobility is viable. Here, human achievement should be evaluated by the amount of *difficulty* involved in making such an achievement as well as the achievement itself. As we discussed in the opening chapter when we drew the analogy of comparing Beethoven and Picasso, human achievement will loom larger when the achiever perseveres against unusual adversities and makes sacrifices. Wanting something naturally and innately desired and being able to obtain it must not constitute a barometer with which to measure human development. In fact, overcoming culturally determined desires should be regarded as a sign of human maturity. An irony of development has been that in the post-industrial society with its sophisticated mass communication facilities, such motivations have been methodically eroded. In this respect alone, the developed has as much to learn from the underdeveloped as the latter from the former.

Human development must reflect one's ability to sustain autonomy and self-determination. The human desire to belong to a society should not result in the submission of human destiny to social determination. The society consists of its constituent individuals, and as such, it must be the individuals themselves who steer the course of social change, not the reverse. Human freedom is a natural right, and as such, it is absolute and sacred. Man needs to guard his freedom not only against political manipulations but more concertedly against the forces of social and economic development. The absolute value of human individuality will be appreciated when one recognizes absolute qualities of each individual whose social worth should never be measured by his position in the social hierarchy. The yardstick to measure human success must not be unidimensional. Humans should be valued in terms of what they are (quality), not in terms of what they have (quantity). Only when members of the society appreciate one another based on their unique personal qualities will they interact in humility and with respect.

Education should entail the cultivation of such individuality, enabling the learner to define more clearly what he *is*. Socrates' virtue of "Know Thyself" should be brought back to life from antiquity. Social and cultural systems should recognize and reward human achievement by the degree of absolute progress, not by competitive achievement in relation to other members of society. Children should be relieved from competitive learning experiences where they are constantly taught to be smarter, faster, stronger, and wiser than their friends. In the competitive learning experience, they learn to be either arrogant or jealous, which will be reinforced further throughout their social lives. Instead, children should be taught to become better than they are, and be rewarded accordingly.

As clearly evidenced in this book, the globe is becoming an indivisible single unit. In a true sense, every nation in the world is becoming every other nation's business, and every individual's well-being is increasingly becoming everyone else's business. American farmers are as much dependent upon Soviet consumers as the latter are on American crops. Furthermore, world distributive justice has become a focal issue in contemporary society to the extent that those who are deprived of daily necessities have come to claim their fair share and to blame the more fortunate ones for their miseries. It is becoming apparent that we need a world management system for the maintenance of a distributive justice if the world is to avoid mounting tensions among peoples and nations, which may easily lead to chronic conflicts. The idea of a world government is not new in intellectual history. What is new is the fact that the idea is proposed for empirical necessity, not as a philosopher's ideal. As such, a world government is not a utopian solution. It is only an inevitable alternative which could turn out to be another dismal institution.

In the meantime, a massive and structured campaign for a cultural revolution is in order if the perpetuation of global imbalances and human self-destructive propensities are to be alleviated; a cultural revolution in which humans reassert their legitimate claims as the masters of human history, free themselves from self-imposed quantitative competition, and search for a self-identity as absolute beings whose *raison d'être* is established apart from social hierarchy. Then, and only then, can the course of development toward a fearful future be redirected.

The problem of underdevelopment is a challenge, but the problem of development is a dilemma. We need to be honest about telling the "success" stories to the aspiring and underdeveloped world. It is a human obligation for the developed world to concede its problems, agonize over its dilemmas, and warn the rest of the world not to make the same mistakes. Otherwise, there will be no twenty-first century to look forward to.

INDEX

ABOUT THE AUTHOR

Han S. Park was born in China and raised in North and South Korea. He obtained much of his higher education in the United States. In 1971 he received his Ph.D. from the University of Minnesota. He has since published extensively in areas such as modernization, Asian politics, and social science methodology. He has also presented numerous professional papers in several countries, including Yugoslavia, China, Japan, Korea, Mexico, and Canada.

Currently he is associate professor in political science at the University of Georgia.